MY LIFE
AND GOOD TIMES

SIMON & SCHUSTER
New York • London • Toronto
Sydney • Tokyo • Singapore

Swifty

BY *Irving Lazar*

WRITTEN IN COLLABORATION
WITH ANNETTE TAPERT

 SIMON & SCHUSTER
Rockefeller Center
1230 Avenue of the Americas
New York, NY 10020

10 9 8 7 6 5 4 3 2 1

Library of Congress Cataloging-in-Publication Data
Lazar, Irving, 1907–1993.
  Swifty : my life and good times /
by Irving Lazar, written in collaboration with
Annette Tapert.
      p.   cm.
    1. Lazar, Irving, 1907–1993.   2. Literary
agents—United States—Biography.   3. Hollywood
(Los Angeles, Calif.)   I. Tapert, Annette.   II. Title.
PN149.9.L39A3   1995
070.5'2—dc20
[B]   94-47215   CIP
ISBN 0-684-80418-2

Acknowledgments

IRVING LAZAR did not live long enough to thank those who helped him with his memoirs. But I know he would have wanted to thank his early collaborators and his devoted staff. They include: the writers Chris Chase and Michael Shnayerson; his longtime secretary, Linda Jones, who assembled his taped reminiscences into a cohesive script; his devoted assistant, Cindy Cassel.

I, too, am grateful for the help I've received along the way from: Chuck Adams, George and Joan Axelrod, Betty Bacall, Glenn Bernbaum, Tina Brown, David Brown and Helen Gurley Brown, Art Buchwald, Graydon Carter, Cindy Cassel, Larry Collins, Betty Comden, Janet and Freddie de Cordova, Dominick Dunne, Ahmet and Mica Ertegun, Joni Evans, Harry Evans, Marvin Friedman, Sarah Giles, Judy Green, Kitty Carlisle Hart, Reinaldo Herrera, Barbara Howar, Linda Jones, Howard Kaminsky, Gene and Pat Kelly, Garson Kanin, Wayne Lawson, Henry and Pauline Lazar, Karen Lerner, Elizabeth Mackey, Carol Matthau, Sue Mengers, Alan Nevins, Jack Nicholson, Bob and Kathy Parrish, Linda and Stuart Resnick, Kathy Robbins, Barbara Sinatra, Michael Shnayerson, Adam Shaw, Martin Singer, Ray Stark, Wendy Stark, Teresa Sohn, Peter Viertel, Richard Zanuck.

Irving would have had some wry, back-handed compliment for Michael Korda, his friend and sparring partner for two decades. The fact was, he was very proud of his association with Michael and as delighted to have him as his editor as I was.

Finally, it was Irving's wish to dedicate this book to the memory of his wife, Mary.

Introduction

"EVERYBODY HAS two agents—his own and Irving Lazar." Indeed Irving was the universal agent—he once only half-jokingly offered me "Universe Rights" to some book—but he was also to many, many people all over the world the best of friends, understanding, tirelessly supportive, unhesitatingly loyal, fiercely protective.

I was privileged to be one of those friends for over three decades—a short time span from Irving's point of view, but long and rich from mine. That circle of friends regaled each other over the years with "Swifty" stories, hilarious anecdotes of Lazar's behavior, wit, and frequent outrage that the world should occasionally refuse to give him exactly what he wanted when he wanted it. It was like belonging to some exclusive, international club—"The Friends of Irving Lazar"—and wherever you went you were always sure that every door would be open to you with the *"Open Sesame!"* of "Oh, you're a friend of Irving Lazar's too! Have you heard the latest?"

That circle of friends included (or rather *had* included): Bogart, Bacall, Sam Goldwyn, Gene Kelly, Moss Hart, Ira Gershwin, Frank Sinatra, Larry Olivier, Noël Coward, Cole Porter,

Vladimir Nabokov, my auntie Merle (Oberon), my uncle Alex (Korda), Leland Hayward, "Slim" Keith, Jennifer Jones, Willie Maugham, Brando, Irwin Shaw, Johnny Carson, Cher, Faye Dunaway, innumerable Rothschilds, Peter Viertel, David and Helen Brown, Howard Kaminsky, Tina Brown, Dick Snyder, Michael Caine, Jack Nicholson, Joan Collins, and a cast of thousands more, most of them at one time or another clients—for with Lazar there was no gap between friendship and business—and all of them devoted Lazar-watchers, who kept each other in stitches with Lazar's latest doings or sayings, and whose day was incomplete without the phone ringing and a familiar, gravelly voice rasping, "Hi, kiddo, this is Lazar. What's doing?"

To tell the truth, every time the phone rings I still expect to hear it. I can confess: I miss him. He made everybody's life a little richer, touching us all with the fantasy of his high expectations—for to Lazar his friends were always handsome, beautiful, gifted, witty, *special,* as if he had willed them so because anything else would be beneath him, a kind of irascible Fairy Godfather with an 18-carat-gold magic wand and big tortoise-shell glasses.

For years he talked about writing his story, while all his friends begged him to. The truth is, despite all their urging, he wasn't really sure he wanted to. Lazar was the master of the unspoken word, the great anecdote, but at the same time he was his own creation. His friends were all "creative" people, artists, writers, actors, but Lazar created *himself,* a work of art which he spent a lifetime perfecting, from the way he dressed to the way he spoke, which explains why from certain angles he looked like a dazzling and grotesque *objet d'art* that Fabergé might have carved out of some Siberian semiprecious stone and set with diamonds for the amusement of the Czar.

He had doubts about committing all this to print, though he cavalierly recommended the process of autobiography (however ghostly) to his clients. Part of the problem was simply that there were two Lazars, one who set out to grab everything out of life that he wanted and succeeded, the other the later Lazar, friend to presidents, counselor to Pulitzer Prize–winning authors like McMurtry, sophisticated international *bon vivant,* the Lazar with the fake English accent and the Saville Row suits and the tiny, gleaming thousand-dollar Lobb shoes.

The great stories were about the first Lazar, but Lazar—and his loving, loyal, and long-suffering wife, Mary—were anxious to see that it was the second Lazar that saw print. For years Lazar wrote, dictated, tried one collaborator after another, trying to reconcile these essentially contradictory personalities, and rejecting each draft as it came closer to the truth—for the truth was that these two Lazars were one, had always been. Even as a tough, brawling street kid, using his fists against bigger guys, taking on Mafia hoods in speakeasies on behalf of his clients, getting stabbed (yes, a true story—read the book!), coming back for more, Lazar had always sought "class," recognized it, respected it, regarded it as the highest compliment he could pay others or receive himself. When he read the book I wrote about my family, *Charmed Lives,* Lazar called me and said, "It's a class act, kiddo," and I knew it was the highest praise he could give, even though Mary had probably read it for him.

But reconciling the two contradictory Lazars in one book was only part of the problem. The other was that at heart Lazar really believed that once he told his story—revealed himself at last in print—his life would be over. In a very real sense, he regarded his autobiography as a sentence of death—he would play with it, gathering endless boxes of notes, but the idea of *completing* it scared him.

In the end it was Mary's illness that finally turned him to completing a book that had quite literally been ten years in the writing. He had always expected that Mary, so much younger than he, would outlive him, but when he found that she was dying, he at last perceived his own mortality—which he had never, I think, truly believed in until then. He turned to his autobiography as a way of holding on to what little of life remained to him, and had the good fortune and good judgment to choose, as last collaborator, Annette Tapert, who had the patience, courage, and sympathy to transform, at last, Lazar's ever-growing collection of rejected drafts, notes, index cards, and correspondence into a book, or to be more precise, *the* book he had always talked about, but always pulled back from at the last minute.

Now it *was* the last minute, and Lazar knew it, so with the help of Annette, and the encouragement of friends like Larry

McMurtry and myself, he gave her—he gave us—his story, in his own words: *Swifty*.

We have chosen to call it *Swifty* deliberately. Lazar never used the nickname himself and allowed very few other people to. He was "Irving" to his friends, or "Lazar," but the admiring, affectionate nickname, invented by Bogart, stuck, much as Lazar disliked it. "Swifty" was the public man, the deal-maker *extraordinaire,* the host of his annual Oscar party, Olympic gold medal–class celebrity, and the story of that man is here. The story of the other one, "Irving," is here too—a far more sensitive, caring, and articulate man, who will be remembered by his friends, and always missed.

Still, Irving always enjoyed his public face. "Swifty" too was his own creation, and as his life slipped away, he enjoyed working on—and even reading—this book, with its hilarious, cutting-edge stories of the great and famous, and its sly self-revelations, in which the real man, sometimes with a roguish wink, sometimes with just the hint of a tear, appears. He would have had a great time promoting it, too, had he lived.

Lazar was not a philosopher, but he had a philosophy, which he shared with me before he died. "The way I see it," he said, "you get to do what you want to do and have a great life, then you have to die—that's the deal."

It was the best deal he could make, so he took it, with both hands.

—*MICHAEL KORDA*

Prologue

MY FRIEND Freddie de Cordova says I'm a legend and that I've been one for a long time. I say nonsense. Legends are dead, and I'm still kicking. But I know what he means. Every spring, for the last twenty years, I give a party on the night of the Academy Awards. I only invite friends and a handful of people I don't know but happen to admire. Can I help it that most of my friends happen to be stars and that the newcomers often arrive clutching Oscars?

Well, all that draws the press. It's gotten to the point that on the Oscar shows themselves, which are seen by millions of people around the world, there are jokes and references to "Swifty" Lazar's Oscar party at Spago. So outside of the movie and literary community I'm this "legendary superagent" who gives the party of the year.

I don't think of myself as that man. Nor do I see myself as an answer on "Jeopardy," or a clue in *The New York Times* crossword puzzle, or a little bald guy with over-sized eyeglasses in caricatures of so-called Hollywood celebrities. Do I like giving parties? Absolutely. I've been giving them for years, and if truth be told, I've hosted a number of parties far more glamorous and memorable than the event which so rivets the public on Oscar night.

But Hollywood isn't what it once was, and so my party is regarded as the year's high-water mark for insiders. You would think that in that case everybody would be on his or her best behavior. Not so. The first year Michael Jackson showed up, he had to hide in the ladies room because so many superstars were bugging him for autographs. Marvin Davis, the billionaire, was miffed when I told him to park his bodyguards outside. Director Michael Cimino insisted that he be served Cristal champagne, so I asked him if that's what he drank at home; when he admitted he didn't, I threw him out.

None of that annoys me as much as the people who think it's their right to come to my Oscar party and won't take no for an answer. One year, Michael Ovitz, who is a friend of mine and always gets invited, called me on behalf of some big-shot producer and asked why I wasn't including him.

"Because he's a bore," I said. "And boredom, in my view, must be avoided at all cost. I'm telling you, Mike, boredom is the single greatest threat to my continued existence."

Ovitz said he understood, but a few days later when I ran into him at a dinner, he had a proposition for me. "Irving, this guy is so rich," he said, "he'd give fifty thousand dollars to any charity of your choice if you'd just invite him."

"Not enough," I said.

"How about a hundred thousand?"

"Way too low."

"How about two hundred thousand?"

"Mike, he hasn't got enough money," I said. "The thing is, I just don't want him around."

I much prefer Ovitz's direct and businesslike approach to that of the movers and shakers who just show up uninvited. I remember one who not only crashed but compounded his rudeness by arriving at my black-tie party in an open-necked shirt and no jacket.

"Why are you here?" I demanded.

"I'm the head of ———," he said, naming a major talent agency. "I deserve to be here."

"How would you like it if I just appeared at your house and announced, 'Hi, I'm here for dinner'?"

"I hadn't thought of it that way."

"Well, why don't you?" I snapped. "And while you're at it, why don't you leave?"

What outsiders just don't understand about this party is that I go way back with almost everybody there. Jimmy Stewart, Gene Kelly, Kirk Douglas, Betty Comden and Adolph Green, Angie Dickinson, George Burns—I've known all of them for decades, and some for half a century. Michael Douglas, Liza Minnelli, Angelica Huston, Richard Zanuck—I met them when they were kids. Seeing them arrive at Spago with their Oscars, I feel almost like a parent. And I'm reminded of the long sweep of my own life.

Here's the thing. I've been an agent for almost sixty years. I've never handled actors—although many of them are friends, they're really a pain in the ass to represent and need constant reassurance that their stardom isn't fading—but I've represented some of the century's biggest literary and musical talents. How's this for a client list: Cole Porter, Noël Coward, Moss Hart, Irwin Shaw, William Saroyan, Truman Capote, Vladimir Nabokov, Larry McMurtry, Herman Wouk, Neil Simon, Richard Nixon, Edna Ferber, Alan Jay Lerner, Ira Gershwin, and I could go on.

I didn't just make deals for these people. They were my friends. Agents don't usually socialize with their clients, but I did all the time. In Hollywood and in New York, my business life was my social life. Because of this, being an agent became an adventure for me, a nonstop party. And I had the best seat in the house.

That's why this legend talk amuses me. I rode into Hollywood when stars still dressed for dinner and people gave glittering parties with no connections to charities or to political causes. I came to know the real legends, and I knew them in ways that the public never got to see. Along the way, I fashioned a life for myself that I'd always dreamed of—you could say I planned my own happiness.

Usually, when an octogenarian produces his memoirs, you get a story of adversity and struggle followed by success and wealth, with intermittent bouts of self-doubt and tragedy. You won't find that here. Nor will I bore you with the wisdom I've gleaned along the path. "How would you like to be remembered?" interviewers ask me. I just look at them and shrug. It's not about me leaving something of myself behind. People will think whatever they want, and no book is going to change that.

Ten years ago, when I first started gathering the material for this book, that might have been my motivation. But I'm eighty-six now, and I'm a little more mature. It's not about leaving a legacy. It's about sharing stories that have never been told about some of the greatest talents of our century.

You want to talk about a party, that's the real one.

At home in Los Angeles.

That's me on the left, next to Jimmy, followed by our mother, Stari, our father, Sam, then Murray, with Henry in front.

*Left, me at age twenty-four.
Below, on graduation from Brooklyn
Law School.*

CHAPTER

One

F YOU LOOK in *Who's Who,* you'll read that I was born on March 28, 1907, in Stamford, Connecticut. Only the date is accurate. I said I was born in Connecticut because that sounded classier to me. The truth is, I was born in a tenement on Houston Street on Manhattan's Lower East Side. When I was eight, my family moved to the Brownsville section of Brooklyn, another rugged neighborhood. And I now thank God that I wasn't born in a Yankee town and raised behind a picket fence.

A lot of people eradicate their roots to make themselves seem grander. I chose to reinvent myself a different way—by presenting my Mean Streets childhood as a great adventure, with characters so colorful you would have thought I was the Huck Finn of Brooklyn. The stories themselves were true. And the people were real. What I added was a new character: the narrator.

When I first went out to Hollywood and started representing playwrights of great culture and composers who were the ultimate in sophistication, I found myself at dinner parties that were light-years away from Brownsville. In those rooms, it didn't matter how much money you had, it was how witty and bright you were. I realized if I was going to run with this crowd,

I couldn't be just another 10-percenter. And so I packaged the stories of my youth until I established myself as a colorful raconteur.

I had a big repertoire of hilarious stories. How I learned to be tough because I was the smallest boy at school. How I became a dandy by observing the fancy clothes of the neighborhood gangsters. How I survived my rough-and-tumble days as a band-booker. How tiny me had a meteoric career as a soldier.

I took great care to make sure that all my stories had a common theme—the joke was always on Irving Paul Lazar. That self-deprecation served me well. In addition to being the person who could get unheard-of sums for his clients, I became known as a fun guy to have around, a life enhancer.

Were there times when I preferred to remember cool summers I had spent in lush Connecticut with my aunt and uncle? Many. It was during those childhood visits, in fact, that I learned about a more genteel life and began to aspire to it. And there were times, I admit, that I emphasized my summers and downplayed my winters. Those summers gave me a true sense of being an American. Unlike Brownsville, where Yiddish was the dominant language, in Connecticut you actually spoke English to everyone! But in the end, I always knew it was growing up in the tough world of Brownsville that made me who I am.

I know very little about the lives my parents left behind in Russia. Neither of them liked to talk about the past. I don't even know my father's real name, for surely he couldn't have been born in Vilna, Latvia, as Samuel Lazar.

What I do know is that around 1904, my father was drafted into the Russian Army and stationed at the German border. His job was to roll cigars for the officers. While rolling tobacco one day, he looked out of his tiny workspace and noticed that the guard wasn't there, so he slipped across the border and kept on going. He made his way to Hamburg and landed a job with a Jewish cigar merchant until he had saved enough money to get to England, where he bought a passage on an emigrants' boat to America.

And so he sailed to New York and became one of the two million other hopeful Jews to pass through Ellis Island (where his name was probably changed). Typically, he settled in the central immigrant hub: Manhattan's Lower East Side. To avoid the sweatshops where most of the refugees worked, my father stayed in the cigar business. Later, he apprenticed at a wholesale food market and learned the butter-and-egg business. When he'd put enough money aside, he sent for my mother, whom he had married in Russia when she was still only seventeen. In 1907, I was born. Three more sons—Murray, Jimmy, and Hank—would follow.

Of my first eight years on Houston Street, I remember nothing. Later, my parents told me of the noise, the unrelenting crush of humanity packed into cramped living quarters, push-carts that blocked every square inch of the street, and school classrooms so jammed that getting a seat was an achievement unto itself.

My childhood recollections begin after we crossed the East River. Like so many Jewish immigrant families, we moved to the Brownsville section of Brooklyn. Brownsville was supposedly a more inviting environment—wide streets, fewer people, and better housing. But like any community with rapid growth, the people who moved there brought much of what they hoped to leave behind. Soon enough, Brownsville became another version of the Lower East Side, only bigger; this small village that was considered the "country" at the turn of the century became the largest and most densely populated section of Brooklyn. Although there were gentile enclaves of Polish and Italian immigrants, Brownsville was 95 percent Jewish.

And not "desirable" Jews. Those were the German Jews who lived in Brooklyn Heights or Flatbush and had assimilated into American ways more readily. The German Jews wanted nothing to do with their Eastern European counterparts. To them, we were a lower class of Hebrew, poor and uneducated.

The German Jews were right about one thing—Brownsville was, in many ways, an unattractive place. The streets were dirty and crowded, and there was a constant clamor of sirens and police whistles, as fire engines and cops fought their way through a sprawl of junk shops, tinsmiths, stables, and garages. The residential areas were almost as grim; speculators had arrived there in the late 1890s and erected countless rows of dreary brick tenements. We were lucky—we lived in a Victorian-style, two-family wooden house on Osborne Street.

By Brownsville standards, this was the top of the heap. Although we were poor, we were—by the standards of the poor —middle-class. When we moved to Brooklyn, my father opened his own business as a wholesale distributor of butter and eggs and set up his store on the first floor of our two-story house.

I was taught from the moment I arrived that you had to be street-smart to survive—a lesson that I'd come to find was equally true in much grander neighborhoods. Like every other boy in the neighborhood, I was a street kid; I lived on the stoop, the roof, and the sidewalk. All social life was conducted in the streets. Every afternoon after school, I'd head for the corner candy store, where the older neighborhood "toughs" were always primed to fight another gang.

Guns, knives, and drugs didn't play a part in those days. What there was was needling, punctuated by a lot of pushing and shoving. It was always a question of who was more macho, with the big guys up front handling the negotiations about turf. A little guy like me stayed on the fringe, a safe place to be if you had to run, for you had a head start home. Even crossing your own street was more hazardous than Washington crossing the Delaware—the toughs were always waiting in the middle of the street, at the end of the block, lurking on the steps, suddenly appearing out of nowhere.

In Brownsville, you were in combat training from the day you learned to walk. By the time you were school age, street fights were a given. It was the Osbornes against the Stones, the Amboys against the Blakers. I hated it, but it wasn't as if I could say, "Excuse me, I don't want to fight today." There was no room for a sissy here. Being a shrimp, I was natural prey to begin with; if I'd ducked a fight, my life really would have been miserable.

I figured out early on that I could make my height work for me. What I learned was never to say "step outside" to a bigger fellow, otherwise I'd get creamed. Instead, because my prowess as a battler was unexpected, I'd catch my opponent unaware and deal him an unexpected blow. Even if he didn't go down, at least he was dulled. Then I'd run like a son of a bitch, and make sure I didn't surface for a couple of days.

Whether you were fighting or not, the whole relationship between guys was macho. Talk was rough and so were manners. Almost everyone had a nickname: "Izzie the Weasel," "Hymie the Pimp," "Joey the Hit Man." Then there were the slurs: "Hey, Jew-Boy!" or "Kike," or, if they really didn't like you, "Sheeney." Years later, I was reminded of this when Mohammad Ali threatened Joe Frazier on the morning of their great fight with "Coon, I'm gonna knock your block off!" After the fight, a reporter asked Frazier, "Weren't you annoyed when he called you 'coon'?" He said, "No, that's just ghetto talk." Well, that's all this was in Brownsville. Ghetto talk.

Of course, people didn't just talk. When you encountered a friend, "So, how are ya?" was met with a shove against the chest. It was necessary to return that shove, so you'd thwack the guy on the shoulder or the lapel and reply, "I'm great!" And stance! Now, that was all-important because if you didn't have your feet planted solidly, you'd get knocked over.

If we weren't fighting, we'd indulge in some hard physical play. A favorite was to line up twenty-gallon milk cans on their sides, get a running start off the curb, and try to leap over them. Some of the guys were agile enough to soar over four or five cans without getting hurt, but if you missed, you could count on getting your balls caught between the cans—now that was a wringer! In the summer, when we weren't playing stickball, we spent our days at the Betsy Head swimming pool. But as I grew older, the greater joy for me lay in exploring.

Brownsville was more like a New World version of an Eastern European *shtetl* than it was a ghetto. Yiddish was spoken at home and in the streets. I was so fluent that I was put on the stage of the Yiddish Theater to make campaign speeches for my father's lawyer, Emanuel Celler, who later became a distinguished member of Congress.

Having mastered the world of Osborne Street, I'd make forays. I visited dark Russian tearooms, smoke-filled from the Turkish cigarettes that the old regulars puffed. When I was nine, I remember a commotion outside the storefront at 46 Amboy Street, where Margaret Sanger had opened her first birth-control clinic.

And then there was Pitkin Avenue, Brownsville's main

thoroughfare. Nothing was more pleasurable for me than this mile-long walk, for Pitkin was Broadway and Fifth Avenue combined, with hundreds of stores displaying every imaginable consumer item in brightly lit showcase windows. If you had money, Pitkin Avenue was the place to shop. Rich or not, you had to speak Yiddish; if you didn't, you'd end up with the wrong size. Also on Pitkin Avenue were the theaters: the Loew's Pitkin, where you could see silent movies and vaudeville acts for eleven cents a ticket (the odd penny went to the war effort), or the Yiddish Theater, where my parents took me to hear Jacob Adler (the father of Stella).

If Adler was in a play, he was on stage all the time. And at the end of every one, he died. The green light would change to red, the red to blue, the blue back to green, and there would be Adler, still on the stage, still dying. One story about Adler that always amused me was that he'd induced some actress to sleep with him, only to have her hit him up for money. "Mr. Adler," she told him. "I need bread!" To which he replied, "Then fuck a baker. Fuck an actor, you get theater tickets."

Pitkin Avenue also offered food. When I started going to Broadway, I was always amazed at how the Jewish-American playwrights were able to capture my own upbringing so vividly in a brief line. In a Clifford Odets' play, for example, a character says, "Let's go eat Chinks." Now that's a phrase that would not have sounded exotic to anyone in Brownsville.

Jews are crazy about Chinese food—or least they used to be. And Pitkin Avenue was loaded with Chinese restaurants that served cheap and tasty fare, not the fancy sanitized stuff you get now. Today, if you order chicken chow mein, the waiters look at you with contempt. I once tried to order it at Mr. Chow's and was told they didn't serve it. "Why not?" I asked. "Because it's a middle-class dish," the waiter sniffed. If you want Chinese food like in the old Brooklyn days, Ah Fong in Los Angeles is the place. It's a total throwback. There you'll see Milton Berle, Don Rickles, Red Buttons, George Burns—they know the kind of food I'm talking about.

The best part of Pitkin Avenue for me was the delicatessens. Derma, marinated herring, stuffed sausage, pastrami, hot spiced corned beef on New York rye, stuffed kishke, chopped liver, matzo-ball soup—and, always, a pickle barrel to dip your hand in and fetch up the one you wanted. I could never understand why one pickle might be better than another, but I think the owners used to mix old soft ones with new crisp ones, hoping to move as many of the old ones as they could.

This food was expensive and not found in the regular grocery stores, so the big treat was to eat deli on Saturday night. We'd order hot dogs smothered with mustard and heaped with sauerkraut, and eat them standing up outside the store, savoring every bite. To us, that was Maxim's. Unlike Maxim's, though, this meal was inevitably followed by heartburn. That meant a trip to the drugstore for Dr. Brown's Celery Tonic.

Heartburn. There was a lot of that in our neighborhood, because even at home you were most likely eating stuffed cabbage. Buddy Hackett used to do a routine where he said that after he went into the Army and stopped having heartburn, he got scared: "I thought my fire had gone out."

Reading was my favorite pastime. To anyone who knows me, that last line will produce a lot of laughter—I'm famous for being the agent who doesn't read. But as a child, I did. It wasn't just pleasurable, it was also an escape from the neighborhood roughhousing. I was particularly partial to reading the dictionary. I could sit happily for hours and dissect all the large, wonderful-sounding words that would never be uttered in Brownsville. And, of course, I read biographies, especially the inspirational stories of Horatio Alger—books that reminded me I wasn't the only boy who dreamed of being rich and famous.

In the 1940s, Humphrey Bogart bet me that I couldn't get three deals for him in one day. When I did, he tagged me with "Swifty," a nickname that's followed me around ever since. What Bogie didn't know, however, was that I had *always* been in a hurry. That's how it was if you were brought up in Brownsville. Everything moved fast.

During the day the streets were bustling with comers, eager to make some sort of deal. The aggression you felt all about you was sheer volatile ambition. Everyone was trying to be his own boss. The idea that someone would *want* to work for anyone else was completely foreign; we all dreamed of getting out and being our own boss. Some, like Lepke and the Amberg Brothers, decided crime was the way to escape. For others, it was show business—in my era, Jews from the ghetto seized on that the way that many young African Americans today seize on athletics. As for me, the neighborhood groomed me from the very beginning to be some kind of wheeler-dealer.

A lot of my drive was inherited from my father. In order to make sure that his four sons would get a college education, he had two businesses. After distributing butter and eggs all day, he would put on a three-piece pinstripe suit, heavy gold pocket watch, and derby hat, and stroll over to the Saratoga Mortgage and Loan Company, a financial enterprise in which he and five other men were engaged.

These weren't banking hours, and this wasn't any ordinary bank. It was a loan-shark operation, but no one called it that. Every other block of the neighborhood had a Belmont branch in a corner of some store where you could borrow as much as fifty dollars. When the interest rate was quoted, the debtor might complain, "You didn't charge my friend that much!" If so, he'd get the loan for less. The threat of not being lent money again usually insured its being paid back within a week or two. But if it wasn't, "representatives" would be assigned to remind the borrower of obligations, and, if necessary, to cause him problems in walking or reaching for his knife and fork. These reps were the neighborhood toughs, and nobody would dare take them on then, or later, when they became famous as gangsters. Few borrowers defaulted. They'd return and say, "Look, I don't have it. We need to buy the kid a pair of shoes." So they'd repay ten dollars, but borrow another fifteen.

Around 1914, my father and his associates got a license and started storefront operations with teller's windows. But Saratoga's interest rates stayed high, and eventually the government informed them—by way of subpoenas—that they were in the usury business. My father's lawyer handled it so deftly that my father and his partners were not incarcerated, but the Saratoga Mortgage and Loan was forever closed.

I learned about entrepreneurship from watching my father operate his butter-and-egg business. As soon as I was old enough, I went with him to the Hudson Street Market on the Lower West Side of Manhattan to pick up the produce. This was my favorite adventure. My father owned three Auto-cars—frontless trucks with the motors underneath. There were usually two truckers and myself. As I was only thirteen, they would only let me drive part way to the market; then I'd help direct our driver into a momentarily freed space that other truckers were vying for. We'd jump out and load the crates of eggs and heavy tubs of butter.

Everyone was there for the same purpose and it wasn't "Boy-Meets-Girl Time." There were a lot of bashings; the truckers were recognizable hoodlums in their own fraternity, who wouldn't hesitate to pick up a hunk of wood from a crate and club you on the head. After the goods were stowed, I would extricate the unwieldy truck out of the path of scores of others, taking off with a screech. One driver would jump up front with me as the other directed us out of the traffic. When we got back to the store, the men would carry the cases of eggs into the candler, who carefully juggled three eggs in each hand in front of an electric bulb apparatus, checking for blood and black spots while my mother kept an eye on the drivers to make sure that they didn't steal anything.

Despite the harshness of his business, my father was worldly in his way: dapper, shrewd about people, quick with a joke. That was in public. At home, he was a no-nonsense guy who never had much to say. He didn't have to say much for us to know what would cause him to be annoyed. He never struck us, but we knew that he could lay it on if warranted, so we did as we were told.

Stari, my mother, was invariably good-natured. Unlike my father, she asked very little of her children. I adored her, and I was continually devastated by her poor health. She was a victim of high blood pressure complicated by diabetes—and in those days the only remedy was by injection. Because I was the eldest son, because she knew how much I loved her, and because I was her favorite, I was the one who had to administer the required two shots of insulin a day. She trusted no one else, so each day she'd hold out her arm, close her eyes, and tense with dread as I filled the syringe and looked for a vein.

Nothing in my parents' marriage can account for my decision not to marry until well after my fiftieth birthday. The only flare-ups I ever saw between them were when she found lipstick on my father's handkerchief. Although his neighborly assignations were always in the afternoon, my mother caught him. Every time. He'd promise to behave, but he was a virile man and women were attracted to him, so he felt compelled to give it a whirl.

There was no doubt, however, that my father loved my mother deeply. They never spent a night apart. They were always together working, shopping, and, with books under their arms, going off to night school together to improve their English.

Most of my Brownsville friends, despite their eagerness to leave some distant day, rarely ventured beyond the neighborhood. Not me. By the time I became a teenager, I was actively seeking opportunities to escape.

I began taking the subway to downtown Brooklyn to see vaudeville at the Bushwick or Albee theaters. I had one pal, Mickey Black, who'd come with me if he had the change. For twenty-five cents, we saw vaudeville's greatest stars. Who could resist Owen McGivney, the quick-change artist who would play all the roles in scenes from Dickens novels, flying through trap doors and windows and emerging a split second later in another original costume? Then there was Smith and Dale and their Avon Comedy Four, later immortalized by Neil Simon in *The Sunshine Boys*. And Harry Rose, who rushed on to the stage wearing his little straw hat cocked to one side and calling out, "Harry Rose sat on a tack. Harry rose!"—his opening line for thirty years. He'd rush out from offstage onto a platform over the orchestra pit that had been built just for him. One day the stagehands forgot about the platform, and Rose rushed out and landed smack in the pit, hurt too badly to get up. "Well," said the orchestra leader, looking down at him, "should I play your entrance again?"

The managers of the Keith-Albee circuit wouldn't allow a performer to change his act one iota. Because of that, I knew every vaudeville routine by heart. For Mickey and me, the real fun was that after we had memorized every gesture and inflection, we would mimic our favorites as we took the subway home. Gallagher and Shean, Buck and Bubbles—Mickey and I felt as close to these performers as if they were our very best friends.

I couldn't have found a better companion than Mickey, for he had a real live vaudevillian living next door. I thought he was very grand. Little did I know he would have looked odd any place but Brownsville. He wore wide pants, a black silk cravat, shiny pointed patent leather shoes, and long sideburns that he trimmed with a straight razor. He used to describe his exciting life in show business, embellishing his tale, I realize now, for himself as well as for us kids.

To these impressionable eyes, any performer was the height of sophistication—the theater and everything connected to it made it possible for me to dream of a bigger life. Even from my cut-rate perch in the balcony I gave equal attention to the actors and the denizens in the orchestra seats. On both stages, I learned a way of dressing, behaving, and talking that, taken together, could form what you might call a personal style. It was there that I became aware of the importance of looking like you belonged.

And so, when I was thirteen or fourteen, I started wearing a jacket, tie, and a freshly ironed shirt. My mother wouldn't let me have a clean shirt each day, so I'd wear it once, hang it up very carefully, and, the next morning, I would iron it out a little and put it on again. Soon I started washing my own socks and underwear so I could have fresh ones twice a day. By fifteen, I was wearing a kerchief in my breast pocket. And because I would have given anything to have been six feet tall, I wore tailored suits to look and feel taller.

I'll never forget the first time I went to a Broadway show. I stopped first at the local barbershop for a trim and proudly mentioned that I was going to the Plymouth Theater to see *What Price Glory?* The barber said, "Louis the Lug was here yesterday. Let me give you the same haircut." That meant a center part. I knew the fancy guys in Brownsville all had manicures, so I ordered one of those up as well. The manicurist not only buffed my nails but polished them to a high gloss.

What I remember most about that evening is not how great

the play was or that it was written by Maxwell Anderson, a future client, but how the people on either side of me in the second balcony nudged each other when they spotted me. It seems that when I put my hands on my knees, my nails shone in the dark.

Preposterous as I may have appeared to others, my look was part of my great undefined plan. Whether I realized it or not, I was looking for billing—I wanted to be a presence. And so I changed my name. My birth certificate says Samuel, but that must have been an accident; my father's name was Samuel, and as anyone who is Jewish knows, a son is never named after his father unless he's dead. The doctor who delivered me probably just heard the name in the house and wrote it down. I didn't like the name at all, and, at thirteen, I changed it to Irving—that sounded much more theatrical. My mother then told me that she had intended to call me Paul, so I adopted that as my middle name. Irving Paul Lazar. Now that had a classy ring to it.

No one else I knew was dressing up as I did. I got a lot of flak in the neighborhood for it; because no one could really relate to it, I became a loner. Except for Mickey, I had no close friends. This didn't bother me. I had my family, my biographies, and vaudeville. It also bothered me not at all that I knew no one when I transferred to Commercial High School—I chose it because it was a subway ride away, which got me out of Brownsville. Nor did I hesitate to run for class president.

People like to say there's a lot of luck in any success story. Not in mine. What happened to me later in life was no accident. I wasn't a shy child who suddenly emerged; I went after what I wanted. This self-confidence stemmed from the fact that I believed completely in the immigrant's dream of pushing hard, distinguishing yourself, and being rewarded. In the election for class president, for example, I figured if you gave the best speech you'd win. I did, and I did. Everything flowed from my awareness that if I upgraded myself, I'd find a place where I belonged.

That's why, despite my diminutive height, I wasn't shy around girls. In our neighborhood, girls were considered a nuisance. Still, we were curious about sex. You'd say to a guy, "Have you ever done it?"

"Yeah," he'd say.

"How do you do it?"

"I can't explain it," he'd reply with a shrug.

But when I was fifteen, I scored. Two sisters in their twenties who lived in a house across the street began inviting me over for soft drinks. One afternoon the three of us started tickling each other, and before I knew it I was in bed with my clothes off, being seduced. What really excited me was the black eyeliner and red lipstick they wore. I had never seen that before—not that I'd seen their other equipment.

With my virginity out of the way, I wasn't interested in pursuing the neighborhood girls. They dressed badly and they all had mustaches. Why girls from the ghetto had mustaches I don't know, but they did. Why I hated facial hair so much, I don't know, but I did.

My interest was in a girl I'd met at Commercial High. Her family had moved to Deal, New Jersey, a prosperous town of green lawns and gabled houses. When my father gave me a Chevrolet convertible on my sixteenth birthday, I had an escape route to a life that fit in perfectly with my social ambitions. The only glitch was that there was a lot of trouble with cars being stolen or tampered with, so I'd attach a string to the steering wheel, stretch it across the sidewalk, under the front door, and into her house, where I'd hold on to it. If anyone messed with the car, I'd feel the tug.

My biggest thrill came when this girl invited my brother Murray and me to a Saturday night dance at the local country club. We had never heard of a country club, but we knew it meant putting on our best suits and ties for the occasion. We didn't know how to dance—there were no dancing schools in Brownsville—so we just sort of hopped around. Other than Stamford, this was the only exposure we had to the high life and to people who were not only well-dressed and well-groomed, but who didn't use four-letter words or hit each other on the head! We had never seen people so genteel.

"I think they're all queers!" Murray whispered to me.

When we got home, we told our parents about the evening. My father had a matter-of-fact response: "That's the way it is in America." We started going to the country club regularly, and cottoned easily to this respectable way of life. Most of these evenings were spent near the refreshment table, drinking an orange-flavored punch that tasted like nothing we'd ever had before and seemed to make dancing so much easier. We didn't realize it was laced with vodka. Murray and I may have known about gang fights, but we were Jews from Brooklyn—and back then, just like the cliché that "Jews don't drink," we couldn't understand why we were getting sick only on Saturday nights.

The Brownsville of my generation brought forth more than its share of talented entertainers: Henny Youngman, Phil Silvers, Sam Levinson, and Danny Kaye. Impresario Sol Hurok was a Brownsville boy; and out of neighboring East New York came George and Ira Gershwin.

If there was one thing that my father impressed upon his four sons, it was the value of an education. His belief was that if you didn't go to college you'd miss your chance at the American dream. In fact, this maxim was true in most households. Immigrant parents were fixated on their children becoming professionals—occupations that would bring in money with some immediacy. And most immigrant sons tended to take their parents' advice: "Become a lawyer. You'll always make a living."

On the strength of that advice, I enrolled at Fordham University. A Catholic school was definitely an odd choice for a Jew, but I'd heard the Jesuits were great teachers and tuition was cheap. Best of all, classes were held only in the evening. Not only did that leave the afternoon free for a part-time job, but more important, I had established my lifelong habit of never rising before 11 A.M.

Classes were conducted on two floors of the Woolworth Building on lower Broadway. That was the campus, if you could call it that—no trees, pretty cheerleaders, or football games, just a lot of earnest kids trying to better themselves under the tutelage of stern Jesuit priests. Father Monahan ran the place. When we had elections for class officers, he held up my hand and said, "Let's elect this Jewish lad treasurer," which I happily accepted. Make what you will of that. It was 1925.

To help out with my expenses, I took a day job that luckily didn't require my presence in the morning—I joined the stenographers' pool at Guggenheim, Untermeyer and Marshall, a prestigious law firm. I'd wait for my number to appear on a sign and then march off to any one of the firm's 150 lawyers to take dictation. One day I got Samuel Untermeyer himself. When I turned in the brief he'd dictated, he asked for my name. "I'll call you again," he said gruffly, and he did—I became his personal stenographer.

Untermeyer was a famous trial lawyer who later became a Supreme Court judge. Taking dictation from him, I got a first-hand view of the agility of his mind and his superior intelligence. And what a dresser! He wore elegant dark suits with a fresh orchid in his lapel every day. I began emulating him by wearing striped, heart-fronted dickeys—starched inserts, simulating a shirt-front—with a separate stiff collar of the same fabric. I thought striped pants would work well with dickeys, so I wore them almost every day. For Sundays, I added a morning coat and spats. I must have looked like quite the dandy, or rather a concierge at Claridge's. When I had a date, God knows what the girl's parents thought. Even after buying these extravagant clothes, I had extra money to buy tickets for Broadway shows or see a star-studded bill like George Jessel and Eddie Cantor at the Palace. I bought cut-rate tickets for Edna Ferber's *Show Boat,* George and Ira Gershwin's *Lady Be Good,* the Marx Brothers in *The Cocoanuts,* written by George Kaufman, and I was lucky enough to see Noël Coward play the piano in *The Vortex.*

An idea began to percolate: somewhere along the line, I'd be involved in show business. I never imagined that two decades later I would represent the people whose talents I had so savored —Ferber, Gershwin, Kaufman—or that, many years later, Coward would write in his diary, "I've turned my affairs over to Swifty and I think I've done the right thing." The fact is, back then, I had no idea what it meant to be an agent.

After Fordham, I enrolled at Brooklyn Law School. Again, classes were held only in the evening; again, I ran for office the minute I arrived, and was promptly elected president of my class. I held that position for three years, but it proved much less important than a scheme that I hit on.

There was at that time a famous cram course for students who were about to take the bar exam. This professor had quite a business—approximately 1,500 students, mostly kids from the Ivy League schools, would pay forty dollars for his review sessions. At Brooklyn Law School, we had Jay Leo Rothschild, a renowned professor who had written several books on torts. No one had heard of Rothschild at the best Eastern law schools, but I knew this other professor couldn't handle everyone. So I went to Rothschild and proposed that I'd organize a cram course for him to teach.

Rothschild got me an office, and I did the rest, hiring reps at other local law schools and meeting with them each day to collect their cash. I charged Rothschild five dollars for each student I enrolled and paid my reps three dollars for every student they delivered—what the hell, they were doing all the work. Technically I had become an agent, with Professor Jay Leo Rothschild as my first client.

It was at Brooklyn Law School that an inside track to Broadway suddenly opened up for me, in the person of one Milton Pickman. We sat alphabetically in those classes, and Pick sat next to me. In my eyes, he was a real Broadway character; before law school, he had worked for Bernie Sobel, who was Florenz Ziegfeld's publicity agent. That connection was quite a thing; Pick could take friends backstage to the Follies or any of Ziegfeld's other shows.

Right off the bat, Pick introduced me to his friend, Pat Mann, an understudy in *Show Boat*. Well, that was spectacular! Since Pat could hardly thrive on his salary from the show, he moonlighted. He was a great raconteur and he played stag parties. I'd tag along and watch him tell a few dirty stories before the nude girls came on. It wasn't the big time, but at last I was behind the scenes.

All this was a lot more interesting than law, but I dutifully graduated from law school in 1931 and apprenticed for the obligatory year with the firm of Emil K. Ellis, one of the best private law firms in the city. From there, I did a dreary stint as an assistant district attorney, dealing mainly with pickpockets, small-time burglaries, assaults, and prostitution. I wasn't making much money and it didn't seem like I was going anywhere, so after four months I left and went into private practice, taking an office in the Flatiron Building on Twenty-third Street and Broadway, a singularly unattractive building, filled to the square inch with perhaps one hundred lawyers. Each one had a desk, a

phone, and a business card—credentials that impressed only the unknowing.

I specialized in foreclosures, an astute choice in 1932. It was fast, dirty work. A sheriff would phone me, and I'd rush off with him to preside over what was called "distribution of assets." Without warning, we would swoop down on some storekeeper, cobbler, or dressmaker at closing time and declare the city was locking his doors because the poor fellow had proved himself completely unable to save his business. Wives and children were always weeping in the background—it was a sad business.

And a crooked one. The next day, I'd show up to oversee the sale of assets, so the creditors would get at least a fraction of what they were owed. But by the time the sheriff, the conservator, and I took our cut, there was very little left for the creditors. Usually, in fact, there was nothing—the sheriffs were crooked, and there was a good deal of stealing.

By then, I was long gone. I took my fee, emptied my pockets onto my mother's kitchen table, and left it to her to deposit it in her account. When I needed money, I asked her for it—an arrangement that may seem strange. But I liked living with my parents and having my mother look after me. Even after my younger brothers began to marry and leave, I stayed on.

My mother took such good care of me that I was a very immature twenty-eight-year-old when she died. Her death was a horrible experience for me, not only because of the sudden and unexpected loss but because my father felt we should be at her bedside as she died. Her bewilderment and fright—the knowledge that she was dying, but couldn't communicate except through her eyes—was as terrifying to me as it was for her. When she died, I cried for the first time in my life, then ran out of the room to call Milton Pickman. I desperately needed to make sense of this, but I couldn't get out the words. I simply couldn't believe my mother had died.

For a while I continued to live at home, but when my father announced that he'd married the housekeeper, I figured enough was enough. I took a room at the Wyndemere, a service hotel at Ninety-second Street and West End Avenue. The second act of my life was about to begin.

CHAPTER

Two

FORECLOSURES were what I did during the day. But that lamentable labor was vastly eclipsed by my social life, which was revolving more than ever around Milton Pickman. By 1936, Pick had joined the Music Corporation of America, which was just beginning to organize its New York office. There were only about six other agents working there: Sonny Werblin, Willard Alexander, Manny Sachs, Lou Mining, Harold Hackett, and Billy Goodhart, who was a full partner with MCA's founder, Jules Stein.

It was because of Pick's new job that I got my first professional taste of show business. He told me about an MCA client, a juggler, who had refused to pay commission for a booking. Now the agency was suing. MCA had its own lawyers, of course, so I convinced the juggler to let me represent him. When I won the case, Sonny Werblin decided it would be better for business if I'd represent MCA in the future.

Pick also introduced me to Ted Lewis, vaudeville's highest-paid entertainer and an MCA client. What started out as a social relationship ended up becoming a professional coup when his wife, Adah, asked me to be the family lawyer.

Lewis started out in Circleville, Ohio, where he demon-

strated instruments in a local music store. In 1917, he achieved a huge success with his clarinet and a five-piece band at Rector's, one of New York's swankiest jazz joints. Lewis was so intimidated by the swells that he looked coyly at the audience and asked, "Is everybody . . . happy?" The place broke up, and Lewis had his signature line.

One night toward the end of that same engagement, Lewis walked onstage with a top hat, and again everybody laughed. They recognized the hat as belonging to a cab driver named Sippi —short for Mississippi—who parked in front of Rector's every night, and they laughed even more when Lewis told the audience he'd won it from him in a crap game. That too became part of his act, along with his showstopper, "Me and My Shadow," with a black dancer named Eddie Chester acting as the shadow.

For me, the real show was at Ted Lewis's sprawling apartment at the Majestic on Central Park West, where Adah ran a salon. There you found the great Jewish mafia of vaudeville: Jack and Mary Benny, the Eddie Cantors, George Burns and Gracie Allen, Joe E. Lewis, and Sophie Tucker. Once Pick introduced me, I became the other extra man.

On one hand, I was dazzled—I was twenty-nine years old, just getting my feet wet in the agency business, and here I was hobnobbing with my childhood idols. On the other hand, I was so completely at home that I would perform for them the routines I'd memorized as a kid. Jack Benny roared at my rendition of his early performances: fencing with his violin bow, taunting the orchestra leader, engaging him in duels with his baton.

Most of the time, though, I was content just to listen and watch. Ted would play his clarinet, Sophie Tucker might sing a song she was about to introduce, or Eddie Cantor might spin a great tale. They had so much in common, and what they shared most is that they were all divorced from the mainstream of life.

One night Adah went to see Henny Youngman, an obscure stand-up comedian at a club on Fifty-second Street. As a warm-up act, he had rocked the joint at a benefit a few nights earlier at Madison Square Garden. Afterward, he told Adah he needed an agent. "Talk to Lazar," she said. "He'll take care of you."

When I met Henny, he told me that Ted Collins—a resourceful radio producer who guided Kate Smith, then one of America's top attractions—wanted to meet him. He didn't know how to handle it. I was new at this game, but I realized I had a live one in Henny. I said, "I'll go with you." Meeting Ted Collins was a big deal for me, too.

Collins wanted to sign Youngman for thirteen weeks on Kate Smith's show, starting immediately. "What commitments do you have?" he asked. "Just a moment—I'll see," Henny said. And he started pulling little bits of paper from every pocket of his coat and trousers. It turned out he was heavily booked for Bar Mitzvahs, weddings, and other one-nighters, some for twelve dollars a date, some for twenty, no more—the guy was so busy, he was really unavailable to go on Smith's hit show. Collins, who was a very shrewd fellow, said, "Let's pay these people off. They can get someone else." And that's what we did.

Now that I had my first real client, I had to build his career. Collins wanted to hire some good writers for Henny, so I looked around. I found Izzie Ellinson, an important contributor of one-liners to Walter Winchell's column, and Joe Quillan. They had just written a radio show that had scored quite a hit as Eddie Cantor's summer replacement. Cantor wasn't crazy about someone else putting up big numbers in his time slot, but was astute enough to want these fellows to write his show.

Fortunately for me, I met them and turned them into clients a day before Cantor's agent—Abe Lastfogel, of the William Morris office—told Pick that he was looking for them. Would they go to Los Angeles to meet Eddie Cantor? "Certainly," I told Lastfogel, realizing that these guys could make much more writing for Cantor than for Henny. "But William Morris has to spring for three round-trip tickets."

Lastfogel asked, "Who's the third fellow?"

I said, "They won't go without me."

That's how I got to California for the first time.

Meeting Eddie Cantor was a remarkable encounter. He was living in a beautiful English Tudor mansion on North Roxbury Drive in Beverly Hills. When I arrived, the butler asked me to go right upstairs as Mr. Cantor was expecting me.

Indeed, he was, and in a darkened room. His backside was the only thing I could see that resembled Eddie Cantor. Only after he emitted a succession of groans did I realize he was stretched out nude, being massaged. He occasionally lifted his head as he kept up a running monologue about his greatness. It took a while for me to slip in a word about these two talented writers.

"What do you do—write with them?" he asked.

"No, I'm their agent."

"What do I need you for?"

"Because of me, you got them."

"Well, thanks for coming to see me," he said, beginning and ending his relationship with me. "Tell the fellows to report to my office tomorrow morning at eleven o'clock."

The boys and I shared a two-bedroom suite—our idea of heaven—at the Knickerbocker Hotel on Vine Street in Hollywood. On Friday nights, when they got paid, I cashed the check, brought the money to the hotel, and divided it into two neat stacks, taking 10 percent from each. It was a solemn ritual.

I didn't drink, but Ellinson did a pretty good job of it, and Quillan was even better. On Friday nights, they'd send out for a case of champagne; it lasted a day or two. While fueled, they had a good deal of fun at my expense—apparently, they had never met anyone fastidious before.

I concede that I would spend a half an hour just in deciding the right combination of shirt and tie. I still wore dickeys which, though old-fashioned, continued to strike me as stylish in the extreme. One evening, Quillan and Ellinson placed a dozen or so of these shirt-fronts on the living room floor, then called me in. "What did you do that for?" I yelled. "Now I have to send them out to be laundered!" They explained that they wanted me to have an "overview" of the shirts and be able to choose one quickly without having to look through all of the drawers.

I had an old friend in California in the person of Mickey Strange. He had been a fellow assistant district attorney and was now working as a criminal lawyer; as a result, he knew a gambling fraternity. Knew them well, in fact—Mickey represented the owners of the Clover Club on Sunset Boulevard.

The Clover Club was practically a Hollywood institution. Moguls and stars went there to play for especially high stakes. I went to look, and, maybe, place a small bet. But the crap games and chemin de fer were out of this world: ten thousand on the line, ten thousand back of the line. I stood in the corner with my hundred dollars in chips and timidly placed it on "don't pass," figuring that if they were going to get anybody it couldn't be me.

"Put it on the pass line," whispered a gravelly voice with a bit of an English accent. He sounded so authoritative that I did as he said. David Selznick made seven on the opening throw, doubling my money for me.

"Keep it there and take the odds," the guiding voice urged. I followed his directions for about four rolls. Then he said, "Take your money away." I did, turning from the table with five hundred dollars in chips. "You owe me twenty percent," said the man, who, I now saw, was imperious-looking and impeccably dressed. I gave him one hundred dollars and asked his name.

"Prince Michael Romanoff."

This encounter began a friendship that lasted thirty years.

I looked around while I was in California, and saw that it really was the land of opportunity. This was 1936, remember, long before MCA came to the West Coast and ran the agenting business like a business. There were only individual agents. I felt I might do well here—particularly if I could affiliate with a classy guy like Leland Hayward, the first agent to bring eminence to a profession in which the practitioners were generally called flesh-peddlers and hustlers.

Hayward came from a distinguished family, had attended Princeton, was handsome and well-dressed. When I saw the picture in *The New York Times* of him attending some fancy ball, I thought, "That's the kind of agent I'd like to be." I *had* to meet him, so, sans appointment, I went to his office, which as I expected was a stylish building, with a stylish secretary who explained he couldn't see me but asked if I would return the following day.

The next afternoon, I was shown into Hayward's antique-filled office, where he was sitting at a large oak table, devoid of papers. I found this surprising, as he was one of the town's busiest agents, representing such stars as Greta Garbo, Katharine

Hepburn, and Fred Astaire. But Hayward seemed easygoing and
confident—he greeted me as if he had all the time in the world.

I explained why I was in California, that I wanted to become
an agent, that I admired him. At length, I got to the point:
more than anything else, I wanted to work for him. Hayward
explained that there was no place in his office for me at that
moment. Still, he thought I should meet his associate, John
Swope.

I knocked on Swope's door. No one answered, so I hesi-
tantly entered. No one was there. But the window was open,
with a head peering over the sill from the outside, steadying a
camera—Swope was photographing me. "Sit down behind the
desk, stand up, walk to the door," he ordered, before I'd said a
word. I thought this was fairly strange behavior, but he was so
totally Ivy League and high-bred that I went along with it. Even
his rejection—he said I should get back in touch with them after
I had gained more experience—was elegant.

"I don't think I'm going to represent MCA much longer as
a lawyer," I told Sonny Werblin when I returned to New York.
"I'm being paid one hundred dollars a week to be Ted Lewis's
lawyer while MCA is earning ten percent of ten thousand dollars
a week. I think I'm going to California and try my luck as an
agent."

Werblin, the classiest agent around Broadway, stopped me
cold. "If you want to be an agent, don't go to California," he
said. "Stay in New York and work for MCA. I'll run the ball
with you and you'll learn fast."

Having Sonny as a mentor sounded good to me, and you
couldn't do better than MCA. About twelve years before, Jules
Stein was a medical student in Chicago who played fiddle in jazz
bands to earn his tuition. But medicine was too time-consuming.
Rather than cut back on his engagements, he hit upon the notion
of having other bands take his place. These bands were happy to
pay him a modest commission, Stein was free to do his medical
work, and the profits began to mount up—by 1926, Stein had
decided to give up medicine and form the Music Corporation of
America.

The company remained based in Chicago, where Stein ran

The original MCA staff. I'm on the right at the bottom.

it. The New York office was run by Billy Goodhart, who had an ice tong for a tongue and reverence for no one. Four-letter words, bitter denunciations, and threats were his common verbiage. He was a little man, five feet three, and a hunchback. All his energies were focused on profit. He'd be in the office by eight-thirty in the morning, often trying to get into your desk and see what you were doing. Everyone resented him, but because the pay was good and there weren't many alternatives, everybody stuck it out.

As well as handling singers, I was, at Jules Stein's direction, to begin MCA's representation of actors. Goodhart hated the idea (but then, he hated everything about Stein). To him, actresses were tarts and actors were bums. If he'd had his way, MCA would continue to handle only orchestras and singers.

Goodhart had a point. He had lined up key hotels as a circuit for MCA's bands, and insisted the hotels let MCA book exclusively for them in return for getting top talent. The bands, in turn, were asked to sign exclusively, too. Then MCA booked the bands into hotels for one-night stands. This was a shrewd way to earn double commissions. More important, it prevented hotels from making season-long bookings that paid the bands less money and made the hotels (and the bands) less dependent on MCA. As a result, MCA now represented more than half of America's major jazz bands, including those of Benny Goodman and Ted Weems. And when the agency signed Guy Lombardo to an exclusive contract in 1928, it gained a lock on the best hotels in Manhattan—and beyond.

Music was a fantastic business for MCA, much bigger than the stage could ever be. A band would play Hershey, Pennsylvania, finish at midnight, get on the bus, and be off to play Scranton the next night. When Tommy Dorsey, Harry James, Gene Krupa, and Benny Goodman were playing these dates—earning five thousand dollars a night and paying their own expenses—MCA would collect five hundred in commission. Here I was, booking some actor for sixty bucks. Clearly, it made sense for me to get as far away from actors as I could.

Goodhart was only too happy to let me book bands. His other agents had the big hotels sewn up, but no one was booking nightclubs from upstate New York to Florida, and west as far as Cleveland. And MCA had no connection with the Mob-connected clubs on Fifty-second Street. Goodhart and his team only knew a lot of fancy-pants guys running the hotels.

In my college years, I had discovered Harlem, and nights when I wasn't walking around Broadway, I would take the A-train uptown and hang around the Harlem clubs. Handling musicians I admired would be a joy, not work—even though I'd have to put up with the mercurial personalities of each bandleader and ingratiate myself with the nightclub owners.

Goodhart drove us like a drill sergeant; we'd do all the preliminary work, and then he'd step in and close the deal. He liked to pit one man against the other. If you didn't return with the contract for a deal that you had described to him as a possibility, he'd send—unbeknownst to you—another agent to contact the same customer.

Which is what happened with one of my first gigs, a one-nighter for Hal Kemp and His Orchestra at the Astor Roof.

Goodhart asked me, "Have you gotten a signed contract yet for Kemp?" I said, "Not yet, but I'm pretty sure to get it this afternoon." He said, "Forget about it." Well, I was fit to be tied because I knew I had the deal and didn't want anyone else to close it. Not only would it be an affront to me, but it also would disturb my relationship with the club owner. I knew that Goodhart was going to send Manny Sachs up there, but all I needed was one more hour with the owner and I'd close the deal.

So I said to Manny, "I'm having trouble with the owner of a hotel in Philadelphia. Why don't you go down with me, and you can see your family while you're there? I'll come back tonight, and you can come back tomorrow." He thought that was a great idea.

Off we went to Philly. While we were having a drink, I left the table and asked the waiter to deliver a note I had scribbled: "Dear Manny, I just called the office and I have to get back right away. Can't say good-bye. Please excuse me. I'll see you tomorrow." As the waiter delivered the note to the bewildered Sachs, I was rushing for the train to New York. I ran over to the Astor Roof, had the owner sign the contract I'd been carrying in my coat pocket, and was back in the office before five o'clock.

I slammed the contract on Goodhart's desk. "*Now* are you happy?" I asked.

"I thought you were in Philadelphia," he snapped.

"I was."

"Where's Manny?"

"Still in Philly."

Well, he started to laugh. He got the gag and it was a momentary victory.

The competition was fierce wherever I went. If I wasn't up against my own guys, I was up against GAC—the General Artists Corporation, our main rival. They had Jimmy Dorsey, we had Tommy. Like us, they tried to talk places into booking exclusively with them, and they tried to beat us by selling under scale.

Once I was up in Albany trying to sell a combo, and I was staying at an old-fashioned hotel that had transoms above the doors. A GAC agent who stood six feet three inches and weighed 250 pounds, heard about me and decided he had to take action. While I was out, he climbed over the transom, found my suitcase with all the photographs of bands I was pitching, and simply ran away with them!

I wouldn't have climbed through any transoms to steal a book, but I wasn't above making the other guy look bad in a club owner's eyes. Like the time I stopped by a summer resort in New Jersey to book an act, and the owner said, "Geez, you're too late. Abby Gershler was here, and I got a break. He gave me the Nicholas Brothers."

"How many did you get?" I asked.

"What do you mean?"

"There are three of them, but sometimes one of the guys doesn't show up, you know? He's a very irresponsible fellow."

Naturally, when the two Nicholas Brothers showed up, the club owner bellowed, "So where's the third?"

"There is no third," they told him.

"You're lying!"

It was a big beef, and the club owner never bought an act from that agent again. I guess it was a dirty trick, but so what? We were all living by our wits. This was dog-eat-dog, and either you got the scratch or you were out of business.

Later, as GAC was going under, I heard an amazing rumor that turned out to be true: Jules Stein was secretly keeping his rival afloat with MCA money, in order to create the appearance of competition and not bring the government down on MCA for being monopolistic. Long after the dust had settled, I asked Stein about it. A bit sheepishly, he admitted it had been true.

The heart of the club circuit was one city block of Manhattan: Fifty-second Street between Fifth and Sixth avenues. A decade before, it had been a street of speakeasies. The five-story brownstones that lined either side were perfect for that, and Mayor Jimmy Walker had allowed the street to be commercially zoned, in part to compensate for Rockefeller Center, which was going up nearby and displacing honest businesses. After the Crash, more and more once-rich families on the street found they liked the rents they could get from bootleggers. And with sociable gentlemen like Jack and Charlie Kriendler of the "21" Club running the speaks, it almost seemed respectable.

You heard jazz in the speakeasies sometimes, but it was

pretty impromptu—a couple of players gathering around the piano to play Dixieland. It wasn't until the repeal of Prohibition, in late 1933, that speakeasies could become legitimate clubs and start attracting the kind of crowds that brought in enough money to pay first-rate bands. For musicians, it was a natural. Some would wander over from the nearby radio studios of NBC and ABC, where they'd just done live broadcasts, and jam with each other for drinks and tips. For black musicians who'd spent the last decade playing Harlem clubs, Fifty-second Street was worth the trip; it was their one ticket to fame and money.

I was getting into the band-booking business just as Fifty-second Street crested (which was how I'd catch other waves later on). I'd start on my rounds at noon, stopping in on club owners, trying to pitch them one of our clients. Nothing looks so dreary or as fetid as a nightclub at midday, especially a second- or third-rate one, with its chairs stacked upside down on the tables and a busboy pushing a broom around.

I did my best work on days when the weather was bad. The club owner would be sitting in his office, glumly looking out the window at the rain or snow, knowing he had a long and unprofitable night ahead. "What the hell are you doing out in this weather?" he'd say, but I knew he was flattered that a cheerful, enterprising band booker was seeking him out.

"Hey, a little rain can't keep *me* away," I'd reply. "Besides, it's a good time to talk."

I made a lot of sales that way.

Art Tatum, Erroll Garner, Fats Waller, Dizzy Gillespie, Maxine Sullivan, Jimmy Lunceford, Count Basie, Louis Prima, Tommy Dorsey, Artie Shaw, Harry James, and Chick Webb were just a few of the artists who were working on "the Street." And for a fellow like me who idolized them, to be paid to hear them, to talk to them, to book them, was bliss—I was almost in a state of ecstasy hearing them. I knew many of their arrangements by heart. I waited for certain solos and knew where the riffs were.

We had quite an operation. Willard Alexander, Manny Sachs, Sonny Werblin, and I were out there signing these bands. Talk about the Gang of Four, we worked day and night. There was no letup. It was hustle and muscle all the way.

We wouldn't have done so well if we didn't have "Shitheel"

The only one in this crew who really knew music was Larry Clinton, the bandleader. I know I didn't, and I don't think Milton Pickman did either (he's the one in the hat). We did, however, know girls.

Goodhart exhibiting the kind of toughness that was more typical of a Frank Costello than an agent. No one but Billy could cope with Tommy Dorsey, the epitome of the superstar who became too big for his britches. Dorsey was feeling his oats at the time because he was appearing with Frank Sinatra at the Paramount Theatre—a formidable duo. Tommy told me that he was being wooed by other agencies. Naturally, every carrot stick was more and more enticing. So he wanted out of his contract with MCA.

"Tommy, the only one who can give you a release is Goodhart," I said. "Tell him what you're telling me. It will be more convincing coming from you than from me."

"Okay," Tommy said. "I'll be there tomorrow at eleven before the first show at the Paramount."

Everybody in the office was primed for this confrontation. I waited at the elevator for Tommy, who arrived with his lawyer and one of his buddies. I escorted them to Goodhart's office. Billy was sitting on the edge of his desk, facing the door. Dorsey never got a chance to open his mouth.

"Tommy, if you continue this bullshit, making everybody miserable, you see these balls?" Goodhart began, bending over and grabbing his own groin. "I'm gonna cut yours off. Not only won't you be working for MCA, you won't be working for anybody else for maybe the rest of your life. You have something to say, put it in writing. Now get the fuck out of here—you irritate me."

Dorsey was thrown for such a loss, he turned to his people and said, "Let's get out of here." We didn't have any more trouble with him for a time, and he became much easier to manage.

Booking hotels was almost genteel compared to what you went through working with clubs. Every last one of them was owned, directly or indirectly, by the Mob. You needed entrée. For me, that meant cutting a deal with an independent agent named Willy Sherman, who was kind of a gangster's pet.

I suggested to Sherman that since MCA had the bands and he had the connections, we should do business together; he'd get half the commission, or thereabouts. Sherman liked that idea because I went a little further and gave him a guarantee of at least ten thousand dollars a year.

I never told Sonny about this arrangement. I figured it would work out, and, luckily, it did. I wouldn't have wanted to think about failure in this case. Sherman had numerous ways of breaking your arms and legs, all learned from past masters.

Life with Willy Sherman was a little dangerous, but you met a lot of interesting people. One night, for example, he said, "Let's check on some clubs in Philadelphia. I'll drive. Do you mind if my brother-in-law comes along?"

That was fine with me, so we went by Lindy's to pick up this guy, who slipped silently into the back seat, a grey fedora covering his face. I couldn't get a word out of him. Not a peep!

Finally, I turned to Sherman. "Willy, what's the matter with him? Doesn't he talk?"

"Nah," Willy explained. "He's kind of a shy guy."

When we got to Philadelphia, the gray fedora got out and disappeared. Sherman and I made our rounds, and headed back to New York about midnight. At 2 A.M., I picked up an early edition of the *Daily News*. The headline read: "MAN IN GRAY FEDORA KILLED." The story revealed that an unidentified man who had sold cocaine to musicians had been whacked getting out of a taxi in Philadelphia.

It didn't occur to me that the coke dealer was Sherman's relative until two FBI men came into Lindy's looking for us the next night. Before I knew what was happening, we were handcuffed together and marched over to the Forty-eighth Street precinct for questioning. I told what I knew and was released. Sherman said that he didn't know anything either, but they tied him into the crime somehow and he actually served time.

Another Mob favorite was Taps. He was getting on in years, and he liked it that I not only split commissions with him but covered his beat so he could turn in early. One day Taps told me about a kid in Havana who sang and played drums: "I hear he's great. He looks and moves wonderfully. Let's pay for his transportation and bring him over."

MCA could afford that, so we brought Desi Arnaz over and booked him into a little club. He was a big hit, he was very good-looking, he could sing well—nice assets to have in the middle of a vogue for Latin bands. It was the era of Enric Madriguera, and the king of the Latin bandleaders, Xavier Cugat. It was also, if I may say so, the era of Irving Paul Lazar, because you couldn't book a Latin band for a hotel without coming to me—I had just about signed up everybody who had a pair of bongo drums.

Sometimes you book people, other times you invent them. That happened to me when I crossed paths with Monte Proser. He was an old-time press agent who wore black-framed glasses with very thick, round lenses through which he could barely see, but he didn't have to see well—he knew how to get a buck.

Monte thought that Don the Beachcomber's in Hollywood

was a terrific spot: lots of bamboo, a fake thatched-straw ceiling, water dripping onto tin to make you think you were in a jungle, and drinks like Zombies and Missionary's Downfall that could turn your brain to mush in record time. He decided to open a Beachcomber-type spot on Broadway and serve those violent drinks. With a twist—he'd advertise one per customer. If a guy could handle a second, it was on the house.

Not long after the place opened, Monte realized atmosphere wasn't everything. "I need a Hawaiian band," he told me.

"I've got a fellow who is sensational," I said, not missing a beat. "His name is Johnny Pineapple."

Monte said, "I love the name. Get me that band."

Well, I had a small combo at the Lexington Hotel that could play any kind of music.

"What's your name?" I asked the leader.

He told me.

"No, it's not," I said. "Your name is Johnny Pineapple, and tomorrow you audition for Monte Proser."

He didn't care what they called him. He'd only been getting scale at the Lexington. He got almost twice as much from Monte —and quite a run as Johnny Pineapple and His Orchestra.

In the early days, there was a place called the Club Abbey on the first floor of a hotel on Fifty-third Street. Gangster money had put the place together—one of the owners was Dutch Schultz. I gave this place first-class attention.

The afternoon before Henny Youngman opened at the Abbey, I prudently suggested that we go there and check the acoustics. As we waited for the band to finish rehearsing, we sat at the bar, which was deserted except for the bartender and one other chap.

At last, Henny made his way to the stage. He was just starting to go into his routine when two men burst in the front door, bearing machine guns. I fell to the floor. The bartender ducked. And the gunmen proceeded to mow down the chap two stools away from me with so many bullets that the back of his coat looked like an imported Swiss cheese. Henny and I made a beeline for the door, and went over to Lindy's.

"Do you think I ought to open tonight?" Henny asked.

A reasonable question.

"You *gotta* open tonight," I said. "They're expecting a big crowd."

We weren't at Lindy's long before detectives arrived. They questioned Henny and let him go, but they took me into custody because I said I had seen the guys with the machine guns. When they asked me for a description, I thought it was wise not to recall too much about a man I vaguely knew as "Nigger" Harris. The incident took care of itself; I didn't see the killer again for fifteen years, until Zeppo Marx innocently introduced us as we sat by the pool of the Flamingo Hotel in Vegas.

When he left, I had a question for Zeppo: "What's that fellow's name again?"

"Harold Smith."

"Any possibility he used to be 'Nigger' Harris?"

"He might have been," Zeppo said noncommittally.

For all my street smarts, I was so naive I once asked Nicky Blair if the Mob bothered him.

"No," he said.

It wasn't until later when we became friends that I discovered he *was* the Mob!

Blair ran the Paradise, the Mob's favorite hangout in New York. I liked to stop by for the 2:30 A.M. show. The public wasn't there for that one, but the insiders sure were. It was a short show, nominally intended to get some people in and sell some booze, but really for the gangsters who rolled in to pick up the dancers.

I first met Frank Costello at the Paradise. I know the books say he was a killer and the head of the Mafia in New York, but to me, he was a mild-mannered gent. When I talked to him about the Copa, in which he had an interest, he couldn't have been nicer. If I was with a girl, he would be extremely polite and ask, albeit in a gruff voice, "What would the little lady like to drink?"

If you booked these clubs long enough, you were bound to be on the receiving end of a love-pat from someone like Three Fingers Brown, Tommy Luchese, Frenchy Demange, or—my personal nemesis—Longy Zwillman. I entered his orbit in a roundabout way. There was a place in New Jersey called the Meadowbrook, which was a big spot of our rival, General Artists Corporation. GAC had Jimmy Dorsey and several other orchestras playing there, but I always had high hopes of cracking the club, and the owner, Frank Daley, always encouraged me to come out and have dinner and tell him about my bands. He never told me he had an exclusive contract with GAC. He was a beast.

While I was driving back to the city from the Meadowbrook one day, feeling like a sucker, I passed a place called the Chicken Coop. It was well-named. What I didn't know was that Longy Zwillman, the Mafia kingpin in New Jersey and one of the most feared gangsters for two decades, not only liked it that way but made his headquarters there.

I walked into this dreary place, which resembled an old Warner Bros. movie set, and asked the barman if I could see the owner. He gave me a look you wouldn't want to meet on a clear day on Fifth Avenue, let alone in a dilapidated, cheerless establishment like the Chicken Coop.

"What do you want to see the boss about?"

"Well, I'd like to put a big band in here to compete with the Meadowbrook."

"What kind of big band?"

"Tommy Dorsey or Harry James."

The heft of those names obliged him to announce my presence to Longy. He went upstairs, returned, and said, "Okay, the boss will see you."

Upstairs I found Longy, a tall, skinny guy, sprawled out on a brass bed with three or four guys standing around. I told him my plans. I felt that, with Sonny Werblin's help, I could ask Harry James to do us a favor and go in for a week or two at scale, between bookings. So I told Longy that if he would let me put in air-conditioning and fix up the place, I'd open with Harry.

His eyes widened. "Okay, kid. Go ahead."

This was too easy. "Don't you want a contract?" I asked.

"I don't need a contract. If you don't do it, I'll break your ass."

We put in air-conditioning, gave the place a facelift, and

tried to shake up the help so it didn't look like a hoodlum joint. Before you knew it, the place was jumping with Harry James and, in subsequent weeks, with other hot bands.

Then Goodhart said to me, "Listen, give Zwillman a smaller band. So far, we're losing money."

"Who've we got?"

He said he had a guy named Lang Thompson, who was then playing at the Village Barn. And he told me to ask for two thousand dollars a week for the two weeks. I went back to Longy and dutifully told him he was getting a great band the next week in Lang Thompson. "Fine," he said. He didn't know the name, and he didn't care. He was relying on my judgment.

Lang Thompson opened, and the place died. Now it was a fancy empty club, instead of an empty dump. I didn't know that Longy was pissed until I dropped in one evening and the bartender said, "The boss wants to see you upstairs." I went up. There was Longy—and six of his friends.

"How much are you charging us for Lang Thompson?" he began.

"Two thousand a week."

"What did he get at the Village Barn?"

"He must have gotten two thousand, because Goodhart told me that's what he'd have to get here."

With this, two of the boys got up and held my hands behind me. Then one of the other guys hit me so hard that I doubled up. The only reason I straightened up was because he next gave me a shot to the jaw.

"Never lie," Longy said, leaning in close. "Thompson got a thousand at the Barn. This gives you an idea of what'll happen to you if we catch you in another lie."

A week later Zwillman called and said, "Come out here. I want to talk to you."

I said, "I'm going to get hit again."

"No, you're not. Just come out and talk to me."

I went out there and he said, "Why did you lie to me?"

"I didn't lie. Billy Goodhart told me the band got two thousand dollars there and that's what they'd have to get here."

He repeated that Thompson had only gotten one thousand. I suggested he tell that to Goodhart. Longy liked that idea.

"Tell him I'll be in to see him tomorrow morning."

I was sitting in Goodhart's when Longy and his entourage arrived. "You'd better leave me alone with these fellows," Goodhart said. "I'll take care of them."

I assumed that Billy would be pretty tough. What really happened, Longy told me later, is that Goodhart cringed and said, "I'm going to fire this kid for lying to you." At which point, Longy said, "If he gets fired, you're not going to be in this office two hours later. You'll be in a road or in a riverbend. Don't talk to me about firing the kid. You're a fucking liar, and I want him back booking the Chicken Coop."

They left. I went back to see Goodhart. He was quaking. He didn't dare tell me why.

Even the biggest stars weren't immune from the hands-on relationships with the Boys. In fact, they were lucky if they were only threatened and humiliated. That's what I kept telling Sammy Kaye, one of the biggest stars of the big-band era.

One night after Sammy finished his stint at the New Yorker, I suggested we stop by the Famous Door. We walked in and Frenchy Demange was there. Frenchy's idea of fun was to bang two heads together. He was a two-concussion man; if he gave only one, it was a waste of time.

Frenchy looked at me and said, "Hello, kid."

He'd never met Sammy, so I made the introduction.

"What's he do?" Frenchy asked.

"He's a big bandleader," I said. "Don't you listen to the radio?"

"No," he said.

"Frenchy, Sammy's a star!"

"Is he?" he said, and with that, he stood up, took a look at Sammy's toupee, put his big paw on Sammy's head, and ripped the rug off, taking some skin along for good measure. Poor Sammy stood there in pain, baffled, full of anguish. Wisely, Sammy ran out. Sammy instinctively understood that was just a little joyful moment for Frenchy.

You don't make it in show business without a big break. Mine came in 1938, when I booked Louis Prima and Count Basie at the Famous Door. Benny Goodman had heard Basie on a local radio station, thought he was great, and loved his band, which included Jo Jones on drums, Lester Young on tenor sax, and Walter Page on bass. Goodman induced John Hammond, the foremost discoverer of jazz talent, to sign Basie to Columbia Records. Goodman then got Willard Alexander, my associate at MCA, to manage Basie and bring him to New York.

Still, it wasn't easy for Basie to crack New York. Size was part of the problem—he'd added four sidemen and Jimmy Rushing to sing. But the bigger hurdle was that Basie wasn't Mob-owned and couldn't get gigs in places like the Cotton Club. "There is no band in America that can jump like Basie's band and still play soft," Willard suggested. "Let's try and put him in the Famous Door."

Easier said than done. Basie now had sixteen musicians, and the Famous Door only held seventy-five people. There was no air-conditioning, and this was summertime. Hammond and MCA loaned the owners the money for air-conditioning units, with one proviso—they'd have to let black patrons in for this gig, so the CBS radio broadcast that Basie would be doing would be even more authentic and exciting. And then Willard gave me something precious: I was to handle Basie at the Door.

At the last rehearsal, Basie threw me a curve. Because it was a small club, we'd decided to mute the brass. Basie thought that would hurt the radio broadcast. His solution was for the band to play the brassy numbers at full volume—while the customers stood outside. God knows that was unconventional, but I went along with it. One thing I couldn't put up with, though, was Basie's outfit. His shirt was wrong, his tie bothered me; I even had trouble with his socks. So I ran out and got him some new clothes.

The evening was a great success, but my work was far from over. I still had to contend with the club's owners, Jerry Brooks and Al Felshin. Brooks was about five feet two, but was a tough guy; Felshin was about six feet one and weighed about three hundred pounds. Quite cleverly, they always managed to sit on either side of the person with whom they were doing business; no matter your size, you always felt dwarfed between them. More than once, I had to shake Felshin and Brooks off my elbows.

They were slow in repaying MCA for the loan that had

made air-conditioning possible for them, and they were slow in paying Basie. Goodhart told me to get the money any way I could, so I'd go to the club late on Saturday night, when I knew there were at least a few thousand dollars in the cash register. Just before closing, I'd put my hand in the till, grab the money and run out. Primitive, but it worked.

It got to be a routine. I'd clean the register on Saturday, and Felshin and Brooks would show up every Monday morning to complain to Willard. "He's embarrassing us," they'd say. Willard would look at me quizzically. And I'd explain, "They make it so tough on me." At that, Brooks would jump up and say, "I'm going to kill Lazar."

They waited to take their revenge until I arranged a one-night stand for Basie at the University of Pennsylvania that would pay him more for that one night than he was making for the entire three weeks at the Door. When I told Brooks about it, he was positively mellow. Realizing that the band was working for scale, he said, "Okay. Take them out that night and put another band in."

About ten days before the Penn gig, I reminded Brooks of our agreement. "Fuck you," he said.

"I need that band and I signed the contract," I pleaded.

He said, "Let's go to the kitchen."

Brooks said that not only couldn't I have Basie, but that he didn't want to see me in his club again. With that, he hit me on the jaw! I hit him back so hard he must have flown ten feet. He picked himself up, then grabbed a foot-long knife and cut me across the belly. I wrestled the knife away, punched him again, and then passed out.

When I awakened, I was at Roosevelt Hospital with fifty stitches in my gut. Brooks and I became good friends after that. He liked me for surviving. I had no choice. He had the Famous Door and I had to book bands. Being aloof wouldn't have gotten me very far on Fifty-second Street.

After I had been at MCA for about a year, Jules Stein came in from Chicago to visit the New York office. Although I'd come to know him well, he came across as a no-nonsense fellow on first meeting. As soon as I explained that I booked talent as well as bands, small talk ended. "There's a show called *Straw Hat Revue* with a wonderful comedian. You ought to go and sign the comic."

I went to see the show, and thought Jules was so right. Imogene Coca was marvelous, as was a young dancer named Jerome Robbins. I went backstage, had a chat with her, and convinced her to sign with MCA.

The next day I reported proudly to Jules: "I went to see that show, and I was able to sign the girl."

"What girl?" he asked.

"Imogene Coca."

"I don't want her, I want Danny Kaye."

"I didn't think he was very funny," I said. "I thought he was too special."

That's how I lost Danny Kaye, much to my pleasure.

I made amends the next night, when I took Jules down to Fifty-second Street and showed him that there wasn't a single place on the street that I hadn't booked and from which MCA was getting commission. At that moment, there was Louis Prima at the Famous Door, Maxine Sullivan and John Kirby at the Onyx, Hazel Scott as the relief pianist at the Door, Milton Berle at Leon & Eddie's, and Lee Wiley down the street at the Hickory House.

There was jazz and then there were fads. Like the Beachcomber-type spot. Once Monte Proser drank the profits and Johnny Pineapple lost his novelty, the place went under. Fortunately for Monte, a buddy of his had just come back from Rio raving about a place called the Copacabana Hotel that had indoor palm trees, samba dancing, and a performer named Carmen Miranda. Monte was off again: "Let's open a place like the Copacabana."

We found a deserted barn of a club and made a deal with the landlord. Now came the tricky part: financing. After discovering that Monte had none, we went to see Jules Podell at the Kit Kat Club. Jules was a product of Hell's Kitchen, and he never let you forget it. He wore an enormous ring on the pinkie of his left hand, and if he saw something in his club that didn't suit him, he would not too gently tap the ring on his onyx-top table. That

would cause two muscle-carriers from Brownsville to material-
ize. Jules would nod in the direction of whoever annoyed him,
and those folks would promptly be tossed from the premises,
their money and valuables having first been extracted. But then,
Jules once broke his wife's nose with one shot. And that was
after fasting all day on Yom Kippur.

Jules put up enough money to get the place open, and I
went out looking for talent. This was a particularly pleasant
assignment because Monte's theory was that what the club most
needed was girls.

It was rare that you found a local girl in a New York show.
Mostly, these kids were from little towns in the South or Mid-
west. They had read movie magazines and taken dancing lessons
in their hometown—although there were some who were just
quick studies with great figures.

If they were pretty, getting a job was fairly simple. Tall
beauties became showgirls. Shorter ones became chorus girls, or
"ponies." If they appeared topless, breasts-a-ho, they'd earn an
additional ten dollars a week. But there was a strict limit to
nudity. You couldn't let the showgirls romp around knockers-
up. They had to stand perfectly still. Now that was art!

Monte and I sat deadpan as hundreds of kids went by. After
arduous auditions, we picked eight beauties, none of them older
than eighteen. We were convinced that there were no more beautiful showgirls in the world than the Copa girls in their Brazilian
costumes, with simulated fruit headdresses.

I told Monte that I wanted to put Don Loper into the Copa.
He wasn't a great dancer, but he was tall and elegant. He came
off like a Spanish nobleman, a style that appealed to audiences.

"Okay, kid," I told Loper. "I got you a job."

He said, "I have no tuxedo."

"Rent one," I suggested.

He said, "I'd never rent one. It's too déclassé, and I can't
spend fifty dollars right now. When I was at the Casino de Paris
in London, I wore a brown suit. Nobody complained."

I went back to Monte and said, "I have a great idea. The
guy is going to be in a brown suit."

He said, "Never. Never will anyone work the Copa without a tuxedo."

I couldn't change anybody's mind. Loper lost the job. And a dance act called Mario & Sylvia opened instead. Mario was a bad-tempered Greek, and if his partner, who was also his wife, made a mistake on the floor, he'd give her a jab and she would go sailing.

One night when she missed a step, Mario gave her such a shot to the ribs that she fell to the floor in a faint. Somehow they got off the stage, but she couldn't continue. There they met Monte, who was, by this time, drunk. He said to Mario, "You brutal son of a bitch, hitting that woman!" You didn't talk to Mario that way—he gave Monte one shot to the jaw and knocked him out cold.

So now I'm between the eight and twelve o'clock shows, with nobody to go on while the showgirls are making their change. When Monte came to, I asked, "How do you feel now about Don Loper in a brown suit?"

He said, "I don't care what the fuck he wears."

Loper liked that response. In fact, he built on it. The minute he had his foot in the door, he said, "You know, the choreography here is appalling!" By that time we were using a Broadway choreographer who was giving us the back of his hand. I suggested to Monte that we let Loper try it for one show. His choreography was okay.

Thus emboldened, Loper next turned his attention to the costumes. Naturally, he thought he could do them better. We had him bring in some sketches. They were also okay. Now he was in the show, doing the choreography and the costumes, and making a lot of money.

One evening Loper said, "My father is coming to see the show, and I'd like to take him to a club after the Copa closes." I was going on afterward, so I said I'd take them with me. Well, his father arrived. And Don, who always carried on as though he'd been left on the doorstep of the Duchess of Marlborough, introduced me to this *alter kocker,* who had a beard down to his navel and could only speak Yiddish.

Walter Winchell referred to beautiful girls as "Great Legs." The girls I used to go out with were "Great Legs." You had to be a musician or an agent or an Olympic athlete to wind up with one of those girls. It wasn't a question of attraction, it was a matter of endurance. These beauties worked late. And that's what I needed in a companion. I couldn't be bothered fussing around with some college girl who had to study at night or wake up early to go to school.

Chorus girls all seemed to live in pairs or foursomes, so taking them home was a problem; you had to separate the wheat from the chaff, so to speak. It was too tough taking them to jazz joints, because some of these girls didn't think it was necessary to go home and change clothes or take their stage makeup off. When you were stuck with a chick who looked like a clown with her makeup on, it was all right to take her to the Hickory House or the Famous Door because there were a lot of other clowns there. If you lucked into a girl who had a greater sense of what was appropriate, you could take her for a drink at a fancier place.

During the Copa years, one of the few endearing memories I have is of Shannon Dean. Shannon appeared in many of Mike Todd's shows; she was one of the prettiest girls I'd ever met, and easily one of the nicest. All chorus girls had to send money home to Mother, and if she didn't have it and you were her guy, you gave her the money. I made a lot of mothers happy during those years, but the only one I met was Shannon Dean's.

One summer, Monte suggested we put a little show into a casino at Saratoga, New York. I immediately recommended Shannon: "She can be the captain of the line and get a little more money for keeping it organized."

"Fine," he said. "Put her in."

I went up early the day of the opening and checked in at Shannon's hotel. We spent such a happy weekend together that I bought a new car when I returned to town, thinking I'd be driving up every weekend. You can take the girl out of the chorus, but you can't take the chorus out of the girl. The following Friday, I drove up for the first show. Shannon was kicking away, looking absolutely divine. I sat down at a table, ordered a martini, and waited for Shannon to finish.

I hadn't eaten all day, so the drink hit me a little harder than booze usually does. The first show ended, and, a few minutes later, the other girls came out, dressed casually. Then Shannon appeared—in an evening gown. I looked at her kind of surprised.

She saw me, nodded, and waved. I expected her to join me; instead, she went over to the table of Alfred Gwynne Vanderbilt, the owner of a racing stable and a very attractive guy.

Soon they were talking and flirting, and I was wondering what the hell was going on. I sent her a note via the waiter, but she tore it up without opening it. I ordered another martini. With two martinis on an empty stomach, I was barely sitting anymore. Finally, I got ticked off and went over to another club.

As I pulled up, a guy said, "Mmm, nice car. Want to sell it?"

"No, I just bought it."

"I'll give you more than you paid."

I went inside, ordered another martini, and went over to the casino table, where I lost eight hundred dollars in about four or five minutes. Now, I was ticked off and *three* martinis to the wind. I went outside and sold the car.

I took a taxi back to the hotel. Who do you think was outside tapping her toes, looking beautiful but outraged?

"Where have you been?" she said.

I said, "Where have *I* been? Why the hell did you let me sit upstairs while you were making time with Vanderbilt?"

She said, "Do you know what I have won this week at the races? Eight thousand dollars."

"I don't buy that."

"Alfred and his friends know a lot about horses; I know nothing. They told me what to bet. And I kept winning. When they invited me for a drink, I told them I had a date with you but they said, 'Put him on hold.' I figured you wouldn't mind."

I couldn't knock that because when I took her home she showed me the money hidden in a hatbox under the bed.

I said, "Why don't you put the money in the bank?"

"It's safer here," she said.

Well, she wasn't a chorus girl for nothing.

One night I was sitting with Monte Proser at the Stork Club when, lo and behold, Walter Winchell walked over. I had seen Winchell there many times—the eccentric owner, Sherman Billingsley, reserved the corner table on the lefthand side in the Cub Room for him, with two phones installed there so he could receive tips—but I'd never introduced myself. He had tremendous power, not only in his newspaper column but with club owners. I knew if he took a dislike to me he could ruin me with four phone calls. On the other hand, if someone else introduced us and he liked me . . .

Winchell wore his usual dark suit that night. I remember how lean he looked, and how tight and drawn his face was. There was a hunger about him. But he was handsome, too, in an unexpected way, with this distinguished, prematurely gray hair. That night, he was flanked by journalists and press agents, all of them listening to him talk. After a few minutes with him, I realized that nobody else was going to get a word in. Winchell talked incessantly about people and places, interrupting his monologue to take calls.

These tips might come from sources in high and low places —even from J. Edgar Hoover. But just because Winchell was on the phone didn't mean you could start a conversation with anyone else at the table or even look away. Monte had warned me: "If you tune him out, that's okay, but if he sees your eyes glaze over, he gets mad."

I kept my eyes glued to Winchell, and it paid off—he started asking me to pick him up at his apartment and have dinner. He liked eating at a deli or Dave's Blue Room. He may also have liked me because I'd pick up a check. He, on the other hand, was an incredible tightwad, with a great way of not reaching for a check. He'd feign a move toward it, but if someone made the slightest protest, he'd redirect his hand and pick up his water glass. In all the years I knew him, I never saw him pay for a meal. And I figured out something else about him: he never wanted to be alone.

One very good reason I spent time with Winchell was that he could give my acts great plugs. I'd take him up and down Fifty-second Street so he could hear Maxine Sullivan or Louis Prima or Basie, and the next day, there they would be in his column. A plug like that had incredible clout; you could count on selling out the room for the rest of the run. I had to pay for it in time and anguish, but it was worth it.

Also, the man fascinated me. I remember being struck by his physical grace; he walked on the balls of his feet like a dancer.

Yet he was utterly lacking in inner grace. He had terrible manners and no consideration for others, which he justified with a lot of sanctimonious talk about the news coming first. In his sharp, uneasy look, I thought I could see the scrappy New York street kid he'd been so many years before.

Women were, at best, a secondary passion for Winchell. He took a liking to a social girl named Mary Lou Bentley, who had aspirations as a nightclub singer. Inevitably, he asked me if I could find a job for her. The best I could do for her was put her in the 2 A.M. show at Nicky Blair's Paradise—she had no talent whatsoever. I mean, she was so bad that the band had to play louder while she mimicked the role of a singer getting drowned out. But Winchell liked her, so I put up with it.

Winchell's real passion was danger. Squad cars frequently came by the Stork Club after midnight to take him to some god-awful place where there was a shootout or a knifing. A couple of times, he asked me to come along. I didn't have much choice, as I didn't want to appear a coward. He carried a gun, but he didn't know how to use it; it was just part of his macho routine. He'd take the gun out in the back of the car, then sit back and wait while the cops checked the scene out. If he stepped out of the car, two cops flanked him so he didn't get mangled. Nobody in blue wanted to read this headline: "POLICE FAIL TO PROTECT WINCHELL."

Eventually he got a car of his own, and had it outfitted with a siren and a police radio. But he hated getting to a crime scene before the squad cars did. So he'd kill the siren and lights and drive around the block. It didn't take a genius to understand that, beneath his bluster, he was more scared than I was.

Toward the end of his life, Winchell was a pitiful man. One night at the Coconut Grove in Los Angeles, I noticed him standing by the entrance. By this time, he had lost his prestige and his power—and he was in his stocking feet.

"Where are your shoes?" I asked.

"I lost them," he said, launching into a pitch for a girl he thought he could turn into a star. The same old bravura, but you could tell he was a toothless tiger. We spent the evening together, with Winchell talking a mile a minute, but he was a goner. He died a few months later.

☐

In 1941, people of any intelligence were reading the news and shaking their heads. But when you stood on Fifty-second Street, all you heard was jazz, and the music that went round and round showed no signs of coming to a rest. In the five years I'd been working there, almost every day had been a party.

In those years, I don't remember examining my life at all. I just thought this was the way it was. I liked living in a good hotel, I liked room service and chicks whenever you wanted them, and I loved what I was doing. Every night was action. I just wanted the party to go on—ideally, with me holding a bigger piece of it.

So in 1941, while the world was going to war, Sonny Werblin and I started talking about going into business for ourselves. I was close to Tommy Dorsey, Harry James, Xavier Cugat, and Sammy Kaye; Sonny had Eddy Duchin, Guy Lombardo, Gene Krupa, and Benny Goodman. Because MCA's contracts with bands were generally of short duration, it was conceivable that Sonny and I would wind up with most of the big names and eventually have the most important music agency in the business.

That sounded great to me, and I was ready to move. It was my understanding that Sonny felt the same way. And so, when "Shitheel" Goodhart was being especially mean, I told him off in a series of four-, five-, and six-letter words, plus with gestures. It was the kind of language he understood but wasn't used to hearing from subordinates.

He sat back, almost enjoying it, and said, "Okay, now that you've gotten that off your chest, stop acting like a nut. I'll give you a raise."

"I don't want a raise. I'm leaving. I've had it."

I walked into Sonny's office to celebrate, certain that this was the moment to launch our new enterprise.

"Sonny, I've just quit," I announced. "What do you want to do?"

"Well, Jesus, I'm not ready to quit," Sonny said. "You shouldn't have done that without talking to me first. I'm not ready."

Well, he was probably right. Still, there I was with no job.

I had no idea what I was going to do. Luckily, I got a job offer the next day from Abe Lastfogel, the major stockholder in the William Morris Agency. Two days later, I was booking Sophie Tucker, Ted Lewis, Joe E. Lewis, and Harry Richman.

And, ironically, I was representing Eddie Cantor. This was the period when his career was not going well and he thought he'd like to return to Broadway. I not only saw his face for the first time, I helped raise the financing for a musical called *Banjo Eyes*. It was just like the old days—the writers were Quillan and Ellinson.

There was a lot of publicity, and opening night was a smash. The audience was filled with Eddie's vaudeville pals, who cheered as if he were the Second Coming. I went back to his dressing room to express my delight and accept his thanks. But he turned to me and, in his high-pitched voice, asked, "How the fuck did you get me into this?"

"Eddie, you were such a big hit tonight."

"Yeah, but it's cold and I'd like to be sitting by my pool in California."

I said, "What the hell are you talking about? You wanted to do a show, and now you're a big hit again. Isn't that marvelous?"

"No, it's cold, cold, cold," he insisted.

Eddie quit the show and the backers lost their money. He was a real scoundrel—but then, I'd never been the greatest fan of his personal charm.

But I had a more pressing problem than Eddie Cantor. The five hundred dollars that Lastfogel had agreed to pay me turned out to be more than any other agent's salary at William Morris. Nat Lefkowitz, who ran the New York office, felt that Abe had made a mistake, and that other agents would soon be demanding raises. The Morris office had a reputation for grooming their people. Sometimes it seemed to me that they took so long to groom an agent that by the time he was well-groomed, he was too old to work.

When I got my paycheck, I discovered they had cut my salary in half. I refused to deposit it. I tried to corner Lefkowitz to discuss the situation but he was never available. I kept on refusing to deposit checks, he kept on avoiding me.

One day, I barged into Lefkowitz's office and grabbed him by the lapels—he was a rather dignified little fellow, and not used to the Fifty-second Street treatment—and said, "Are you going to pay me or not?"

He said, "I've never been hit before."

"Are you going to pay me or not?"

Lefkowitz muttered a bit and made excuses, so I tossed him into his chair and walked out.

About five minutes later, Lastfogel called from California. "Why did you hit him?" he asked.

"I didn't hit him. I picked him up so he could listen better."

"Why don't you come to California and work for William Morris out here?" Lastfogel suggested.

"I don't want to come to California."

Which was the truth. I'd loved my one visit there, but Los Angeles couldn't compete with Fifty-second Street. If I couldn't work on that street, I didn't want to work anywhere else. And, as it happened, there was now a useful alternative.

For the last few months, I'd been doing my bit for the war effort as a civilian: producing talent shows at Fort Monmouth, the Signal Corps training base in New Jersey. It was easy enough to ask top stars like Joe E. Lewis, Harry Richman, Ethel Merman, and the cast from Broadway musicals or the big nightclub revues to do shows at the camp. On Sundays, when theaters and clubs were dark, the performers would meet in front of Lindy's for the two-hour ride to camp, perform, and get back to town about 11 P.M. Along the way, I'd become friendly with the general who ran the camp, and though I had decided he was short on stature, brains, and administrative ability, I was pleased when he put me in charge of Special Services.

So now it seemed time for the next step. I was well past draft age, but I could still enlist in the army. Two of my brothers had already signed up, and my father had been urging me to do the same. And so, on March 28, 1942, that's what I did. The date is easy to remember: it was my thirty-fifth birthday.

CHAPTER

Three

ONE MINUTE I was enlisting, the next I was being issued a G.I. uniform big enough for two of me, with sleeves so long I looked like an orangutan and a hat so oversized that it covered my eyes. That would never do.

My first free day, I went to Brooks Costume, owned by my friend who outfitted all the Copa girls, and ordered a custom-made uniform that was a cross between a dress Army suit and that of an officer. If I could have carried a swagger stick, it would have been perfect. I didn't know how to salute, but I didn't have to—everybody saluted me. I looked better than the general.

For the obligatory weeks of training camp, I was assigned to a barracks with forty other recruits: row after row of Army cots, and no privacy whatsoever. For a meticulous chap who liked to sleep alone, get his sheets changed every day, and have the largest bathroom at the Madison Hotel all to himself, this was not home.

After the first night, between the yelling, fighting, and farting, I knew I wanted out. In the morning, I learned that the shower was a pipe across the ceiling with seven or eight guys under it at one time. Worse, the toilets were all open, and in a row. The conversation in there was enough to make you ill, though my colleagues had a great time as they sat, stool by stool, enjoying what was, for some of them, the first indoor plumbing they'd ever seen.

After my second night, which I survived only by taking a Seconal, I decided to seek out my good friend, the general, and set matters to right. Imagine my surprise when the general, whom I'd buttered up with trips to the Stork Club and the Copa, was suddenly unavailable. I sent him an angry note telling him off, which got me a meeting but little else.

"Look, General," I said, "I can't sleep and go to the can with twenty other guys."

He said, "Well, you'll have to get used to it. You're in the Army now."

I was to find that out again a couple of days later when the sergeant asked, "How many of you can type?" When I raised my hand, he ordered, "Okay, you clean the latrines." I never volunteered again.

When the training weeks were over, I was at last free to spend nights in New York. I still had an apartment at the Madison Hotel, so I ate at Toots Shor's, went to the Paradise, and kept in touch with my former clients. I didn't know how long the war was going to last, but I didn't want to be forgotten.

During the day, I had to participate in the camp drills, but I was still head of Special Services, so my only other job was to line up acts for the camp's weekly talent shows. I was having a grand time, until a tall, thin, gray-haired gentleman was introduced to me as the new Captain of Special Services. He promptly announced that he wanted Abbott and Costello for the next week's show. I explained that Abbott and Costello were in California.

He said, "Son, don't you know there's a war going on?"

"Who's going to pay for them to come to Fort Monmouth?" I asked.

"They will," he answered.

"They won't."

"Then cancel the show."

I quickly suggested Kay Kyser.

Very reluctantly, he said, "If you can get Kay Kyser, okay."

I called Kay at his home in South Carolina and he offered to hire a special train at his own expense and to bring his band up to do a show. He was a hit, which mollified the captain for about two weeks. Then he returned to the subject of Abbott and Costello. I knew I was in trouble with this character. To my delight, we went out on maneuvers soon afterward, and as we were crawling with real ammunition going off, the head of the Abbott and Costello fan club raised his ass too high and got shot. And for that, he got a medal!

I figured the best way out was through the Army Air Force Officers Candidate School. I liked the idea of the Air Force—its OCS was in Miami. I'd spent a lot of time booking bands there, and I had friends there. I knew it wouldn't be easy competing with young bucks just out of high school, but I preferred that challenge to dealing with idiotic Army captains. Even though most of the material on the qualifying test was unfamiliar to me, I used logic and scored third in a class of two hundred. It was July 1942.

Just by enrolling, I became a corporal, which pleased my father so much he started to cry on the phone. I couldn't see what he was so excited about. To me, the real payoff was a bathroom of my own.

It was tough for a thirty-five-year-old character like myself to go through the rigors of becoming an officer. I was on my own, a little middle-aged guy among a lot of giant-sized kids with no bellies who actually seemed to enjoy climbing walls, shimmying up ropes, and jumping from hilltops. Every day, there were sergeants standing off to the side, ready to yank anyone they decided didn't have the right stuff. For me, it was a question of survival; I was determined not to be yanked. In four months, I shed thirty pounds, gained some muscles, and lost the rest of my hair—I looked like a different person.

The days were severely hot in Miami, and there were periods when you had to stand at attention for hours in the hot sun; you couldn't move even if the kid next to you dropped to the pavement on his face. The marches were even worse—three miles or more, with a rifle on your shoulder. As the shortest man, I was always at the rear, so far behind the six-foot-plus giants that I felt like I was marching alone.

Some of the kids tried to help me by carrying my gun. For the return trips, I came up with another solution. I figured the only way to survive was to hire a limousine and have the driver follow us. When we were allowed to fall out, I'd throw my gun into the back of the Cadillac, get in, and ride home in style.

A week later, the colonel called me in. He wasn't alone—the three men in his office identified themselves as being with the FBI.

"What were you doing in that black Cadillac?" they wanted to know.

"It's transportation for my gun."

"What are you going to do when you get overseas?"

"Get another Cadillac."

Word began to get around that I'd hung out with stars like Tommy Dorsey, Harry James, and Count Basie. For my celebrity-dazzled comrades, that made me a star, too. But they couldn't believe their ears the day a very excited first lieutenant came in to announce, "There is an Eddy Duchin here to see you. Do you know him?"

"Sure, kid," I said. "He's a friend of mine."

I went downstairs and there was Eddy, dressed in his naval officer's uniform, looking like an ad for enlistment. Nobody looked better in blues than Duchin. "C'mon, Lazar," he said. "We're going for a drink with Jack Rose."

I knew Jack very well because I'd booked a lot of bands and singers into his Miami hotel. I'd always found him easy to deal with, although he was, of course, thick with the Mob. Over drinks, Jack was eager to make my time in Miami more pleasant. I wasn't quite sure what he had in mind.

A few days later, I got a visit from a very agitated second lieutenant. "The general wants to see you," he said. "There's a car with three stars parked outside waiting to take you over to Jack Rose's hotel."

I was sure I was about to be sent back to the Army, so I decided to go out in my fancy uniform. But when I walked into what had been Jack Rose's office before the war, the mood was decidedly informal. The general was in his shirtsleeves, and Jack had his feet on the desk. Looking at them, you wouldn't have known that the government had requisitioned Jack's hotel as a

Me as a lieutenant, circa 1943.

headquarters. The general wasn't getting any money, but ladies were delivered and booze and luxury items were supplied in exchange for letting Jack keep some of his enterprises afloat.

"Hey, kid," Jack said. "Meet the general. General, this is my buddy. I'd hate to see him go overseas and get hurt. What can you do for him?"

I felt sorry for the general. He was an older guy, and he was embarrassed by the way Jack flouted military protocol. He was even more embarrassed because he couldn't object. He knew I knew he was on the take.

"Look, Jack," I said quickly. "I appreciate your concern, but I've got to get through school legitimately. I can make it on my own."

"Don't be stupid, kid. General, what do you say?"

"I think the soldier is right," the general replied. "He seems like a very intelligent young man, and although it's sometimes harder for an older man to keep pace with the young ones, I'm sure he can make it." Then, with a nod to me, he added, "If there's anything I can do to help you, let me know." He couldn't resist a skeptical look at my uniform, and one wry shot: "I don't know who you're fighting for, but try and conform with the rest of the fellows."

Jack wasn't satisfied. He took me into the next office. "No matter what happens, you're getting through," he said. "And here's one thing I can do. The food here is awful, and they don't know about the chicken place I own around the corner. We'll make up some baskets of chicken. Around ten o'clock, Joey Bigmouth and the baskets will be in a black limousine, with the Gimp at the wheel. They've got a guard patrolling your barracks who carries no ammunition. When he turns away from your building, put the best catcher in your barracks at the window. Joey has a great arm—he'll throw the baskets up to him. If we see the guard coming, we'll fire one shot in the air. That'll scare the shit out of him, and he'll run like hell."

I thought he was kidding, but at ten o'clock, the limo came around the turn, and when the guard disappeared around the corner, the chicken baskets came flying up. There was more than enough for the three guys I was billeted with and me, so we broke the extra chicken into little pieces and flushed it down the toilet. This routine went on for about a week until the toilet overflowed and we had to report it to the lieutenant. The puzzled plumber reported that the pipes were a veritable chicken grave- yard.

"Where did you get the chicken?" the lieutenant demanded.

We said, "What chicken? It must have come up through the pipes."

He may have a gotten a clearer idea of the truth at the party Jack threw when we graduated. Every mobster and hooker in Miami was there. I brought some of my chums, who couldn't believe it when they saw these tough characters wearing paper party hats and carrying real guns in their holsters. They looked more scared of these guys than they were of the Germans.

Lieutenant Irving Lazar's orders were to report to the Spe- cial Services Division at Mitchell Field, on Long Island, which was close enough to Toots Shor's to sound beautiful to me. I moved into the Gotham Hotel, drove to camp every day, and waited for the Army's pleasure, making sure I softened up my commanding officer with some late-night field trips to the Stork Club.

One day he showed me a directive that had just come from

General Hap Arnold, the commander of the Army Air Force in Washington. The note said Arnold was looking for a Special Services officer to produce a benefit show for AAF Emergency Relief that would be like Irving Berlin's hugely successful benefit for the ground forces, *This Is the Army*.

I told the captain I could give him a show that would make Berlin's production look tame. The next day, I submitted a very carefully worded proposal suggesting that Jimmy Stewart, Clark Gable, Henry Fonda, Josh Logan, and a number of other Hollywood stars who were in the Air Force should be asked to participate. I knew none of them. Nor did I promise that I could deliver any of them. Anyone with any knowledge of show business whatsoever would have realized that it was merely a list of top American talent that any fool could compile. But the general wasn't in show business, and that's what I was banking on.

Several days later, the captain in charge of Special Services came in shaking with excitement. In his hand was a telex asking that I go to AAF Headquarters to see Colonel Fairchild. My précis, it seemed, had pleased General Arnold.

Off I went to Washington, where Colonel Fairchild had enlarged a copy of my letter to a 4' x 4' format with all the famous names circled. "I think you have just the right approach," he enthused. "So does General Arnold. He wants to see you right away."

General Arnold was a very impressive man. He spoke in deliberate and precise terms, and he looked through you, not at you. I turned around more than once to see if there was anyone behind me.

"Lieutenant, do you think you can do this show so it will be a credit to the Air Force?"

"Yes, sir!" I answered in a quivering voice. There was nothing else to say. It was too late to back out. All that was left for me was to salute and get the hell out of there.

Outside, the colonel informed me that I had carte blanche. I could go anywhere I wanted to seek out talent for the show. Only later did I learn that the money I would need to rent a theater and pay for the show would *not* be paid for by the AAF —I'd have to raise it.

The first move I made was to take on a partner, a second

lieutenant at Mitchell Field named Ben Landis. Like me, he had
once represented Eddie Cantor. And, like me, he was more eager
to put on a show than carry a gun. Ben would prove to be a
godsend, coordinating the effort from the base while I flew
around the country.

What I needed next was a major talent to get the train rolling, so others would hop on. Josh Logan, the Broadway director, had done *This Is the Army*—he was the ideal candidate. I
didn't know Logan, but I managed to find out when he would
be at El Morocco. When I walked in, Logan was at the bar with
friends, having a few drinks.

"Lieutenant," I began, addressing him by rank, "I have been
authorized by General Arnold to do a show for the Army Air
Force. Would you be interested in helping?"

He looked at me quizzically. "Do a show? For the Air
Force? Are you kidding? I joined the Air Force to"—and here he
pointed his fingers like a machine gun firing at my face—"kill
Germans, not do another show."

I left fairly humbled by this onslaught. Logan had thought I
was imposing. I suppose I was. But what choice did I have?

A few nights later, I was having a drink with Bob Lewine,
a fellow agent, in the Oak Room of the Plaza Hotel. Lewine was
a classy guy; I was not. He came from a very fine family, and
had a first-rate education. As we were chatting, he made a witty
remark: "Look, there's Moss Hart with the future Miss
Appleby."

Moss Hart! In 1942, he was close to being the god of the
theater world. George Kaufman and Maxwell Anderson were
right up there, but Hart embodied the glamour, wit, and charm
of Broadway as its popular best. He'd been an idol of mine since
Once in a Lifetime, and through the years I'd seen every brilliant
comedy he wrote. In my mind, I saw him at the center of the
circle of Broadway's elite: tall, lean, handsome in an angular
way, with a carved wood pipe in one hand and cocktail in another, holding forth with an effortless series of witty remarks.

Never once had I dreamed I would meet him. Hart was
Lewine's turf. Mine was Frank Costello, Dutch Schultz, Nicky
Blair, and Walter Winchell. So it must have been a terrific shock
to Lewine when, without a word, I got up and walked over to

Hart's table. I don't know where I found the courage. It was a confrontation between an immovable body and an irresistible force. "Mr. Hart, my name is Lazar. May I take a moment of your time?"

Hart, as I would learn later, had impeccable manners. He stood up and invited me to join him, even though he was in the midst of a tête-à-tête with a girl who was terribly engrossed in making a pitch!

I explained how Hap Arnold had assigned me to pull together an AAF show. "Something similar to what Irving Berlin did," I added, and then cursed myself for such oafishness. What playwright wanted to be told he was being asked to ape someone else's work?

Hart said the one thing a well-mannered man could under the circumstances: "Call me tomorrow."

I returned to my table in a state of ecstasy. "I can't say what it is," I told Bob, "but I think I did something pretty good just now." Little did I know that Moss was one of the most sophisticated manipulators of boors in the world and very experienced at fending off amateurs.

When I called Moss the next day, I got the brush-off I should have known to expect. He said he'd talked the matter over with Irving Berlin, and Berlin had advised him not to take such an assignment unless the request came directly from General Arnold himself.

I called my colonel and asked if I could introduce Hart to the general in a brief meeting, just to reassure Hart that the project was on the up and up. The colonel was dubious, but he said he'd give it a try. When he called back, he told me all I needed to hear: "Six minutes."

Moss called me the next morning. The tone of his voice had changed perceptibly. "The oddest thing just happened," he said. "I have a wire from General Arnold and he wants to see me."

"Of course he does," I told him. "You're the only one he wanted for this. He's a terrific fan of yours."

I never let on that I had sent the wire and signed General Arnold's name to it.

The plan almost backfired when Moss and I were ushered into the general's office. I had assumed that, if the general didn't know who Moss Hart was, the colonel would brief him. No such luck. As far as Hap Arnold was concerned, Moss was just another show business civilian.

"Do you think you can do this show for the Army Air Force in the dignified way it should be done?" the general asked without preamble.

I could see Moss was taken aback. At the same time, he was impressed by Arnold's charisma and character. This was no lucky West Pointer who had risen through the ranks by accident. General Arnold was the real thing.

"General," said Moss, "if you want me, I'll do it."

"Excellent," the general said, as if Moss's participation had never been in doubt. "I trust that Lieutenant Lazar will fill you in. I'm giving him authorization to go to any encampment of the Army Air Force's to solicit entertainment."

I was a little less scared than I'd been six minutes before. Now, at least, I had Moss Hart. What better seal of approval could there be? I knew I could recruit any star I saw just by dropping his name. What I didn't know was that I had just begun a relationship that would change the course of my life.

I had assumed we'd do a revue of some sort, one talent act after another. Throw in a couple of comedians, a line of chorus girls, and an orchestra in the pit, and we'd have a whale of a show. That's how I'd done it at the Copa and every other joint I worked with. And that's how Irving Berlin had done it in *This Is the Army*.

"I think not," Moss said gently after hearing me out as we rode back to New York on the train. "Revues are boring, and besides, we'll just invite comparisons with Berlin if we do one. What I'd rather see is a full-length, original play about the AAF."

"You're absolutely right," I agreed. I would have said that no matter what. I was a two-bit showman, he was the famous creator. But where was the money for a full-blown Broadway production? Like General Arnold, Moss wasn't worried about that. Wasn't that Lazar's problem?

As a first step, we decided, I would conduct a national talent search, making a grand sweep of all the AAF bases and gathering résumés from the famous and unknown alike. To my shock,

Moss said he wasn't nearly as interested in stars as he was in good working talents who were young enough to be in active military service. He didn't want to produce a star vehicle; he wanted the performers to be subordinate to the story.

Call me old school, but in my corner of show biz, I'd never heard of a director choosing unknowns when he could book stars. Still, I took this as yet another sign of Moss's brilliance and began flying around the country to almost one hundred bases to find the goods. I took a cameraman with me to photograph the better talents while I collected the application forms.

When I had collected a substantial number of prospects, I flew east to review the applications with Moss at his country place in New Hope, Pennsylvania. Moss was still a bachelor— he didn't marry Kitty Carlisle until after the war—and he lived in baronial style with a number of servants in an eighteenth-century stone farmhouse. It wasn't hard to see that Moss delighted in luxury. He was famous for a silver tobacco pouch he'd had made at Cartier to conform to the shape of his backside, so he could slip it into a rear pants pocket without creating a bulge. He had imported dozens of rare trees and planted them in neat rows, prompting his near neighbor George Kaufman to comment, "This is what God would have done, if he'd had the money."

Moss and I couldn't have been more different. He loved running a large country house; I was still living in a hotel and didn't own a stick of furniture. And yet, we became fast friends, I think because we had both grown up poor and spent our childhoods in third-balcony cut-rate seats.

It didn't hurt that I admired his work with real and knowledgeable delight—although Moss never let on that praise had any effect on him. He never talked about his work, and had no interest in hearing other people's comments. It took me years to understand that under his surface confidence and charm was a man so profoundly insecure and anxious that he went to a therapist several times a week, convinced that he would never write anything decent again. If he was impatient with praise, the real reason was that he simply didn't believe it.

Moss didn't hesitate to introduce me to the likes of George Kaufman and Alexander Woollcott. Kaufman had heard of me, and like a lot of Moss's friends, he didn't take kindly to a new-comer—particularly one in uniform. So when he first saw me he greeted me with a baleful stare. As Moss would do time and again for me, he made the introductions and left no doubt that I was a new and respected friend. By the end of the evening, I could feel the ice thawing.

This, as it turned out, was only a prelude to the first Califor-nia visit I made with Moss. I was still on my talent search, and Moss had volunteered to come along to help. As soon as we checked into the Beverly Hills Hotel, Moss said, "Let's go over and see Barbara Stanwyck and Bob Taylor."

"Right," I said, acting as if I'd met dozens of movie stars. We drove to North Beverly Drive, and sure enough, there was Barbara Stanwyck, absolutely delighted that Moss had stopped in on her. I tried to act nonchalant, but the act was pretty trans-parent. I was overcome.

I soon realized that whenever Moss arrived in Los Angeles, the drums began to beat and the calls commenced, inviting him for breakfast, lunch, dinner, or drinks. Indeed, the first night we were in town, we found ourselves at a huge party given by Harry Kurnitz, the Hollywood screenwriter. I met everyone that night: David Selznick, Bill Goetz, Joseph and Herman Mankiewicz, even Ira Gershwin and his wife, Lee. In the midst of all the revelers was Groucho Marx, singing bawdy songs from his vaudeville days as Harry's wife joined him at the piano. I couldn't imagine a happier couple than the Kurnitzes. It came as a great shock the next day to pick up the newspapers and read that the Kurnitzes were going to be divorced. I couldn't believe it. "Man," I muttered to myself, "so this is Hollywood!"

Our piles of applications and photos were growing larger every day, but we still needed $150,000 for the theater, scenery, and orchestra. My first stop was Juan Trippe, the chairman of the board of Pan Am, whom I'd met at jazz clubs. Trippe felt sort of obligated, and I certainly did nothing to lessen that feel-ing. I may even have pointed out how embarrassing it would be for Pan Am if word got around that it had stiffed the Air Force in wartime. For all I knew, people might boycott the airline. I didn't need to take Trippe further down that path. He got the point, and we got a hundred thousand dollars.

I raised fifty thousand more through Gilbert Miller, the impresario whose rich friends were delighted to serve as backers. And the Shuberts agreed to rent us a theater for less than the going rate. In the summer of 1943, Moss and I rented an office on Fifty-seventh Street. We were in business.

From then until the curtain rose in late November, Moss and I were together every day. For the story he was creating, our cast needs were huge: three hundred people. Of the final choices, none was a major star, and only a few—Karl Malden, Red Buttons, Mario Lanza, Martin Ritt, Peter Lind Hayes, and Edmond O'Brien—had known any professional acclaim.

In his writing, Moss had stayed absolutely clear of speechifying and propaganda. Nor was he interested in cold facts. His focus was on the human stories behind the statistics. In two acts and seventeen scenes, he followed a handful of raw recruits from home to training camp, showing how they matured as they became responsible members of a bombing crew headed for the South Pacific. Meanwhile, their girlfriends, wives, and mothers appeared in scenes at home, worrying over their loved ones and fearing the worst. The name of the crew's plane became the name of the play: *Winged Victory*.

The only point I felt strongly about was that the play should have music. After some hesitation, Moss agreed. I got David Rose, one of the best composer-arrangers in Hollywood, to sign on; he chose the show's theme song, "Off We Go, into the Wild Blue Yonder."

It was astounding to watch Moss as a director. He never yelled. If something bothered him, he would always go up to the stage, pull the actor aside, and speak to him privately and gently, acting out the lines the way he thought they should be delivered. That technique turns a director into a father-figure; overnight, we all became Moss-clingers, telling him our sad stories and sharing our fears. Which wasn't to say that Moss couldn't be brusque. One day, as we were walking down Fifth Avenue, a guy grabbed Moss by the sleeve. "Hey, remember me? We went to grammar school together," he said. Moss politely said that he didn't. "Come on, you *must* remember me," the man persisted. Finally, Moss stopped short and faced him squarely: "Oh, yes. *Now* I remember—you were a boor then, and you're a boor now."

As we worked on the production, it became increasingly

odd to think that we were in the military. It was as if we were all actors in military costume. But one day, a new colonel was assigned to us, and, incredibly, he ordered me to get the men out marching to keep them fit; after all, who knew how long the show would run. "No problem," I said, and with eyes straight forward, we marched from Forty-fourth to Fifty-ninth Street, then through Central Park and back to the theater. As we carried our rifles, pedestrians lined the sidewalks, waving their handkerchiefs and getting choked up as one hundred men strong sang "Off We Go, into the Wild Blue Yonder." If they only knew—we were going to wind up at Sardi's.

November 20, 1943, was unlike any other opening night I would ever experience. You could sense an extraordinary feeling in the air; this was a theatrical event and then some. I was in the wings as the curtain came up on three recruits and they began reading the letters that told them where to report for duty. They went on to voice their fears, as well as their determination to serve their country with honor. It was a powerful moment, and I cried for sheer joy that Moss had created this incredibly meaningful show, and that I had been part of it.

The reviews were about the best I'd ever seen. I was particularly pleased when Robert Garland, in the *Journal-American,* told the story of the show's birth. Moss, he wrote, had been approached in the Oak Room of the Plaza by a Lieutenant Lazar, who said he was the only man for the job: "The Lieutenant, a combination of Little Eva and the Bethlehem Steel Company, meant what he said."

After that, it was a piece of cake to convince Moss's great friend, Darryl Zanuck, to buy the screen rights to *Winged Victory.* I helped hammer out the terms—my first movie deal as an agent, and perhaps the only time in my entire career that I took no commission. Moss wrote the screenplay, George Cukor directed, the movie was a big hit, and, adding up the profits from the play and the film, the Air Force Emergency Relief made $4 million.

Every production has a nemesis. Mine was our commander, Colonel Dunham, who kept badgering me about what I was

Getting to work with Moss Hart on Winged Victory was a pivotal point in my career. My friendship with Moss was one of the highpoints of my life.

Dear Irving—

At liberty next season. As you can see, will travel anywhere — with or without beard — good dresser on and off and will follow animal acts. Have worked for Lew Wasserman, Jules Stein, and Norman Korne — in that order. Salary no object but will only go to one Doris Stein cocktail party per week.

Moss

doing. By the time we were in Los Angeles making the movie, he was completely impossible—wondering why I was on the set so much, and, finally, demanding that all business go through him. This man knew nothing about show business; his one brush with it had occurred in Waco, Texas, where he had been the organist at Mrs. Hap Arnold's church.

Eventually, I lost my temper. "Listen, you know nothing," I told Dunham. "Why don't you stay out of this, and let Ben Landis and me take care of the company's problems? You're having a good time, aren't you?"

"I know how we can get along even better," he countered. "Without you!"

"But you've just recommended Landis and me for captain!" I pointed out.

"Start packing," Dunham snapped. "You're moving out within the hour."

I could smell those orders, and they were indeed vibrant. I was to report immediately to Greensboro, North Carolina, a large depot for officers who had no prior overseas experience. The entire cast and crew of the film lined up to say good-bye. I turned to Dunham and said, "Good-bye, Colonel Gummo!" He didn't look up.

When I arrived in Greensboro, I discovered that there were no special quarters for officers because everybody was an officer. You were simply given a footlocker and a bed. And then you waited for your orders, which could take as long as two weeks.

Two weeks in a barracks wasn't for me. I nosed around and learned that Greensboro had one great hotel, the O'Henry. I engaged a two-bedroom suite, then went over to the liquor store and bought a case each of scotch, bourbon, and champagne. Finally, I went to the officers' quarters and introduced myself to four of the best-looking young soldiers you ever saw.

"What's the action here?" I asked.

"Oh, there are some beautiful girls here, some really beautiful girls," they said.

"Great! Let's have a party at the O'Henry—I've got a suite there and all the booze you want. All you have to do is invite all the pretty girls you know in town."

Well, they were crazy about that idea. It was the best offer they'd had since they'd left home. In fact, they'd never had an offer like that at home. And at six o'clock that evening, they had thirty knockouts in the suite. By the time ten o'clock rolled around, there were very few sober people on the premises. Overnight, I was the talk of the camp. Every officer wanted to get in on my party, but I kept it down to my quartet.

Everything was going absolutely splendidly, until I got a call to report to the general. I had hired a limousine just to pick up the girls and drive them home, so I had the chauffeur take me to camp. When I arrived, the colonel who was the general's aide was waiting for me. "Is *that* how you're going to fight this war?" he asked, pointing at the limo.

"There are three ways of getting out here, Colonel," I said, not bothering to be too nice about it because I was, after all, going overseas any day now. "Either I walk, take the bus, or come out in comfort. I don't see anything wrong with driving out here in a limousine."

I walked into the general's office. There were four men in civilian clothes sitting with him. They were, the general said, from the FBI.

"You're living at the O'Henry Hotel?" one asked.

"Yes, sir."

"What are you doing there?"

"Well, there's nothing for me to do here. I thought it was pointless to sit around on these hot days, so I went into town."

"That's against orders. Whether you like it or not, you were supposed to stay in camp. Nobody knows when you're supposed to ship out. If they'd come in the middle of the night, you wouldn't have been here."

I answered that I had it all staked out with the boys. Had anyone wanted me in the middle of the night, they would have known where to reach me and I could have been over in less time than it takes the other fellows to dress.

"Dammit," the general barked, "you weren't supposed to get that undressed."

"What are these telephone calls all over the country?" the other G-man asked. "The list from the hotel shows that you've called California, Virginia, Florida, Cleveland, Chicago, five and six times a day. Who the hell are you calling?"

"My office."

"What are you selling?"

"I'm selling bands and acts all over the country. There's no law against that, is there?"

Then they got to the short strokes.

"Do you know that you gave one of the girls fifty dollars, and she went to the drug store and bought some sleeping pills, and now she's in the intensive care unit at the hospital?"

"No, sir."

"Do you know a girl by the name of Elizabeth Randolph?"

"Yes, I think I do."

"You *think* you do? Didn't you pay her hotel bill?"

"It's quite possible."

"Do you know that she's under surveillance as a possible spy?"

I then realized that this was getting serious.

"Have you any idea how many men there are in this camp?"

"No, sir," I said. "I've only been here four days."

"Do you have any knowledge where you're going?"

"Yes, sir."

"How do you know?"

"One of my chums is part of the team in the Office of Strategic Command, which issues the orders. He called me from Washington and told me I was going to Foggia, Italy."

"Do you know what happens at Foggia?"

"I know it's the base for operations between Russia and England.

"You're not going to Foggia any more," the general said. "We have some other plans for you. You're going to be shipped out tomorrow morning. We have just assigned five hundred men to you. I'm giving you three second lieutenants, one first lieutenant, and a sergeant. You're to lead these five hundred men to Newport News, Virginia, and then embark from there."

"Yes, sir. Where are the men?"

"Not far from here."

"Where are their credentials?"

"You'll find out. Now get the hell out of here."

To console myself, I visualized myself becoming a major in the field . . . machine gun in hand . . . ready for action. I went over to the camp and looked over the credential cards of my new unit. They were appalling. All of them had been in the brig for two years for such infractions against officers as stabbing and killing. One officer got off lucky; the soldier had raped his wife.

As I reviewed the cards, I saw that most of them had never worked. When asked how much money they had earned the year before entering the Army, they wrote in "nothing" or "paid in kind," which meant they were getting potatoes or turnips for their efforts. All had a prior criminal record before they'd reached the Army.

This was a beautiful bunch—more dangerous than the enemy because they were closer. But orders were orders. Bright and early the next morning, I took my associates over to the barracks. There were one hundred men in each, and all of them were sleeping. As Army regulations precluded an officer from laying a hand on a soldier, we had to shake them awake ever so gently.

"What do you want?" the first soldier asked.

"It's time to get up."

"Why don't you go fuck yourself, toy soldier? I'll get up when I feel like it." And with that, he pulled the covers over his head. I wasn't going to disturb that chap further.

Eventually—with the help of thirty military policemen— we got them awake and lined up beside their bunks.

"Anyone who makes a move to strike an officer or an MP will have sufficient cause to be shot," I announced, as the MPs leveled their guns. Then my five officers and I went through the footlockers of the first one hundred men. You wouldn't believe the implements that they had brought with them: antique flintlocks, broken guns, and a lot of collapsible knives. They really whimpered as we took their weapons from them. We continued through the five barracks, allowing no one to leave and no communication.

It was now time for Captain Lazar to address his troops. I wouldn't have seen them from the ground, so I stood on the highest boulder. There they were, five hundred killers glaring at me, hatred permeating the atmosphere. As I began to speak, a rock whizzed past my head. I bravely kept on talking, telling them we could be friends or we could be enemies.

"There's no point putting any of you into solitary confinement," I said. "You might as well cooperate—you're going overseas in any event. How about it? Let's shape up and be friends."

With that, a mud-covered rock flew by. The rock didn't strike me, but the mud did.

"That, gentlemen, is very unfortunate. If we find out who did it, or catch a man raising his arm to throw anything in the direction of your captain, you *will* get solitary."

This inspired loud booing, but for three days they behaved themselves fairly well. I held on to the leader, promising him a promotion in the field. In order to establish some discipline, I found one soldier in each barracks who could control the group and gave him twenty dollars. Things were looking up.

We had to go by train to Newport News, where we would be shipped out. As the captain, I was given the only single compartment on the train. When we boarded, I went to my quarters, stashed my gear, and went to see the adjutant; when I returned, everything was gone. I didn't even have shaving equipment. Fortunately, I had kept four or five sleeping pills in my pocket, in a little Tiffany pillbox.

The adjutant rushed in and said there had been a fight in the car ahead of ours. One guy had been slashed with a broken beer bottle and was bleeding profusely. I told my aide to arrange for an ambulance at the next stop. He said, "You'd better go back there yourself."

"Not me, brother," I said. "By now, the guy with the beer bottle is looking for his next victim."

My aide went back, but everyone wanted Captain Lazar. I wasn't that crazy. I took one of my sleeping pills and nodded out. When I woke up the next morning, the train seemed a lot quieter. The cook explained why: a lot of guys were missing.

"Go and count the men," I told him. "They'll think you're planning the food. Then come back and report to me."

The cook's report was grim—three hundred men had deserted. I cabled the next stop and advised them to be on the lookout for my AWOL troops. But by then, more men had fled, bringing the number of deserters to four hundred.

In Newport News, the plan was for the officers to alight

first, with the troops following. A few miles before we reached town, we could hear a band playing patriotic airs. We had a regular welcoming committee—what a surprise they were going to get.

At the station, the three of us marched onto the platform. Our troops were outnumbered about three-to-one by the musicians. A colonel had been sent to the station by the commandant of the camp.

"What happened?" he asked.

"It beats the shit out of me, Colonel. We started out with five hundred men and we're down to a hundred."

"Where the hell did they go?"

"I don't know."

"What do you mean, you don't know?"

"All I can tell you," I said, "is that I'm more confident we're going to win this war without those guys."

"Why didn't you call for the MPs?"

"I did, but they disappeared, too. Out of thirty, we only have six left."

"Your job was to get these men here. You'd better come with me to the general."

The sleeping pill hadn't quite worn off, so I was starting to warm to the idea of solitary confinement. "This is the worst performance I've seen in my entire career," the general said. "This could only happen to civilians who don't belong in the Army."

"I did the best I could with those crazy guys," I replied. "My choice was to be standing here talking to you or lying in a box."

The day we were to ship out, I was doubled up in pain. X-rays revealed a duodenal ulcer. For some reason, I was sent to the hospital for a spinal tap. To compound this peculiar treatment, the doctors neglected to tell me I wasn't supposed to walk around afterward. I fell, passed out, and couldn't be revived for three days.

They sent me to a military hospital to recover. In a few weeks, when the effects of the ulcer and the spinal tap had subsided, I appeared before a board of medical corps officers. They gave me some happy news—because there was no evidence that

I suffered from an ulcer before I enlisted, I had a potential claim against the Air Force.

I was given the choice of staying in the service, or, because of my age, being honorably discharged. If ever a decision could be made quickly, this was it. "Not only will I accept an honorable discharge," I said, with heroic stoicism, "but I will waive all medical benefits."

Walking on wings, I went to my quarters and called my father. He had envisioned all four sons doing their duty on the fighting fronts, and then coming home to tell all about it. The news that I was leaving the Air Force ruined that script for him.

Then I caught a plane for New York. I checked into my old hotel suite and took the walk of a free man on Fifth Avenue.

CHAPTER

Four

I DIDN'T HAVE to think too long or too hard about my future. The very next day, Sam Goldwyn called and offered me a job.

"We'll give you a five-year contract and you'll be in charge of the studio," Sam told me. "You'll have an interesting experience, and you'll be a great producer. And I'll give you a cut of the profits of the pictures we make."

"Well, it sounds terrific, Sam," I said, trying to sound both excited and noncommittal. "I haven't even considered moving to California. Let me think about it."

"There's nothing to think about. You're not going to do anything else. You're exactly the fellow I need. We'll talk money when you get here."

I was definitely flattered. In theory, I didn't see how I could pass up the chance of working for Goldwyn. But I had to run the proposition by Moss Hart, who had introduced me to Goldwyn—and to Jack Warner and Darryl Zanuck—when we were in Los Angeles to do preproduction work for the *Winged Victory* film.

I strolled over to the Henry Miller Theatre, where Moss was rehearsing a Norman Krasna play, and briefed him over a cup of coffee. Moss wasted no time: "You and Sam will never get along. I know you very well, and you're a volatile fellow. The two of you will have an argument the first week you're there, and you'll quit, and it will have been a waste of time. Don't do it. Go into business for yourself. If you need money, I'll lend you some to get started, and I'll be your first client. From there, you'll work it out. I know you'll do great, just great."

I had often been the recipient of Moss's concern and generosity, but this was overwhelming. I didn't have to consider his suggestion for too long, however—within a day of Goldwyn's offer, Sonny Werblin called and asked if I'd like to return to MCA. I reminded him that no one who had left MCA had ever been invited back. "We all want you," Sonny insisted. "Let me come over to see you."

I was happy to see him. Sonny represented an important period in my life, and I felt I owed a lot to him. But I told him the only way I would consider rejoining MCA was if Jules Stein called me personally to tell me that he wanted me back.

Sonny had no sooner left than Jules was on the phone.

"Listen, come on home," he said.

"Jules, are you *sure?* I don't want to find myself out of a job a couple of weeks from now."

"No, no, no. You come back. What kind of salary do you want?"

"Five hundred a week, and two hundred and fifty for expenses."

"No problem. Go to work."

"Great, Jules, but I want you to know that I have gotten an offer from Sam Goldwyn. I'll call right away and tell him I'm not going to accept his job, but he's going to be very much annoyed about this, especially when he finds out that I'm going to work for you. You'd better be prepared for some kind of beef, because it apparently doesn't take much to anger Sam."

Then I called Goldwyn. Our conversation was pleasant—until I told him I wasn't coming to work for him.

"We have a contract!" he shouted.

"Sam, we haven't got a contract. We never even talked out the terms. We've just been talking." And then, because there was no way around it, I dropped the bomb. "Jules called and asked me to return to MCA," I said, "and I decided I'd rather go back into the agency business."

"I'll sue Jules Stein!" Goldwyn screamed. "And I'll sue you! You're not going to work for MCA—I'll get an order stopping you. I'll put you in jail! And that goes for Stein, too!"

Jules called an hour later. "My God, what have you done?" he said. *"Did* you have a contract with Sam? He's threatening to sue me, MCA, and you for damages!"

Goldwyn never sued. Neither did he completely forgive me. To the end of his life, he would refer to that blowup as "the incident."

In 1945, when I began my second stint in MCA's New York office, the agency was getting out of booking bands and into the business of representing actors on both coasts. At the time, many of MCA's New York clients were getting offers from Hollywood, but they all wanted to be sure that before accepting any film offers that they could return to Broadway. Under the supervision of Kay Brown and Edith Van Cleve, I was to help actors like Richard Widmark tailor film deals to fit their love for the theater.

Widmark wanted it clearly understood that he'd be back on a Broadway stage after two years in front of the cameras. Gregory Peck and Patricia Neal took the same position. In fact, only Kirk Douglas and James Stewart would make good on the escape clauses in their movie contracts—once they got to Hollywood, the others found the life too pleasant and the salaries too big to leave.

In addition to helping Broadway actors make a painless transition to film, I was taking on such challenges as negotiating a raise for the likes of Marlon Brando, who was then making his Broadway debut in *I Remember Mama.* Marlon was having a rough time getting by on sixty-five dollars a week. The extra ten I got him made a difference.

Even if I had only gotten him five dollars more, I suspect that Brando would have kept coming to my office with his girlfriend, Blossom Plumb. The two of them would arrive—Brando in an old trench coat—and take chairs in opposite corners of the room. They wouldn't speak, just listen to me making deals on the phone. After a few hours, they'd leave. Next day, same routine. It definitely gave me the idea that Brando was taking notes on my "character." Although he did, in later years, develop an agent's instinct for getting his money first and fast, he fortunately never got a part that enabled him to use whatever he learned from me.

That Brando's visits to my office were something of a big deal is testimony that New York wasn't the same to me as when I had left. In the time I'd been away, there were new clubs and owners, and most of the guys I had spent my nights with were gone. At the Stork Club, Winchell was more frenetic and less productive than he'd been in 1939. At Toots Shor's, it wasn't so amusing to see Bert Lahr sitting there when he was in a hit show or to hear Frank Fay's bigoted views on every subject. Even Lindy's wasn't the same.

It wasn't like I was an outsider. It was that, like many veterans, I came out of the Army with a chip on my shoulder, ready to argue with anyone. I was constantly annoyed by civilians—especially men my age or younger who hadn't served. I knew none of this was rational, but I couldn't make myself feel differently. For the first time ever, I felt at loose ends and at odds with myself.

By springtime of 1946, the West Coast seemed the answer. I knew all of the movie people; I was sure I'd click there. So I called Lew Wasserman, head of the MCA office in Los Angeles, to ask how he felt about my moving out.

Lew was enthusiastic about having me in Los Angeles. There was, he said, much for me to do there. That was modesty talking. MCA was riding high. It was the most important of the large Hollywood agencies, with the most prestigious clients and the best staff of agents. Wasserman himself had a sweet deal—because he was answerable only to Jules Stein, he could run the agency pretty much any way he pleased.

The way that pleased Lew was very different than anything ever seen in Hollywood. MCA was more like the Central Intelligence Agency than a talent business. It started with an official uniform: dark suit, white shirt, and a blue or gray tie. But although you could spot an MCA agent at twenty paces, you couldn't learn much from him. We were forbidden to discuss MCA business on the basis that it was really our clients' business.

As a newcomer, I was once again blessed by my connection to Moss Hart. By this time, Leland Hayward had been bought out by MCA, and Moss, his client, was now represented by the agency. Moss thoughtfully requested that I be involved in the negotiations for his motion picture deals, beginning with the contract he was about to sign with Darryl Zanuck to write *Gentleman's Agreement* for Twentieth Century–Fox.

Because of my connection to Moss and the fact that I knew Zanuck from the *Winged Victory* project, Lew asked me to cover Fox. I had no idea what "covering" a studio meant. This was, I soon discovered, one more way that MCA was different from other agencies. To be an agent at MCA was to represent more than your clients—you were also the agency's representative at a particular studio. If an MCA client who was making a film on that lot had a complaint, you were expected to deal with it.

My first day on the lot, an actor hailed me. "Are you the new MCA guy?" he asked.

"Yes."

"My name's Bob Sterling. I don't like the color of my dressing room. It's green. I want yellow."

"I don't handle dressing room colors," I replied.

"But you're my agent."

"I handle contract matters, or any disputes you might have with the director or with your costars," I told him, "but I don't handle paint."

"If that's your attitude, I'm going to fire MCA."

"I don't care what the hell you do, but I'm not going to Darryl Zanuck and ask him to change the color of your dressing room."

When I got back to the office, Lew asked me why I'd been so difficult with Bob Sterling.

"Because he's a horse's ass. He's carrying on about the color of his dressing room, and he's not even queer."

Well, that was certainly not the propitious thing for me to say, but I wasn't accustomed to the lengths to which an agent was obliged to go to help his client. And this was only the beginning of my inability to play by Lew's rules.

Lew wanted to know everything his agents did, so he required us to write a daily report on all our clients and activities. These reports were distributed to MCA executives at the end of the day. At a weekly meeting, Lew would choose highlights from these memos for discussion.

"What were you talking to Norman Krasna about?" he asked me one day.

I thought for a moment, and then, just to be ornery, I said, "I didn't tell him to go to the Morris office, I know that."

"The Morris office? Why would he go to the Morris office?"

"I don't think he will. I told him not to."

Lew failed to see the humor. "I wish you would remember your conversations," he said. "The way I run this office, I need all the information."

I nodded, but I knew his approach wasn't much good for a loner like me. I had been functioning on my own as far back as a kid in Brownsville, and I didn't need anyone to help me. To quote an old vaudeville expression, "I was doing a single."

When the meeting was over, I explained to Lew that I couldn't possibly do it his way. "You have a Mafia-type routine here with all these guys reporting to you," I told him. "I'm no robot. I do my own thing."

Lew disagreed. I disagreed with his disagreement. After that, we didn't get along very well. I wish it had been different —if there was anyone in the business I could have learned from, it was Lew. He was such a brilliant agent that he not only saw the light at the end of the tunnel, he put it there.

After a year of failing to conform, I agreed with Lew that MCA was not the place for me. He offered me a bonus and a tidy sum if I agreed to take the year off and not compete with MCA as an agent. I thought that was more than fair. And I was flattered to be regarded as so competitive that I would be a menace to fifty-eight agents in an agency with about $300 million worth of backing.

The day I left MCA, I felt almost exactly as I had when I got out of the Army eighteen months earlier: relieved, exhilarated, and, best of all, free. Without a job, but with a lot of loot, I went to Romanoff's to celebrate. Sitting in a booth was Brynie

Foy, who had directed the first all-talking film, *Lights of New York,* and who had headed the B-unit at Warners.

Brynie Foy had a gift for knowing what the moviegoing public would go for. And he knew how to get product onto the nation's screens very, very quickly. Jack Warner was crazy about him because he could take major stars, put them in a production for six weeks, and—boom, boom, boom—have a movie. Warner also liked Brynie because they were in accord politically, which was a little right of the Pharaohs. Their only difference was in the expression; Brynie was funny about his politics. He used to say, for example, that he didn't mind hiring writers who were Communists—that way, at least, he could keep track of them.

"I've been looking for you," Brynie said.

"What about?"

"I've been authorized by J. Arthur Rank of Great Britain and Robert Young of the Pennsylvania Railroad to form a company called Eagle Lion," he explained. "I'm going to run the studio for them, and I'd like you to be the executive officer."

"Well, I haven't got a job. You're on."

Before we had a chance to talk about the terms of the deal, Brynie got to his most pressing concerns: "Let's understand each other. You're not entitled to more than one girl under personal contract for three hundred a week, and neither am I. Or, if you like, we can each have two girls under contract for one-fifty. That gives us four girls under contract to the studio."

"That's terrific, Brynie," I said, somewhat startled by this proposition.

"One thing, though—they can't be under contract for more than six months."

"Why?"

Brynie looked surprised. "Because we want to have a change of face."

Brynie rented offices across the street from the Goldwyn Studio and gave me free rein to make deals with actors, directors, and writers. I didn't have to consult with him, which was just as well. It was dangerous when Brynie made a deal.

One day, Mel Cohen, an agent for the Ritz Brothers and other Las Vegas characters, came into my office. Mel was a real "dem, dese, and dose" fellow who was popular with the Mob. If you were inclined to laugh at him, you waited until he'd left the building.

"I made a deal for George Tobias to play the priest in *The Cardinal,*" he told me.

"Mel, you can't have a man who looks so Semitic playing a priest," I said. "It's not the right casting."

"This man came out here from New York with his wife and four children in a trailer. They're sitting out there, and they haven't got a dime. I've been supporting them. I made a deal with Brynie on this. It's closed."

I called Brynie on the intercom while Mel was in my office and asked if this was, in fact, true.

"No way. Who said that?" Brynie replied.

"Mel Cohen is right here. He told me."

"That shit! He doesn't know what he's talking about."

With that, Mel got up without a word, and went to visit Brynie in his office. Three minutes later, I got a call.

"You'd better come right over," Brynie instructed in a panicked voice.

The scene that greeted me was one of Brynie sitting at his desk and Mel holding a cocked pistol to Brynie's head. He leaned over to cue Brynie: "Please tell Lazar that we have a contract with Tobias for two thousand a week for ten weeks."

"We sure do," Brynie replied.

And that's how George Tobias played the priest in a picture which died so quickly that there was no time to embalm it.

Every so often several executives from New York would come to visit us. To each man, Brynie would say, "Why don't you put a girl under contract? Get yourself a beauty." This made me crazy. "How are we going to account for this," I'd ask Brynie, "if someone ever wonders about our string of actresses?" He'd say, "No problem. We'll make two women prison pictures a year. The actresses will be behind bars. They won't have to talk, just scream. They'll never have to act. We'll have no problems." And that's how Eagle Lion came to make two women prison pictures a year.

In the end, we only made one picture of any merit, *T-Men* —and that was an accident. Eddie Small, who had produced *The*

Man in the Iron Mask, The Corsican Brothers, and would go on to make *Witness for the Prosecution,* had been hanging around the office, listening to Brynie and me discuss potential film deals. Small never said a word. I often wondered if he could talk at all. Somehow, he knew that if he hung around Brynie long enough he'd hear something worthwhile. One day we were discussing the plot of *T-Men,* which was a Secret Service project with good action. When Small heard about the cast and the director, he asked, "Can I put up half the money?"

Well, just to hear him talk was a miracle. I thought dust would fly out of his mouth.

"Let's do it!" Brynie screamed.

The picture was such a hit that it almost put Eagle Lion back on the street. Six months after the picture was released, we got a call from Eddie Small's lawyer saying that Eddie wanted to know what we were going to do with the wardrobe from the picture. This was puzzling—*T-Men* was a contemporary picture, requiring almost no "costumes." No matter, the law explained; Small wanted half the money from the sale of the clothes.

At first, Brynie was furious. But as the eldest of the Seven Little Foys, he was an old-time vaudevillian who was trained to find a funny way out of any jam. So he decided not only to send Small the modest wardrobe from *T-Men,* but to ship him all the costumes hanging around from our other prison pictures. And that wasn't all. Brynie had these dusty old costumes packed up in thin cases so they could be easily pushed through a doorway of a hotel room, then called the manager of the hotel where Eddie Small lived and arranged to have them delivered to his room. When Eddie got home that afternoon, he discovered his room was completely filled with his bounty. He couldn't even get to the bathroom except by vaulting the cases. That's the last we ever heard from him about costumes.

In the year I was at Eagle Lion, pranking Eddie Small was probably the most fun I had. Running the studio had quickly become a bore to me. We didn't have enough money to make big pictures, not that Brynie would have wanted to make them. With a year and a half to go on my contract, I quit. And, at last, I did what I'd been dreaming about all along.

□

The Irving Paul Lazar Agency opened in the fall of 1947 in an office that had belonged to Spencer Tracy's brother. It wasn't terribly impressive. Set in an alley just off South Beverly Drive in Beverly Hills, it consisted of two chambers: a tiny reception area for my secretary, Sue Foster, and an eight-by-ten-foot office for the small agent and his smaller client list.

After working at MCA, I knew I didn't want to represent actors—they demand so much attention that an agent working alone couldn't really represent more than three or four of them at a time. Actresses were even more demanding. With them, it was "Where is my hairdresser? Where is my makeup person?" All major problems to them.

At MCA in New York, I had handled well-trained theater actors who were realistic, sensible, and for the most part, able to function on their own. I had seen, however, how all that changed once they'd moved to Hollywood, made a name for themselves, and acquired a battery of advisers: a personal manager, press agent, and business manager. After these sages got together to pay homage to their meal ticket, the actor would start to think, "Hey, I'm worth two or three million." I didn't want any part of those inflated expectations.

No, I saw my niche clearly: to represent East Coast playwrights who were, at that time, in big demand by the movie studios. It's absolutely clear to me that none of these writers would have given me the time of day if Moss Hart hadn't been my mentor. He engaged me to represent him for the movies the minute I opened the agency—which didn't mean much, as he wasn't writing screenplays at the moment. But he did me a great service by introducing me to his talented friends: Maxwell Anderson, Edna Ferber, Arthur Laurents, Garson Kanin and Ruth Gordon, Howard Lindsay and Russel Crouse, George Kaufman, and Cole Porter.

Representing playwrights in Hollywood wasn't a revolutionary idea. But I made myself different from other agents with similar client lists. For one thing, I was soon handling more playwrights than any other agent. For another, I quickly realized that I didn't have to limit my representation just to dramatists. All variations of East Coast talent were an exotic commodity: songwriters, lyricists, costume designers, and directors. Armed with that realization, I brought composer Gian Carlo Menotti, set designer Oliver Smith, choreographer Michael Kidd, and costume designer Irene Sharaff to work at the studios.

Most agents in the late 1940s would look at that client list and feel they'd made it. To me, the list was just the beginning. As I saw it, I still had to prove myself. For it was always my intention to be more than just a flesh peddler who took the service entrance. To do that, I not only had to insinuate myself in the lives of the people I wanted as clients, I had to become a welcome and regular presence in Hollywood's most desirable homes—I had to merge my social life with my professional life.

Once again, Moss's sponsorship was crucial. When I arrived in Hollywood, he introduced me to Lee and Ira Gershwin, who had one of the town's ultimate salons. Moss and Ira had done *Lady in the Dark,* and they adored one another. What was good enough for Moss was good enough for the Gershwins, for they promptly took me under their wing, inviting me for dinner several evenings a week. And what dinners! Their guest list included

Truman Capote and Harold Arlen.

Oscar Levant, Harry Kurnitz, Judy Garland, John Huston, Anatole Litvak, Bogie and Bacall, and George Cukor.

If Moss was like a brother to me, Ira was like my surrogate father. He not only became my client, he asked me to handle the George Gershwin estate. And that led me to even more songwriters, and a broader client list: Howard Dietz and Arthur Schwartz, Harold Arlen, Betty Comden and Adolph Green, Alan Jay Lerner and Frederick Loewe, Richard Rodgers and Oscar Hammerstein II.

Even with Moss at my side, it wasn't easy breaking into this league. To the George Kaufmans and Cole Porters of the world, I looked like exactly what I was: a pushy outsider. But I was so intent on becoming a success that I wouldn't allow myself to be snubbed. I just persisted until I won them over.

Signing these giants was a process of observing and educating myself. Not the hardest work I ever did—just being around them was an automatic good time. And once I learned how to act with the right people, it wasn't so hard to get to the next place.

Take, for example, Martin Gabel, the actor and director who was married to Arlene Francis. I got him a contract to direct a picture for Walter Wanger. When the Gabels arrived in Los Angeles, they became my neighbors at the Garden of Allah apartments, a complex on Sunset Boulevard in West Hollywood. I soon discovered that Martin and Arlene went out to Malibu every weekend to visit their good friend, Irwin Shaw, and a host of other writers, like Peter Viertel and Harry Kurnitz.

Shaw was enjoying a great success with the recent publication of *The Young Lions.* Viertel was a good young writer who had grown up in Hollywood and was the son of the legendary Salka Viertel, who had collaborated on the screenplays of several Greta Garbo films and who also had one of the great intellectual salons in town. Kurnitz was a successful screenwriter and one of the town's great wits.

I knew that Shaw's weekend lunches were where I wanted to be.

I also knew that Gabel had misgivings about taking me out there. Shaw and Viertel were great athletes, and Martin didn't think I'd cut the mustard with these sporty types. Nevertheless, I badgered him for weeks to take me along. When he could no longer avoid the fact that I was responsible for him being in Hollywood—and had to admit that he really liked me—he relented.

Once I got my foot in the door, I did whatever was necessary to be accepted. I was certainly no athletic powerhouse, but I was more than game to join in their athletic pursuits. And my willingness and fearlessness to go out in a rubber raft into the Pacific in a roaring surf or jump on a horse and go full tilt endeared me to Shaw and Viertel.

But I wanted to be more than an occasional guest; I cultivated these friendships. Although I was hardly wealthy, I decided to turn these top-tier acquaintances into clients by becoming the consummate host. So I entertained them, like a Jewish Medici Prince.

This was a novel approach. Writers had never heard of an agent giving dinners for groups of eight to twenty in the most fashionable restaurants and picking up the check. But I did it on a regular basis—what the hell, it was all tax-deductible. My clients became my friends. My friends became my clients. It was interchangeable.

Those dinners, which were really no big thing, turned out

to be a key difference between my competitors and me. As Harry Kurnitz, who was living mostly in Paris in the 1950s, wrote me after I'd visited him, "Paris misses your jaunty frame, the tilt of the homburg, the swing of the cape, the grab of the check. We have all been paying our own way since you left and it's a damned fucking frightening experience, so come back quick."

And I tried to make myself indispensable. When I brought writers out to work in the movies I organized everything for them—apartment, car, servants. "Lazar will take care of everything," was the phrase most often used by the New Yorkers I brought out to Hollywood. So much so, that my client Quentin Reynolds gave me a gold cigarette box with the inscription "Lazar is my shepherd; I shall not want."

Even with an impressive client list, I still had to figure out how to deal with the studios. In the 1940s, agents were the low men on the totem pole, subject to the whims of the all-powerful studios. In that setup, with most talent attached to studios under long-term contracts, agents just weren't very important. There were, however, always one or two agents who were friends of the moguls. L. B. Mayer, for example, had a soft spot for an agent who apparently procured women for him.

Benny Thau, head of business affairs at Metro, was a potentate in charge of hiring, firing, and casting. When Metro folded, he was out of a job. Not for long. Because he had done a great deal of business with the William Morris Agency, Morris president Abe Lastfogel felt obliged to give Thau a job as an agent and pay him more than anyone else at the agency. But after only six months, Thau quit. I saw him shortly after that and asked him why he'd left such a cushy setup. "I can't wait outside," he told me. I understood—he couldn't wait like a supplicant to make a pitch to a middle-level executive.

At that time, agents didn't deal one-on-one with moguls. If they were lucky, they dealt with heads of the story department; if they weren't, they talked to underlings. To break into the top tier of the agenting world when I was the new kid in town was going to be tough. The only way to get there, I knew, was to barge through the barriers.

As it happened, Leland Hayward and Charlie Feldman had left the agency business to become producers just as I was launching my agency. What an opening that created! Feldman had been a majority owner of one of the major talent agencies in Hollywood, with such distinguished clients as Dick Powell, Marlene Dietrich, Tyrone Power, and John Wayne; Hayward had represented Greta Garbo and Katharine Hepburn, along with writers like Moss Hart and Edna Ferber. While their counterparts were scrounging around, trying to talk to the second or third most important guy, Feldman and Hayward were great personal friends of every major studio head. That wasn't favoritism. It was justice—because they were internationally known and received, they really were as influential as any studio head.

Feldman, in particular, had a great influence on me. He was a wonderful host, and his house on Coldwater Canyon in Beverly Hills was filled with fine art. It had been decorated by his first wife, Jean Howard, a former Follies beauty and later a famous photographer. Feldman's eighteenth-century English dining room table could accommodate twenty people, and it often did—with food and wine worthy of the upper echelon of Hollywood. Feldman recognized that these surroundings were superior to any office, so he tended to spend his days in an easy chair next to an antique table on which rested three phones. That seemed like a sensible work ethic to me, and I soon adapted it.

Most of those who represented playwrights were in New York. These East Coast agents—Brandt and Brandt, Audrey Wood, Annie Laurie Williams, Kay Brown, and Edith Van Cleve—had a big edge, so I began to travel between both coasts, seeing all the plays in New York and rushing back to California to give my reviews. Because I saw the plays before the producers and studio heads had a chance to hear much about them, I figured my opinions would make me indispensable to them.

We come now to one of the charges most frequently leveled against Irving Paul Lazar. Let the record show that he pleads guilty. That is, of course, guilty with an explanation.

It wasn't lost on me that virtually all of the New York playwrights I courted had agents. Nonetheless, I was determined to get a piece of the action. So I devised a tactic that drove the playwrights' agents crazy: I very openly tried to sell—and often did sell—properties that I in no way represented. This tactic was what prompted Harry Kurnitz to deliver his famous line: "Everybody has two agents, their own and Lazar."

Kay Brown called me unethical. That's because she hated the fact that I'd try and sell one of her client's plays to a producer like Hunt Stromberg at Metro when she was already trying to sell it to Metro without assigning it to Hunt. "I don't want your commission, Kay," I'd tell her. "But I can make this sale happen for you. My friend is the producer and he wants to do it." She never accepted that logic. "Get out of my way, just get out of my way. How dare you do such a thing?" she snapped.

I was immune to her screams. It seemed to me that if I didn't interfere with her commission and the sale was made, what did it matter? But all she saw was that I was getting 10 percent from the studio or the producer on a property that she could have sold alone—in effect, burdening the project with a double commission. My cut wasn't anything that ultimately affected other agents, but they considered it a very sharp practice and they were personally offended when I told them the truth: "I can get more money for your client than the studios are willing to pay you."

What Kay Brown really resented—even more than my getting a commission from the producer—was when I'd tell a client like Lillian Hellman, whom I had gotten to know through Moss, that there was a deal in the offing before Kay had mentioned it. When I tried that tactic on Arthur Miller, Kay slapped me down. Well, some you lose.

Why did I go after the top writers—especially the playwrights—who were represented by the top agents in New York? Simple: I found those agents not as well versed about the Hollywood scene as I was. Sure, I had some charm. But the reason I was able to poach so successfully was that I knew more, negotiated harder, and made better deals.

One of the more important agents of the day was Harold Freedman, a rather nice man and a gifted agent, but not made for this kind of street fighting. I was told that whenever he heard my name, he would start to cry, knowing he was about to lose some valued client to me. If only he had gone along with my theory, we could have had a great working relationship. He needed someone on the West Coast to sell Paul Osborne, Maxwell Anderson, and Arthur Laurents to Hollywood, but he hated parting with half the commission. So "Mr. Lazar from Hollywood," as he referred to me, had to take the whole client.

Even in Hollywood, as I try to recall the competition I had in those days, I can think of very few names. My major threat in the 1950s was Ray Stark, who later became one of the most prolific and successful motion picture producers in Hollywood. Ray was murder; as soon as I left town, he would be calling my clients. That kind of solicitation worked both ways—only I didn't wait for him to leave town!

Finally, I found a smart solution. I was going to Europe, so I called Ray and said, "I've told every one of my clients that if there are any problems while I'm away, they are to call you."

He got a kick out of that. "Well, now you've got me," he said. "I have to be a nice boy. Have a good time and if any problems arise, I'll take care of them."

The other felony I am alleged to have committed is a life-long inability to cast my eye upon the manuscripts of my clients. Because of this reputation, my clients sometimes liked to put me to the test. Some sent their manuscripts to me with crisp hundred-dollar bills pressed between the pages—only to find their work returned with the money still in place. Dominique Lapierre inserted love notes to my wife between the pages of a manuscript.

Alan Jay Lerner went furthest: he taped together the pages of his manuscript of *An American in Paris*. When I returned Alan's script, I enclosed a note in which I claimed that he had created "an absolute rare work of art." Alan checked his script, discovered that the pages were still stuck, and told the press I had the nerve of a one-armed paper-hanger.

In my opinion, his finding out that I hadn't read his script was a less than fabulous discovery. I didn't need to read what he wrote because he had already told me his story and point of view. With that much knowledge, I could sell his work without reading it.

Ditto for most of the books I sold. Of course I didn't read them! I never pretended I did. I always got a synopsis, which was all I needed to know. Or I'd go on instinct. When I'd represent a celebrity who wanted to write his or her autobiography, I was, more often than not, fairly familiar with the life story.

It's not as if I was the only one who didn't read. How about the heads of the studios? They didn't read. And the producers? They didn't read, either. The fact is, *everybody* worked from synopses. That's why it was easy to deal with producers and studio chiefs—nobody read.

Of all the moguls, Louis B. Mayer had the most unusual method for judging material. He had the play or book in question read aloud by a drama coach named Lillian Burns, who would act out all of the parts for him. Just imagine the scene: L. B. Mayer sitting at his desk and watching this tiny woman, who weighed about ninety-five pounds, acting the part of babies and the grandparents alike—crying when the script called for it, laughing when she was supposed to laugh. The intensity of her one-woman show depended on how much she liked the material. And that, in turn, influenced Mayer.

In the early days, I was so eager to please and so dogged in my pursuit of sales that I'd go to any length to make it look as if I'd read something. On one occasion I was flying back from New York with a script, and Charlie Feldman, who was now producing, happened to be on the plane. What good fortune: me with an unread script on my lap, and an immobile producer at arm's length.

First, I baited the hook. "This is one of the best things I've ever represented," I said.

"What's it about?" Charlie asked.

"I'm pooped," I said, feigning a yawn. "Let me snooze a while, then I'll tell you."

I didn't tell him I hadn't read it. Because I traveled cross-country so frequently, and always on TWA, I knew many of the stewardesses. On this flight, I recognized one and told her I'd give her a hundred dollars if she read half the script before we reached Chicago and then told me the story. There was another hundred with her name on it if she read the rest before we landed in L.A.

When we took off from Chicago, I went back to the galley and she told me the first half of the story. Then I strolled back to my seat and recited every word she said.

"It sounds great," Charlie said.

"I'm going to take another nap now, but I'll tell you the rest later," I said.

As we were passing over Las Vegas, the stewardess told me the second half. Once again, I quoted her verbatim to Charlie.

"I'll buy it," he said.

North to Alaska was later made into a film starring John Wayne, but Charlie's real interest in the script was that it had a potential role for Capucine, who was then his girlfriend.

Charlie went on to read the script. Give him points. Quite often, producers pretended to have read. They were easy to spot. When a producer who probably hasn't finished college tells me a property I've given him has a "Kafkaesque substructure that would make it difficult to dramatize," you know you're being hosed.

Even Moss Hart succumbed to what he called the "Edna Ferber Literary Test." He named it that because once, as Moss and I were having lunch at "21," he spotted Edna at another table.

"How do I get out of here without Edna seeing me?" he asked. "She gave me her new book to read, and I haven't looked at it yet. She'll be furious. Let's try and sit here until she leaves."

We sat around aimlessly after lunch, but we could see that Ferber hadn't even gotten to her coffee—and Moss had to get to another appointment. As we walked out, Moss tried to dodge behind waiters and captains. Luck wasn't with him. "Moss, I'd like to see you a moment," rang a voice from across the room.

We went over to Edna's table, and Moss congratulated her on the book. "Edna, it was wonderful," he lied. "I just loved it."

She looked at him sternly, and, let me tell you, a stern look from Edna could scare the hell out of anyone. "What did you think about the part of the priest?" she asked. "Do you think I was right to leave it in?"

Moss stood there, sweat forming on his brow. And then, because he couldn't go on, he confessed: "Edna, you got me. I haven't read it."

"I thought not," she said.

For me, the goal wasn't to keep producers honest, but to

Sixty below in Kotzebue, Alaska. Don't be deceived by this smile. Merely cheese, dear Irving. Edna.

Edna Ferber.

get them to buy properties based on scanty information. Most of the time I was selling a book I'd never read to a buyer who was never going to read it either. And the truth was, we were probably both working from the same synopsis.

Harry Kurnitz's theory was that I didn't want my appreciation for my clients' work to be diminished—which would have been the case if I read a book and discovered it wasn't very good. "If I give Swifty something I've written, he tears off to Zanuck or somebody with nothing but enthusiasm," he told George Plimpton in an interview for the *Paris Review*. "If he stopped to read it, he might get sick and throw up all over Darryl Zanuck."

In the same way I preferred to sell plays before opening night, I liked to sell books that not only had I not read but weren't even finished. One of the gems of my career was the time I sold *Ice Palace* to Jack Warner.

One night at a party at Charlie Feldman's, Jack asked if I had any good new books. Now, Edna Ferber wasn't my client then. Harriet Pilpel, a classy New York lawyer, was doing her film deals, but Ken McCormick, her editor at Doubleday, had asked me to handle this one. With my chutzpah, he believed I could make a speedy and lucrative sale before word got out that it wasn't such a great book.

Word wasn't anywhere at that point, so I told Jack that Edna Ferber was finishing a new novel. I didn't have to say another word—Jack had enjoyed an enormous success with Edna's great novel, *Giant*. All he needed to buy *Ice Palace,* he said, was a quick synopsis.

This was not so easily done. I recalled only vaguely what Edna and Ken had told me about the story. It wasn't enough, so, to fill in the gaps, I threw in a few plot points of my own. And Jack went crazy for it.

"Will you sell it to me right now?" he asked. "How much do you want?"

"Four hundred thousand."

"I'll give ya three-fifty."

I told him I'd check with Edna and get back to him. Needless to say, she accepted the deal. Six months later, when the book was published, Warner gave a copy to Delmer Daves, a very fine writer-producer at the studio. He couldn't have been a better choice; his take was that if it's Ferber, it must be terrific. And he continued to feel that way until he read the book.

"This isn't the story you told me," he said to Jack Warner. "You told me a story that's better than the book."

So Jack called me: "The plot of *Ice Palace* you told me—it sounded great, but Delmer Daves says the book isn't the same. Come over here tomorrow so we can sort this out."

Well, I couldn't remember the synoposis I'd given them. This didn't put me at much of an advantage when Warner, Daves, and I met.

"What *was* the story you told?" Jack began.

"The story of the book," I lied.

"Have you read it?" Daves asked.

"No."

"Then where did you get the story you told Jack? That's the story I like."

"I was trying to recollect what Edna's editor had told me. I must have elaborated a little."

"Well, that's the part we want."

"Too bad I can't remember what I told you. Why don't you

read *What Price Glory?* and find out what happens to Sergeant Quirt and Captain Flagg, and follow that line."

"If that's the case, we should have bought *What Price Glory?*" Jack said.

"I can sell you that, too," I said.

"That's been made."

The meeting ended in a shambles. But eventually Warners figured something out, for they released *Ice Palace* in 1960.

"What would you like for Christmas?" Moss asked one December afternoon.

"Cole Porter," I said in jest.

That is what's called "kidding on the level." While it might have seemed an impossibility to have Cole Porter as a client at that point in my career, it wasn't beyond hope. More than a decade earlier, Moss had made a trip around the world with Cole, and out of that evolved their collaboration on *Jubilee,* a big hit on Broadway.

At that time, Cole had a devoted, bright, and capable attorney in the person of John Wharton. But Moss took my request seriously and explained to Cole why I should represent him. Cole called Wharton, who was so busy he wasn't at all displeased if I could take care of some of Cole's career. For him, it was simply a question of whether Cole would like me and trust my judgment.

Moss took me to meet Cole at his apartment at the Waldorf Towers. I was tentative in my approach because I was simply in awe of him—and because Moss had warned me that Cole was quite aloof unless he knew you well. On first meeting, Cole seemed shy and spoke in a low voice. And yet he possessed an uncontrived air of elegance.

I mean something quite specific by this. Noël Coward and Fred Astaire were elegant, but with a theatrical flair; Cole was without artifice. Noël, for example, would inevitably pin a red rose to his lapel and Astaire would sport an ascot, but Cole would only occasionally wear a white carnation. (I learned later he was inventive in certain unseen bits of attire—he had his collar stays and the clips on his garters fashioned of gold from Cartier.)

The day I got Cole Porter as a client was one of the proudest days of my life; for Cole, it was less momentous. Despite his sophistication, he adored listening to the radio soap operas. I was unaware of this. And so, in the early days of our relationship, I was so delighted to have Cole in my stable that I wanted the world to know he was my client—whenever someone came to my office, I'd push the button on the phone and say to my secretary, "Get me Cole Porter." I didn't really have anything to say to him, but I thought it proved to my guest that I was a hotshot agent.

Finally, Cole called Moss: "Mossy, dear, I love that little fellow you got me for an agent, but could you get him to stop calling me two or three times a day? First of all, he interrupts just when I'm listening to the 'Romance of Helen Trent.' And secondly, he talks like an educated Negro."

Moss passed the word down. I shut up. And, in time, I proved myself with Cole and went on to represent him for writing the scores of such memorable Hollywood musicals as *High Society, Silk Stockings, Les Girls,* and *Can-Can.*

By 1950, the clients I represented for motion pictures included Alan Jay Lerner, Johnny Mercer, George S. Kaufman, Charles Jackson, Howard Lindsay and Russel Crouse, Dorothy and Joseph Fields, Betty Comden and Adolph Green, Arthur Laurents, John Patrick, Clifford Odets, and Lillian Hellman. My most prolific client for the next three decades also joined me that year. How I got him is a story—about other people's carelessness more than my overarching scheming.

Irwin Shaw had been represented by Leland Hayward. When Leland sold his business to MCA, Irwin stayed with the agency. But about a year or two after I met him, his contract expired. Before he signed a new one, he paid a visit to Ned Brown, a charming and good MCA agent who was going to represent him.

During their meeting, Ned Brown walked out of the office for a few minutes, leaving Irwin alone. And Irwin spied a stack of copies about three feet high of Norman Mailer's recent novel, *The Naked and the Dead.* He picked up one and began reading. When Brown returned, he was already on page forty, so he asked him if he could take the book. And Brown made a colossal error

—he told Irwin he couldn't spare a copy because they were being submitted to various studios. At that point, Irwin supposedly said, "You mean to tell me that I, who have paid this company thousands of dollars in commission, can't have a book when there are two hundred sitting there?" Brown shook his head.

With that, Irwin left Brown's office and came directly over to mine.

I always say I'm the first agent to have sold the motion picture rights of a play to a studio for more than a million dollars —before the play opened. If I'm not, then I don't know who did.

I began selling plays to the movies for high prices in the late 1940s, but my real contribution was doing it in advance of the opening, thereby obtaining a guarantee for the author whether the play was a hit or not. As the percentage of plays that do well is very low, there is a distinct advantage to selling a theatrical work for the movies before it opens. I convinced Maxwell Anderson, Edna Ferber, and French playwright Marcel Achard, among others, that this was the route to take.

The classic example of this strategy came when Howard Lindsay and Russel Crouse gave me *The Great Sebastians.* When they wrote this play, they already had Alfred Lunt and Lynn Fontanne to star. Lindsay and Crouse, Lunt and Fontanne: What more could a producer want? It was to die for.

The play was a melodramatic comedy. I felt it wouldn't go, but I couldn't say that to them. They had, after all, enjoyed fabulous success with *Anything Goes* and *Call Me Madam,* and had won the Pulitzer Prize for *State of the Union.* Who was I to tell them that their play wasn't very good? All I could do was advise them to make a preproduction deal with a studio.

The Dramatists Guild rule was that if a preproduction deal was not signed before the curtain went up on the first performance, the play couldn't be sold to Hollywood until three weeks after it opened in New York. Lindsay and Crouse believed they should wait; I pressed them to accept a preproduction deal with Harry Cohn at Columbia Pictures.

I was so desperate to have Lindsay and Crouse sign the Columbia contract before the first preview—in Wilmington, Delaware—that I went to see Edward Colton, the Dramatists

Guild's attorney, who had to approve all motion picture sales. "They won't sign this unless you're present," I told him. "And I must get it signed." And then I took him into my confidence and confessed that I didn't think the play would work.

Colton had never gone out of town to get a contract signed, but the Guild got a percentage of the sale—it was in his interest for Lindsay and Crouse to make this deal. It was equally in Columbia's interest to wrap this up quickly, so I got a few studio executives to join us on the trip to Wilmington.

You see, I knew what I was up against. The boys were cocky about the play. They thought it would be a smash on the order of their *Life with Father,* the most successful play in the history of Broadway up to that time. They not only didn't want to sell *Sebastians* to the movies so soon, they were determined to outsmart me. Making agents crazy gave them pleasure; it actually amused them that I was so frantic.

We arrived at the theater about a half an hour before curtain. Lindsay and Crouse were nowhere to be found. They strolled in about ten minutes before curtain, and it was apparent they wanted to get rid of Colton and me. People were streaming into the theater, no one was supposed to be backstage—we were being pressured to be nice boys and let the show go on.

I finally nailed Lindsay and Crouse at the back of the theater. "I have to talk turkey to you guys," I explained. "Take my word for it: there's no time to lose. You've *got* to sign. If you decide after the play opens that you really don't want the contract, I'll try and figure a way out, but meanwhile, you must sign it."

Colton assured them that the documents were okay. I held the contract up on the back wall of the theater. Someone held a flashlight. And Lindsay and Crouse each signed as the curtain was rising.

The play hadn't been on for fifteen minutes when we all "knew" there was no way it could ever run. It didn't. And Columbia never made the movie. But my clients got paid, and handsomely. There is a reason why my cable address was "Cav Emptor, New York."

In the early years of representing screenwriters, there was often a Wild West attitude when it came to negotiating. Many of the writers I handled only wrote when they needed the dough;

by and large, they had great contempt for Hollywood. You couldn't blame them—producers thought they were dispensable.

Jack Warner was one of the worst with writers. His theory was that the less he paid them, the better. As for taking breaks during the day, forget it. Writers weren't allowed to leave the lot even for lunch because Jack thought going to a restaurant wasted too much time.

Goldwyn was almost as bad. Once, after a commissary lunch, my client Harry Kurnitz and I were walking back to the studio. Goldwyn swooped down upon us. "You're walking a little too slowly," Goldwyn told Harry.

"I'm a slow walker," Harry replied.

"I hope you're thinking about the screenplay while you're walking," Goldwyn muttered.

"No, I'm talking to my agent."

"Instead of talking to your agent, who has nothing to say to you that will change your life, why don't you think about the movie?" Goldwyn snapped as he walked briskly away.

But as I recall some of the negotiating episodes I was involved in, it's amazing what some of these writers were, in fact, able to get away with.

No one was better at beating the moguls at their own game than Ben Hecht. The deal I made for him with Sam Goldwyn certainly proves that he had Sam beat.

"I get paid two thousand dollars per day—in cash," Ben told me. "I want it in hundred-dollar bills on my desk, or I don't show up for work the next day. And by the way, there's a very pretty girl who's a wonderful secretary. You've got to get her a contract while I'm out here. She'll make a thousand a week. I know that sounds like a lot, but she's a great actress and a great typist—and I want her to have a part in the picture."

"Can she really act?" I asked.

"*She* thinks she can. *I* think she can. Nobody may agree with us, but I can tell you right now, I'll fight for her."

William Saroyan was another odd bird. One day L. B. Mayer mentioned that he was looking for some new stories. By coincidence, Saroyan had just called me—he always rang when he was broke. I explained what Mayer was looking for and urged him to come up with something. I then told Mayer that I had a Pulitzer Prize–winning writer with a great story. A few days later, I brought Saroyan to Mayer's office. As Saroyan took him through the plot, L. B. began to tear up—he was a real crier. My heart was less moved: I knew Saroyan was making it up as he went along.

"That's terrific," Mayer said, when Saroyan finished weaving his tale. "Now go wait outside, and I'll talk to Irving about it."

Saroyan dutifully strolled out to the parking lot.

"How much?" Mayer asked.

"He wants one-fifty," I said.

"He's got it."

I went to Benny Thau to work out the payment: fifty thousand up front, fifty thousand when he hands in half the story, then a final fifty thousand when he turns in the ending. Elated, I hurried out to the car to tell Saroyan I'd gotten him fifty grand to start.

"What's the total?" he asked.

"One hundred fifty."

"Get me the one-fifty. I need all of it right now."

"You're crazy."

"Tell him I want the one-fifty now, or no deal."

I went back to Mayer's office and explained the situation— and he agreed to give Saroyan a check in full. I raced back to Saroyan and told him I'd deposit the check, take my commission, and give him the rest tomorrow.

"No, I want the money in cash, now."

"You're crazy. Can't you wait two days?"

He apparently couldn't—his bookies had threatened him. Back I went to Mayer, who called Benny Thau. And Thau arranged for the bank to bring the money over to the studio in hundred-dollar bills. I took the loot to the parking lot, and stood with Saroyan as we counted the money out on the hood. With every ten thousand he took, I'd take a thousand for myself, until I had my fifteen grand and he had the rest. Then he went off to pay his bookie.

The next day, Saroyan arrived at my office. "You better give me a thousand dollars," he announced. "I've got no money to get home."

Another wily client was Clifford Odets. One day he called me. He was so in debt, he said, that he'd sold his art collection.

But he had an idea for a movie, *Page One*. I knew he was spitball-ing, but I took him over to see Jerry Wald, who was an easy sell if I had him alone for ten minutes. Odets told him half the story, and Jerry bit. Jerry sent us on to Darryl Zanuck, who had been a journalist as a young man. To him, the title alone of *Page One* was catnip.

I got Odets two hundred thousand, a small fortune for a screenplay in those days. I also got him a cottage on the lot and a secretary. Momentarily, Odets was almost pleased. But nothing really satisfied him—he wasn't what I'd call Charm Boy, not by a long shot.

A month later, Odets invited me to pick up the script. When I walked into his cottage, he was holding a six-hundred-page screenplay—a document about five times longer than a standard script.

"Wait a minute, you're a professional writer. Why are you giving me this?" I asked, staring at all those pages.

"Let them read it," he said.

"If they read it, what can they do with it? There's no way a picture can be made with this much dialogue. Why don't you cut it to two hundred pages and we'll go from there?"

"I'll cut it if they pay me."

I was furious. "I got you this job because Zanuck trusted Jerry and me," I snapped, "and now you're betraying me."

"Your job is to protect me, not Jerry Wald."

I soon realized that Odets had planned this caper. All the same, I went back to Jerry and Darryl and got him some additional money. Odets started cutting away. He trimmed it down to three hundred pages, and then I had to get him some more money to cut it to two hundred. At that point, he announced he wanted to direct the movie. On that one, I told him, he was on his own. I knew what he was trying to do: get as much money as possible. And I knew, if they let him direct, he'd do a lousy job.

But Jerry Wald was overcome by the prestige of Clifford Odets, as was Darryl—they let him direct the picture. *The Story on Page One* starred Rita Hayworth, and just as I predicted, it was a ghastly movie that died on Pico Boulevard and should never have been released.

CHAPTER

Five

*L*OUIS B. MAYER once told me, "A producer will respect you, no matter how tough you are, if he thinks you're representing your clients to the best of your ability. He may not prefer to do business with you, but by God, he'll respect you. If your client is the person he wants, he'll buy him from you, and his agent could be King Farouk."

Well, I wasn't King Farouk. I was someone the moguls had met socially, had grown to like, and then had moved on to do business with without damaging the after-hours friendship.

When I did business one-on-one with Darryl F. Zanuck, Jack Warner, Harry Cohn, Sam Goldwyn, and Louis B. Mayer, I marveled at how much they made decisions on instinct. They weren't as realistic or cautious as their production executives, which is why they didn't usually deal one-on-one with agents. They were lousy businessmen, and they knew it.

Of all these giants, I knew Darryl Zanuck the best. He was short, trim, and iron-hard. He wore a little mustache and had slightly bucked teeth with an aperture in which he could have rested his cigar. He'd stalk his office, frequently holding a riding crop.

For all his toughness, Darryl was a prankster with a flair for slip-on-a-banana-peel humor. I once flew with him from Los Angeles to New York in the days when a cross-country flight took ten hours. Because a late departure meant a night-long flight, there were berths on planes so you could get undressed, put on a pair of pajamas, and go to sleep. But when I flew with Darryl that time, I woke up in the morning to find that my trousers had suddenly become knee pants—Darryl had cut them off at the knees. I looked ridiculous deplaning in New York with my short socks and garters.

I loved to negotiate with Darryl because he was so emotional. If he liked a specific book or play, he had no problem paying more than anyone else. He knew he wasn't a good businessman, so he avoided talking business. In the beginning, I had to siphon my deals through David Brown, head of the Fox story department, or Lew Schreiber, the studio vice president, so Darryl would have time to digest the deal.

But when Darryl was overcome with an insatiable desire to buy a book, nothing could dissuade him—forget Brown or Schreiber, he wanted to close right then and there. Such was the case when he asked me to come to the studio to discuss Romain Gary's *Roots of Heaven,* which he wanted John Huston to direct. I asked for two hundred thousand dollars. He didn't flinch.

"You've got a deal, but you have to sign the contract right now," he said.

"I have to call Gary. I can't sign without telling him about it."

Darryl offered me his phone. I called Gary's office and discovered that as the French Consul General in L.A., he had gone to San Francisco to attend a meeting of colleagues. I tried to locate him at his hotel, then at the convention hall, all to no avail. I didn't want to lose the sale, because it was doubtful that anyone else would pay any real money for the book. Darryl, meanwhile, was eyeing me with a cigar grasped firmly between his two front teeth, looking more like Peter Rabbit than a mogul. He had me exactly where he wanted me.

"If you walk out of here, you can forget the deal," he said. "I don't want you peddling this around."

I knew he meant it. I thought for a moment, then accepted his offer. It wasn't correct for me to do it, and I didn't do it without reflecting on the possible consequences. But I felt in my heart that if push came to shove and Gary was unhappy with the deal, Darryl wouldn't let me swing in the wind.

The next day, I finally got Gary on the phone and asked what he thought would be a fair price for the novel.

"We've been turned down quite a few places, so just do the best you can," he said. "If you could get twenty-five thousand, it would be great."

When I told him to multiply by eight, Gary almost jumped out of the Top of the Mark.

I sold Sloan Wilson's *The Man in the Gray Flannel Suit* to Darryl at Romanoff's, but the next day he didn't remember he had bought it. I had told him the story a few weeks earlier, when we were flying from California to New York. And he absolutely had to have it. I demanded two hundred thousand dollars. He was outraged. But I knew Darryl would come back to me.

When I returned to California, David Brown called. "I wish Darryl would buy that book," he said. "It would make a wonderful movie." I told him of my conversation with Darryl, and David said he would talk to him. That night, I went to Romanoff's for dinner with a client of mine. Darryl was seated at the first table with Michael Romanoff and the director Gregory Ratoff. As I passed by, he motioned for me to come over.

"What will you take now if we close the deal on *Gray Flannel Suit*?" he asked.

"A hundred seventy-five thousand will do it," I said.

"I'm making you a firm offer of one hundred and twenty."

The next day I called the author and told him about the deal. He was very pleased. I immediately called David Brown to accept Darryl's offer.

Very quickly David called me back. "Darryl doesn't remember seeing you last night," he said. Imagine my chagrin. Having closed the deal, I'd informed the author and his publisher. What to do? David suggested that I write Darryl a letter, recounting our conversation in great detail. Darryl then consulted with Ratoff and Romanoff to verify my account. They did, and the deal was honored.

Ethics is not necessarily a word you associate with Hollywood. But during the Golden Era most of these men did deals on a handshake and more often than not lived up to their commitments. Perhaps it was because they were gamblers at heart and understood you paid your debts in full.

In 1946, when I was still handling Moss Hart at MCA, I sat next to Jack Warner at a preview of Moss's play, *Christopher Blake*. For whatever reason, this story of a father who neglects his son had a powerful emotional effect on Jack, and he was soon weeping.

"I want this play," he whispered to me.

I knew I couldn't close a deal because of the Dramatists Guild rule prohibiting the sale of a play that's being performed until three weeks into its run.

"Jack, don't tell anybody," I said at the intermission. "Let's just make a pact. I want a hundred fifty thousand for the play."

He agreed, and we shook hands. I told no one but Moss. Meanwhile, audiences began avoiding the play. It barely made it to the three-week mark. When it did, however, I called Jack to remind him of our agreement. He was more than a gambler, he was a good sport. He knew the play was a flop, but he lived up to his commitment and paid in full.

Of all the moguls, Jack probably had the best sense of humor. He once threatened to bar me from the lot but then relented. "I can't really stick to that," he told me. "I have too much fun with you. Forget it."

"Jack. I never took it seriously."

"Well, if that's the case, you *are* barred. After today, you can't come around any more."

"What about mornings?" I inquired.

"All right. Just mornings."

"You want to give me some time in the afternoon?"

"Okay. You can be on the lot for one hour in the morning and one hour in the afternoon. Otherwise, you're barred."

When I first met Sam Goldwyn, I got the idea that because his accent was so heavy he didn't understand everything I said. So I spoke to him in pidgin-English.

"You like book, Sam?" I would ask. "Book good for you. You have somebody read it, then we talk."

This went on for quite some time until one day he said, "I want to ask you something. How much education have you had?"

I reeled off my educational credentials.

"But you speak strangely," he countered.

That put an end to my talking like an Indian.

Goldwyn admired success in the theater. He always reached out for the best playwrights and was more than happy to pay for them. The fact that he mispronounced the names of the authors or the titles didn't matter—he trusted his instinct. His gut was just as useful when he looked at a film; he knew exactly what wasn't working. He didn't need an audience. His intuition was all he needed to guide him to the making of a successful film.

But Sam was difficult to deal with. During the late 1950s, I had one contretemps with him.

"I cannot tell you what it would mean to me if you found a book that I really cared about," Sam would often say in those years. "I'm anxious to make a picture, but I can't find anything I want to do."

Max Shulman had written a marvelous book called *Rally 'Round the Flag, Boys!,* which was funny, had a great point of view, and was full of Americana. I thought it could bring Sam a success comparable to what he had enjoyed with *The Best Years of Our Lives,* so I sent him the galleys of the book. Two days later, he called: "You've given me a book I'm crazy about, and I want to do it. Let's make a deal right now. I don't want you to show it to anyone else."

"Sam, I haven't given it to anyone. So here's what we want: three hundred thousand for the book, a hundred thousand for Max to write the screenplay, plus a percentage of the profits."

Goldwyn agreed. I went back to my office, called Shulman and his New York agent, Harold Matson, and we all shook hands over the telephone.

Two mornings later, I got a call from Sam's wife, Frances Goldwyn: "We're not buying that book you gave Sam."

"Frances, what do you mean you're not buying it? You already did."

"No, we haven't. It's my money, not Sam's. The book will never make a movie that would sell in Europe. I'm not buying this book, and you can bet on it. Good-bye."

I was startled by this turn of events. Frances had always been very friendly to me. I didn't know what to do next except call Sam.

"Whatever Frances says, goes," he told me.

"I've never dealt with Frances before," I countered. "You didn't tell me the deal was contingent upon her approval."

"Well, that's the way it is."

I wasn't just flabbergasted, I was frantic. That afternoon I gathered up four copies of the Shulman novel and personally visited the head of every other major studio—Mike Frankovich at Columbia, Buddy Adler at Fox, and Jack Warner. I told each of them that I was auctioning the book off to the highest bidder.

Several nights later, I was at Frank Sinatra's for dinner—as were Adler and Frankovich. I asked if they had taken a look at *Rally 'Round the Flag, Boys!* They both said they hadn't gotten to it yet.

"Well, you'd better do it tonight, because I'm selling the book tomorrow," I warned.

When they realized that they were competing with each other, they took early flight from the party. The next morning, Sinatra called and asked me what I had to do with their leaving so early: "It seems to me that after you talked with them, they blew."

"Frank, I merely told them that they hadn't read a book that was going to be sold today."

"You son of a bitch. Try and do business in your own office." Then he added, "Is there a part in it for me?"

Buddy Adler called later that day. "Come on over here. I want to buy the Shulman book." I went over to Fox and got an offer that wasn't as good as the deal I had proposed to Goldwyn; nevertheless, it was an offer.

I called Harold Matson and told him the situation. I had spoken to my lawyer, who felt there was no way we could sue Sam. It would take years before it got to court, and he didn't even think it was a good case. So I suggested that we take the Fox offer because if anyone found out that Goldwyn didn't buy the book, we'd be in trouble selling it elsewhere. Matson wisely agreed.

Weeks later Frances Goldwyn's secretary called to invite me to a dinner party. I told my secretary to tell her I wasn't available. About a week later, another invitation. I declined again. The next time, Sam placed the call himself, but I still wouldn't take it. After that, when I saw the Goldwyns at a dinner party I'd be polite, but I wouldn't let myself get cornered talking to either one of them.

I hadn't told anyone what had happened, but Sam was agitated. He had a great sense of guilt because he fancied himself a man of his word. By his standards, he was. Except that his standards applied only to him. If he made a promise he couldn't keep, he had no difficulty clearing his conscience. My refusal to talk to him made him fear that I would take a stand, perhaps publicly. And that—not his broken promise—was unbearable to him.

One day a distinguished Eastern lawyer called. "I'm in town visiting Sam Goldwyn," he said. "Come over to the studio to see us."

"No, I won't."

"As a favor to me?"

I got into my little Thunderbird, and as I drove along Wilshire Boulevard, I stopped for a light in front of a Rolls-Royce dealership and saw a car in the window that caught my eye. I parked and went into the showroom to look at this beautiful black-and-brown Silver Cloud. It had a custom interior designed for a customer who had put down a five-thousand-dollar deposit and then disappeared. They would sell it to me for sixteen thousand.

At the Goldwyn Studios, I was promptly ushered into Sam's office. Our Mutual Friend was the first to speak.

"Mr. Goldwyn is very, very embarrassed at what happened," he told me. "He doesn't like the idea of your not being friends, and he wants you to reconsider the situation."

"There's nothing to reconsider," I said, not looking at Goldwyn. "I think he behaved very badly. He reneged on a deal and embarrassed me. If I hadn't sold the book to Fox, it would have been disastrous. What Sam did was unconscionable."

"You're right," Sam blurted out. "And I want to make it up to you."

Only now did I turn to Goldwyn. "How?"

"I want to buy you a gift," said Sam.

"What kind of a gift?"

The gathering at my fiftieth birthday party.
Being serenaded by Martin Gabel, Arlene Francis, Joan Axelrod, Kitty
Carlisle Hart, George Axelrod, and Moss Hart.

"What do you want?"

"I just saw a Rolls-Royce."

"It's yours."

Goldwyn pressed a buzzer, and in walked Bobby Newman, his general manager. "Bobby, take Mr. Lazar and buy him the Rolls-Royce he wants."

Newman's eyes popped. I shook hands all around, then Newman and I drove to the Rolls-Royce dealership. I'm sorry to report that, after the first couple of years, the car wasn't much good; at that time, there weren't enough qualified Rolls-Royce mechanics in this country. But when it was out of the shop, my Rolls was a great status symbol—particularly in the eyes of friends and clients who had no idea it hadn't cost me a penny.

"There is one man who is not here who is single-handedly ruining the motion picture business as we know it," David Selznick told an assemblage of the most important people in Hollywood at a dinner at Charlie Feldman's house. "The ridiculous prices he demands for books and plays and writers will surely be the end of us all."

It was later reported to me that everyone seemed stunned at this pretentious statement. Then Audrey Wilder, Billy's wife, spoke up. "You're full of shit, David," she said. "You probably wanted to buy something from Lazar, and he didn't want to sell it to you, and you're just mad."

Audrey had it just right. Selznick's outburst was the result of the somewhat legendary sale of Irwin Shaw's novel *Lucy Crown*. When Irwin finished the final draft, he called me from Klosters to say he was sending it only to Random House. "Forget trying to sell it to the movies," he told me. "It's definitely not a film."

Those words only made me more determined.

Irwin's concern was with a crucial scene, in which a child at camp looks through a window and sees his mother having intercourse with his hero, the camp counselor. Irwin thought there was no way that pivotal moment could be depicted on the screen. But Irwin, who was far removed from Hollywood, was wrong. It was possible to shoot such a scene—though not, to be sure, as vividly as he had written it.

The real issue, I felt, was Irwin's pride. He didn't want the book shopped around and possibly turned down. Nor did he want to make a deal that would result in an emasculated version of his story. Because his feelings were strong, I had to agree with him. And, for once, I sat on my hands.

What I didn't know was that Bennett Cerf, at Random House, had slipped David Selznick a copy of the galleys. Selznick had read it and immediately saw a role for his wife, Jennifer Jones. But even if Irwin wanted me to sell the book, I didn't want Selznick to be the buyer. He was a heavy gambler who played for exorbitant stakes—and at that moment he wasn't in the greatest financial shape.

So here I was in the curious and somewhat contradictory position of trying to dissuade Selznick from making a bid for the book, even as I was working to convince one of my top clients —who was also one of my two best friends in the world—that we could sell the book. True, *Lucy Crown* would have been, in almost any hands, a foolish movie. But if I could get Irwin more money than he'd ever seen before, I felt he could tolerate an embarrassing production.

So when David wrote me a letter stating that I shouldn't interpret his enthusiasm as an opportunity to ask for a lot of money, I told him I'd been offered four hundred thousand dollars. "If you want it, you'll have to pay four-fifty," I continued. "Personally, I don't think you ought to pay it."

"Why can't I buy it for the same amount of money that's been offered?"

"Because you have no preferential status. Nobody does. Whoever buys it has to pay the most money. I'm working for Irwin Shaw."

David asked me not to do anything for a few days. The next day I went over to see Burt Lancaster, Harold Hect, and their partner, James Hill. Under my arm was the manuscript.

"What have you got there?" Burt asked.

"Shaw's new manuscript, *Lucy Crown*."

"Can we read it?" Burt asked.

"David Selznick wants to buy it, so I really can't talk about it," I told them, knowing, of course, that would only pique their interest.

They suggested that I could do them a big favor by letting them read it overnight. As they were big Shaw fans, I let them. And at eight the next morning my houseman awakened me to say that I had visitors downstairs in the living room. Burt, Harold, and James had been up all night reading the manuscript aloud to each other, page by page. They were crazy about it and wanted to buy it on the spot.

"It's a tough way to wake up," I said, "but as long as you're here, let's make a deal."

"Not only do we want to make a deal for the novel, but we were looking at your paintings just now, and our company would like to buy some of them," Harold said, looking lovingly at my two Picassos, a Juan Gris, a Chaim Soutine, and some other large oils.

"The paintings are out. As for the book, I want four hundred thousand dollars, payable at the rate of forty thousand a year for ten years."

"That's an outrageous price—but we'll pay it."

That afternoon Selznick called inquiring about *Lucy Crown*.

"Sorry, David. I've sold it."

"You couldn't do that without telling me."

"It's done."

"I'm going to Switzerland to see Irwin."

I called Irwin and managed to track him down at the ski lodge at the top of the mountain.

"What's the matter?" he asked, thinking it was some kind of emergency.

"Do you still not want to sell *Lucy Crown*?"

"It's not a movie."

"Say it could be. What would be a fair price for it?"

"I don't think anyone will ever make it, but if you could get fifty thousand, that would be terrific."

"Would you take four hundred thousand?"

"If you can get four hundred, I'm not going to ski down the mountain, I'm going to fly down!"

David, in the meantime, was as good as his threat. He arrived in Switzerland the day after I called, told Irwin he was willing to pay more, and asked why he was willing to take only four hundred thousand.

"I don't know," Irwin said. "But Lazar must have a good reason."

As soon as he could shake free, Irwin called to find out why I wouldn't sell it to Selznick. I explained that David was strapped for cash. I knew he could make the first payment, but by the time the contracts were finalized in two or three months he might not have the rest of the money. If that happened, he was too distinguished for us to badger him for money—we'd have to walk away empty-handed. To me, a real four hundred thousand was better than a vaporous four-fifty. Irwin agreed. And he not only made out all right, he did fine creatively—to this day, *Lucy Crown* has never been filmed.

While I got my commission, I paid a certain price; Selznick shunned me for the next couple of years. Then, as if nothing had happened, he called and asked me to work out a deal on some of his properties. I met him at the St. Regis in New York, where, like an Arab sheik, he had taken over an entire floor. Two secretaries followed him with open notebooks, their pencils flying as they took down the gospel according to Selznick.

L. B. Mayer was a great showman who loved and admired talent. If he thought he spotted a potential star in the making, he was like a kid with a lollipop. And when he met someone who had been recognized as a talent, he was an even more formidable champion. Nothing would stop him from putting all of the muscle, power, and money of Metro-Goldwyn-Mayer behind his judgment, and in some cases, his pure instinct.

By the same token, he was destructive and callous if the talent he endorsed and supported didn't observe his rules, his social standards, and his politics. And that was a problem, for L.B. was one of the fiercest leaders in the search for Communists in Hollywood. He felt completely justified in destroying anyone he identified as un-American—that is, anyone who wasn't a friend of Ward Bond, John Wayne, or John Ford, or who wasn't endorsed by Hedda Hopper.

When Mayer was "eased out" of his position at Metro in 1951, he couldn't comprehend that he was no longer king of the realm and had no power to make or break a star. The way he saw it, he had only to press a buzzer and a minion would produce whomever he wanted. Despite his loss of stature, it was still a given that you showed up when Mayer wanted to see you.

Mayer's secretary called late one morning to inform me that he wanted me in his office at one o'clock that very day, so I changed my schedule around and drove over to his house on St. Cloud Road. As ever, the place was so sanitized that it gleamed. The only paintings Mayer could tolerate here were by Grandma Moses; the only photographs on display—of the Pope and Cardinal Spellman—were both inscribed. Mayer, of course, had not called me to advance his spiritual development.

"I want you to give me your best property," he told me. I knew what that meant: I'd better not offer a potential hit book or screenplay to another producer before giving him first crack. I was a little apprehensive about that because I knew he wasn't accustomed to spending his own money, and he was no longer set up to spend other people's money. Money was even a little bit of a problem—considering that he was once reported to be the highest-paid executive in the United States, he didn't wind up with a fortune.

I had to tell him about something, however, so I recommended *The Shrike,* a play starring José Ferrer that was a big hit in New York. I thought it would work well for Mayer, as it had a strong point of view and could be produced with minimal financial risk. Mayer agreed to pay a hundred and fifty thousand for the property. I then made a deal for Joe Ferrer both to star in and direct the film.

Only after the deal was closed did Mayer want to go to New York to see the show. On the day of our departure, however, various crackpots called him to say that Joe Ferrer was a Communist. As a result, we didn't go to New York.

The next day Hedda Hopper wrote in her column that she thought it was outrageous that Louis B. Mayer was buying a play directed by and starring a Communist, and that the play itself had Communist overtones. Hedda's column was all Mayer needed to renege on the deal. After reading the paper, he called to announce that he was not going to see "that Commie play," nor was he going to pay for it.

As I saw it, Mayer had already committed himself—we were, by this point, waiting for contracts to be prepared. Mayer didn't deny that he had authorized me to buy it. His position was that he would never have done so had he known that José Ferrer was a Communist.

Ferrer didn't behave much better. When I ran into him in London, I extended my hand. "Joe, I'm going to do everything I can to fight this injustice," I said.

"You called me a Communist."

"Don't confuse me with Mayer. He called you a Communist. I'm the one who's fighting for you."

"I don't believe it," he said, and with that, he gave me a shove. I shoved him back a little harder.

My main concern, of course, wasn't clearing Joe Ferrer's name. It was to hold Mayer to the purchase of the play regardless of the outcome. And that I achieved.

My career as a literary agent in Hollywood had just reached its peak when McCarthyism hit the industry. Irwin Shaw, for example, couldn't get a job because Jack Warner had spread it all over town that he was a Communist. At one point, Irwin confronted Warner in a café in the South of France and grabbed him by the lapels. "Come outside and call me a Communist!" he demanded.

When Harry Kurnitz was under contract with Metro, Louis B. Mayer wanted to use his politics as an excuse to break his contract. The idea was that Kurnitz was a member of the Communist party. In fact, Kurnitz had, at one point, been briefly active in party discussion groups but that was the extent of his involvement. Hardly a crime, but in those days, you risked being barred from working in Hollywood just for having a drink with "suspicious" people.

Metro couldn't find the modicum of "proof" that would justify breaking Harry's contract, so the studio arranged to have him assigned to a back lot in the midst of muddy flats quite a distance from the Thalberg Building. This was, in essence, Siberia. If you worked here, you were locked up in a bungalow without any heat. It was a singularly unpleasant experience, and that was the point—after the briefest exposure to Siberia, most writers resigned. Harry, unfortunately, couldn't afford to quit: quitting would mean not eating caviar and he liked that too much. I eventually had to sell him to studios under the pseudonym of Marco Page.

By 1953, Red-baiting was at its crest. That year, Jerry Wald wanted Peter Viertel to write a script, but before bringing Peter from Paris to Los Angeles and putting him to work, he requested a report on Peter from the Motion Picture Alliance. According to this report, Peter needed to answer some questions about his mother's and his wife's political associations, even though he was now separated from his wife. And, of course, he would have to sign an affidavit stating that he was not now and never had been a Communist, and had never contributed to Communist causes. Peter, too, needed the work and had no choice but to comply.

CHAPTER

Six

Hollywood is like any industry town—everybody knows everybody else's résumé. It's like kids knowing the baseball stats; if you wanted to know what deals I was making, you could easily find out by asking any of the town's top agents.

In 1949, I lucked into a situation that put me in a different league altogether. I was negotiating with L. B. Mayer, when he suddenly said, "There's only one way to succeed in this business, and you can do it."

"What's the way?"

"Step on those guys. Gouge their eyes out. Trample on them. Kick them in the balls. You'll be a smash."

And that's how I was hired for a one-of-a-kind job. On top of representing my other clients, I now acted as a quasi-agent for M-G-M. What they wanted me to do was find talent for the production unit headed by Arthur Freed, the godfather of screen musicals of the forties and fifties. Talent! If I didn't already represent it, I sure knew where to find it.

Freed had started out at M-G-M as the associate producer of *The Wizard of Oz,* and from then on his name was synonymous with the golden age of M-G-M musicals. Freed helped define the careers of such stars as Judy Garland, Gene Kelly, and Cyd Charisse. *Meet Me in St. Louis, The Barkleys of Broadway, On the Town, Royal Wedding, An American in Paris, Singin' in the Rain, Brigadoon, Gigi*—his credits read like a list of landmarks.

What distinguished Freed from other producers who were doing musicals at M-G-M was that he had an appreciation for theater. Because he knew I went to New York frequently and had great connections in that world, he would tell me what he was looking for. That gave me a tremendous edge in garnering talent.

My days at Metro were very profitable for me. I had so many clients working that I would be dancing through the hallways on the first floor, up to the second, and on to the third, knocking on doors, calling out, "How are things going?"

At one point I had as many as twenty writers, composers, songwriters, costume and set designers, and choreographers working at Metro—Johnny Mercer, Oliver Smith, George Jenkins, George S. Kaufman, John Patrick, Robert Nathan, Betty Comden and Adolph Green, Irene Sharaff, Harry Kurnitz, and Alan Jay Lerner, among others.

Sometimes it seemed I'd brought out so many people from New York to work in Freed's unit that I was, in effect, packaging the talent. I didn't think of it that way because I never took a commission on the gross of the movie. Instead, I got a commission from each element. But what people did not know—and I see no point in omitting this fact all these years later—was that I also got a fee from Arthur Freed.

Freed did this as a thank-you for a favor I did for him. Because Freed produced hit after hit, Mayer thought he deserved some kind of extra compensation. There was no way he could raise his salary or give him a share of the picture, however, because that would affect what Mayer paid other producers. So I devised a plan in which Freed bought a vintage catalog from a music publishing company for about a hundred thousand dollars. A year later, Mayer bought it from Freed for six hundred thousand. That was largesse at its most creative, and you could say it entitled me to a cut.

Arthur Freed referred affectionately to anyone working for him as "the kid." There were exceptions. That ultra-sophisticate, Cole Porter, clearly couldn't be "the kid." Nor could Freed's idol, Irving Berlin.

Years later, on a day when I was in Freed's office, Berlin came in with a sheaf of music tucked under his arm.

"What's that you've got there, Irving?" Freed asked.

"No use talking about this, Arthur. It's a score that I've just finished, but I'm not going to sell it. I want to hold on to it."

Freed pleaded for just a look. Irving hummed one or two songs. By this time, Arthur was frantically jiggling the coins in his pocket with one hand and wiping his brow with the other.

"How much do you want, Irving?"

"One million dollars."

"I'll give you the million."

"Okay," said Berlin.

"Now can I hear the songs?"

"Nope."

"But I've just bought the score."

"I'm not ready for you to hear it yet."

"Let me hear *one*. Play it on the piano," Arthur begged.

Everyone knew that Irving could only play on his custom-made "Buick" which, by the press of a lever, transposed music from one key to another.

"I can't play it on the piano," Berlin snapped. "You know better than that. I'll sing it to you."

When Berlin sang a song to you, he didn't trust you to concentrate, so he sang literally with his nose up against yours, looking into your eyes so that you didn't dare not listen. After you'd endured that once or twice, you hoped it wouldn't happen again anytime soon.

Freed called L.B. and told him he wanted to see him right away. He begged Berlin to stay put, then went upstairs to Mayer's office. "It's all settled," he told Berlin when he returned. "What kind of story are we going to tell?"

Berlin said he wanted the film to tell part of the story of his life. I pointed out that such a film had been made before: *Alexander's Ragtime Band*.

"Don't worry about it. Just give me a good screenwriter," Berlin remarked.

I suggested Arthur Laurents, who had written the book for

West Side Story and *Gypsy*. Berlin thought that it was a terrific idea.

"He won't work for less than two-fifty," I told Freed and Berlin. Berlin was so powerful that Arthur agreed. They seemed to think everything was settled, although I hadn't talked to Laurents yet.

"I have a good job for you. It's to do the story for Irving Berlin's score, and for a lot of money," I told Laurents on the phone.

"I don't want to work."

Arthur Laurents, you see, is a very interesting man and a very difficult man as well. There are many people who think he's more difficult than lovable. He lives modestly but always gets top-drawer prices because he refuses to settle for less.

"Arthur, this is the time for you to consider the gambit of asking for a preposterous sum of money," I said, not at all fazed by his snappishness. "Then, if they don't pay it, you don't do it."

"What kind of money are you talking about?"

"Two hundred thousand dollars."

"It's not enough to turn down. I want to turn down two-fifty."

"You've got it."

"What do you mean, 'I've got it?' "

"Just that. That's what they're willing to pay."

"You have the authority to tell me that?"

"Yes. You don't get it all at once. Fifty thousand to start, fifty thousand halfway through, and so on. But eventually the deal is for two-fifty, plus they'll pay your first-class, round-trip transportation and expenses. You come out and talk to Berlin and Freed, and then you'll go to work—or turn it down, if you like."

Laurents didn't turn it down.

We soon discovered that Berlin's "new" score—*Say It with Music,* the title of a song he had written in 1921—was really about three songs and seventeen old ones that he'd sold about fifty times. Somehow Laurents couldn't get a handle on the project, so I sold another client, George Axelrod, to Freed. And when that didn't work, I made a deal for Betty Comden and

Adolph Green to do the screenplay. That didn't work out either. In the final analysis, the studio invested well over a million dollars in the project, but could never make the picture. M-G-M had nothing to show for that investment—all rights reverted to Berlin after a number of years.

To those who knew Berlin, this outcome was unsurprising. He was one of the smartest businessmen and traders in the business. He was so confident of his longevity that even in the last phase of his career he wanted his earnings spread over a number of years. I thought Adolph Green had him pegged when he suggested to Berlin, "Why don't you take a dollar a year for a million years?"

During the late sixties Simon & Schuster wanted to publish a two-volume edition of his lyrics. Berlin was famous for making his own deals, but I thought that because we were talking about a book instead of a show or film, the time was right for me to make my move.

"Irving, you're much too dignified, much too important to go out and sell yourself," I told him. "You shouldn't be doing that. Do you think I'm a good agent?"

"The best," Berlin said.

"Okay. Let me be your agent. I'll take five percent, I don't care. I just want to represent Irving Berlin. More than the money, it would be the prestige and honor."

"You're very persuasive, but let me ask you something. If you were me, would you get an agent?"

"No," I admitted.

"There's your answer."

One of the first talents that I introduced to Freed was Alan Jay Lerner. It was 1949. Lerner had just finished working with Kurt Weill on *Love Life,* and was considering going out to California. Moss told him to call me if he made the move. And from the moment he arrived in Hollywood until he did his last film, *The Little Prince,* in 1974, I was his agent.

When Lerner arrived, I immediately took him to meet Arthur Freed. Alan didn't have any ideas, but Freed said that he was looking for a film for Fred Astaire. "Stay in town for ten weeks, think of something, and we'll make a deal," Freed advised.

Two weeks later, Alan got the idea for *Royal Wedding,* made a deal with Freed, and wrote the screenplay and lyrics. *An American in Paris, Brigadoon, Gigi, My Fair Lady,* and *Camelot* followed. I'd have to say that Freed was a very prudent choice for Alan's first meeting.

Before Alan cemented his relationship with Metro, I was in Freed's office with the director Richard Brooks, who was also my client. "Why don't you give that fellow Lerner a steady job?" Brooks said. "He's a very talented boy, but apparently he's broke."

Brooks was, it seemed, unaware of the fact that Lerner was extremely wealthy, not only from his earnings and royalties as a composer, but from his family's ownership of the Lerner Shops. Freed looked at Brooks incredulously. "What makes you think he's poor?" he asked.

"Well, he comes to my house almost every night to talk. He looks so thin and pale that I ask him to have dinner. And he always accepts. I figure he comes over because he has no money for food."

Freed explained rather elaborately just how rich Lerner was.

"Then why does he come to eat at my house?" Brooks asked.

Alan later explained to me. "I think Richard Brooks is fascinating and he knows a lot about picture-making," he said. "I can learn a lot from him. I don't even like his food."

I loved those days working with M-G-M and reveled in my clients' achievements. I have been known to say "I did a lot of pictures at Metro," because I took such pleasure in my clients' feats. Naturally, I got quizzical looks from those who felt I was usurping the author's privilege.

When I went to Belmont Park racetrack during the thirties, I used to hear the riders' agents say, "I'm riding in the first and third, carrying a hundred and ten. Next week I go to Kentucky to ride in the Derby." Like me, they were speaking for their jockey clients; unlike me, they talked as though they did the riding and had to watch their weight.

When I say "I did films at Metro," I mean that I was heavily involved in the making of those films. And I was careful to say

that only when it had been a collaborative effort. I don't feel that way about a book. I'd never go so far as to say "I was on the best-seller list." That would be a little too much.

When Arthur Freed and I were in Philadelphia for *My Fair Lady* tryouts, he approached Alan Jay Lerner and Frederick Loewe about adapting *Gigi,* Colette's novella, into a musical film. They were interested, so Freed asked me to go to Paris to purchase the rights from Maurice Goudeket, Colette's widower. Now *there* was a character for you. He was still wearing a black armband ten years after her death. I think it helped the mourning widower get a better table at restaurants on the Left Bank. If he had worn spats, a white-checkered vest with gold chain, and a derby, he would not have looked any more crooked.

I triumphed over my first impressions, and returned to California with a signed contract giving M-G-M the rights for $125,000. But all hell quickly broke loose—Goudeket had also sold the rights to the impresario Gilbert Miller for a Broadway musical. Freed had to pay Miller $87,000 to kill his project.

The first preview of *Gigi* in Santa Barbara was hailed by everyone but Lerner, Loewe, and Freed. At a little restaurant after the preview, Lerner was absolutely brilliant in describing what changes were necessary and Loewe only slightly less brilliant. We returned to Los Angeles full of hope. But the studio wasn't inclined to do any reshooting. Times weren't that good and we didn't have L. B. Mayer backing us up. Dore Schary was head of production now, and he wasn't as sure of himself as Mayer was.

Our meetings with studio executives were unavailing, so it was a question of getting Joseph Vogel, the studio's New York money man, to come to the rescue. Freed prepared a budget that allowed three hundred thousand for the changes that Lerner requested. Vogel wouldn't make any decisions until he came to California and saw the film with an audience. To no one's surprise, he thought it was great as is.

Now Lerner and Loewe put on their dancing shoes, even offering to cough up the dough to buy 10 percent of the film. Vogel told them that couldn't be done. "How much did the picture cost?" Lerner asked. "Three million? We'll buy it and take it off your hands."

At this point Lerner, Loewe, and I went to the men's room, the only place we could speak privately.

"How the fuck are we going to pay three million?" Loewe asked.

"Well, I haven't got three million—I'm not even sure I can put my hands on three hundred thousand," Lerner said. "But doesn't it sound great?"

"You'd better pray that Vogel doesn't say, 'Okay,' " I pointed out.

Well, Vogel was so impressed by Lerner and Loewe's sincerity that he finally acquiesced—that is, he agreed to have the studio pay for reshooting. Now the hard work began. The actors had to return to the studio from their homes and other assignments around the world—making me, at least, nostalgic for the good old days when there were contract players, all on the lot, available for a second call. Vincente Minnelli, the film's director, was now in Paris directing *The Reluctant Debutante*. To replace him, I suggested my client, Chuck Walters, who had directed *Easter Parade*. Meanwhile, Lerner went over the film frame by frame.

In this flurry of activity, *Gigi* was reborn. Lerner transformed this ugly duckling into one of America's most cherished films—and the winner of nine Academy Awards.

With Charles and Doris Vidor, and Audrey and Billy Wilder.

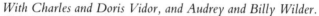

The point of the story is this: if flying twelve thousand miles round-trip to purchase the rights to the story; if having my clients write the screenplay and score; if having another client, Cecil Beaton, design the sets and costumes; if participating in the arduous discussions to convince the studio to finance the required changes; and if having another of my clients, Chuck Walters, direct those sequences doesn't entitle me to say "I 'did' *Gigi* at Metro," what or who can?

But that's not even the high point. The ultimate peak of my career during this glamorous era occurred one afternoon in Philadelphia. I was sitting in a darkened theater at the final rehearsal of *My Fair Lady* with the show's director, Moss Hart; the author of the book and lyrics, Alan Jay Lerner; the composer, Frederick Loewe; Oliver Smith, the set designer; and Cecil Beaton, who did the costumes. Taking in the magnificent spectacle on the stage and the kings of the theater seated next to me, I asked myself: "What more can I ask of my profession?" There was nothing. This was the summit. I represented them all!

CHAPTER

Seven

*W*HEN I FIRST arrived in Los Angeles, I spent most of my evenings at Lee and Ira Gershwin's magnificent house in Beverly Hills. Surrounded by French Impressionist and post-Impressionist paintings, Ira left a continuous trail of cigar ashes everywhere from the rug to his soup bowl while Lee somehow tidied up his debris and maintained a beautiful, spotless household.

The Gershwins lived on North Roxbury Drive in a neighborhood so populated by New Yorkers it was like Central Park West. Jack Benny, Eddie Cantor, Oscar Levant, Charlie Chaplin, and just about every mogul—Selznick, Cohn, Warner, and Mayer—were within a few blocks. These homes were lavish establishments, many featuring staircases that allowed a host and hostess to make a grand entrance. At some point during these Beverly Hills evenings, the ladies—all beautifully gowned— would go upstairs to powder their noses and then descend the staircase, which was a ritual unto itself.

The Gershwins' home was built around a very different idea, that of a transplanted New York salon. Unlike so many other émigrés from the East, Lee and Ira never adopted Hollywood affectations; they not only still talked and thought like

New Yorkers, they were a magnet for hometown friends who craved an intellectual hangout. Charlie Jackson, the novelist, bunked there, as did Sam Behrman. And while Dorothy Parker checked into the Garden of Allah or the Château Marmont, her husband, Alan Campbell, preferred the Gershwins' luxury and grace. Almost every weekend, you could find Maxwell Anderson, Oscar Levant, Lillian Hellman, Judy Garland, John Huston, Harold Arlen, William Wyler, Jack Benny, and George Burns gathered at the Gershwins' for swimming and tennis or dinner.

Lee and Ira never really invited anyone over. Their motto was "Drive by on your way home. If the light is on, stop in." Because Ira and I were both night owls, I'd drop in even on nights when I was otherwise engaged. We'd talk about the theater and music. But we never talked about Ira's work. I'd admired his lyrics long before I ever knew him, but when I'd quote from "The Man I Love" or "Our Love Is Here to Stay" and tell him he was a poet, Ira would only say, "I just put the words together nicely."

Ira was without pretense in every way. I remember one Sunday morning when Lee, Audrey Wilder, Peter Viertel, and I were standing in front of the Del Coronado Hotel waiting to take a limousine to the bullfights in Tijuana. When I realized Ira was missing, I rushed back to his suite—only to find him tearing up the leftover pancakes and waffles from breakfast and flushing them down the toilet. "I was just too embarrassed for the room service waiter to see our great waste," he explained.

We spent a lot of time on the weekends at the racetrack, where Ira had a box on the finish line. He found happiness only in losing, even though he knew a fellow who made the line for Las Vegas. This expert amused me no end for the simple reason that when the Roosevelt Hotel raised his sixteen-dollar-a-day rate by two bucks, he moved out—although he sometimes bet as much as three thousand on a race, he didn't feel he could afford the rent! I used to follow him around the track to try and find out what horse he was going to bet on. If I gleaned a name, I'd tell Ira, thinking he'd follow the tip; instead, he'd bet on such imponderables as three horses in the same race whose first names all started with the same letter. If, by some chance, Ira was winning early in the afternoon, he'd pick an impossible long shot in the eighth race, lose a bundle, and then hum happily all the way home.

As Lee, Ira, and I became closer, we traveled to Europe together: Venice, Paris, London. They were the ones who introduced me to such palatial accommodations as the Gritti in Venice, but because I enjoyed organizing the day's activities, I was the de facto tour guide. Like me, they had high standards and liked living well.

The big difference between the Gershwin and the Goldwyn homes was that Sam entertained primarily for the sake of business, whereas the Gershwins invited those they were genuinely interested in. There was no conflict for me—I loved being with people who were amusing and achievers. And ever since Ira Gershwin pointed me in the right direction with a well-chosen shelf of art books, I liked spending time in rooms with great pictures on the walls. Like, for example, the Goldwyns' home, which was filled with fine French Impressionists, a Picasso, several paintings by Degas, and, over the fireplace, a Toulouse-Lautrec.

The other attractions of the Goldwyn quarters were just as impressive. Inside what looked like an upper-class English country house was a paneled library with projection facilities, a convivial room in which to have a drink before dinner. Because the Goldwyns were as punctual as Swiss trains, you arrived at 7:30, when they began serving drinks, and gulped down whatever you could handle until eight o'clock, when everybody moved into the dining room. If some guests hadn't arrived, their places were left at the table. You didn't know who the missing were unless you were bold enough to inquire—or if Frances was feeling snippy and volunteered the names. Needless to say, few were ever late.

One night, when we were force-marched into dinner, two guests hadn't yet arrived. Half an hour later, the butler opened the door and in burst Rex Harrison, looking terribly agitated, closely followed by his wife, Lili Palmer. Rex was shooting a picture and hadn't been able to leave the studio on time. Sam and Frances arose, greeted the Harrisons cordially, and nodded to the butler to serve them. Not the first course, however. The main course (which, because Frances and Sam had very narrow

*With Sam Goldwyn and
Frank Sinatra, and with
Frances Goldwyn, flanked
by George Axelrod.*

culinary interests, meant either ham or chicken). Had they arrived later, they simply would have been served dessert.

Given Sam's meticulousness, it was daring of Frances to propose a surprise party for his seventieth birthday, but by then, I guess, she figured she had his friends well trained. We dutifully parked our cars down the street at seven o'clock, walked to the house, and, while Sam was upstairs changing from one custom-tailored Savile Row suit to another, we were ushered into the hallway. We hid under the staircase, whispering like children, until 7:25, when we began the final countdown—we knew that Sam's footsteps would hit the top step at 7:28, giving him two minutes to get downstairs to the library for one drink before what he expected to be a quiet dinner with Frances.

Right on cue, we heard Sam. It was fairly dark in the hallway and we were all buttoned up. And so, thinking he was alone, Sam let go a fart that would have rocked the Empire State Building. What could we do but roar with laughter? And then, because this was, despite this strange beginning, certain to be a great celebration, we launched into "Happy Birthday."

The Goetz household also made a big contribution to my social life. Edie was the daughter of Louis B. Mayer, which was a potent factor in her popularity as a hostess right up to the time that her father stopped talking to her. Bill was a very attractive and witty guy, who became even more attractive and witty when he was appointed head of Fox. One of the reasons I liked Billy so much is that he was an iconoclast. No one was safe from his barbs; he had a capacity for maximizing one's frailties. If he didn't like something that Goldwyn, Zanuck, or Selznick had said, he would speak up and tell them what he thought—but in a cute way so no one was offended. Kirk Douglas once told Billy, "I've just done a movie about Van Gogh. How do you think it will do?" Billy came back with "Everybody who's got a Van Gogh is going to see that movie."

The Goetzes were the kingpins of Hollywood society in the late forties and into the fifties. Their house in Holmby Hills was bigger than the Goldwyns' and maintained like a museum, with cozy rooms where you could dine, read, or meet for tea, and marvelous gardens and a vast pool. When Edie and Bill gave dinner parties, you knew that you—and as many as forty others—would see the most polished staff in Los Angeles in action and enjoy a meal cooked by a chef Edie had brought over from Paris. After dinner, Billy might press a button in the living room, causing his great Toulouse-Lautrec to slide into the ceiling and a projector to be revealed; on the opposite wall, a Gauguin would rise and a screen would take its place. Then we'd settle in to watch an as-yet-unreleased film.

Or the guests would perform. That, for me, is the ultimate: when performers perform for one another. Curiously, they do their best on these occasions—no audience to speak of, just a handful of well-lubricated peers who are uniquely qualified to savor the subtleties of a tossed-off phrase, a bent note, or a knowing look. After a typical Goetz dinner, Johnny Green, a fine composer and a conductor at Metro, would sit at the piano playing standards until singers like Kitty Carlisle or Grace Moore felt like offering a song or two. Heaven!

I learned early on that if I was going to spend my evenings in homes where the premiere players hung out, I had to make myself as interesting as possible. In 1947, when I was still pushing to be accepted, I found a way to do that—I went to Europe. For Californians, Europe seemed like a lifetime away; since the War ended, few of them had made the trip. And so, on my return, I got invited out to dinner just about every night.

For the sake of dinner party chat, I improved the story of my trip with some extraordinary details. A countess I'd met became a princess, I was transported by private plane everywhere, I had several rendezvous with Marlene Dietrich—like that. I went too far, though, when I said that I had posed for Utrillo, who, as my listeners knew and I certainly didn't, was not then painting anything remotely resembling a person.

This trip, and the trips that followed, paid off in unexpected ways. Bill and Edie Goetz, for example, loved to travel as much as I did—but by the early fifties, I knew a slew of swells they had never encountered. So Edie and Bill appointed me as their tour guide and let me make all the arrangements—which is how they met the Rothschilds.

You may wonder how a kid from Brownsville was in a position to introduce Hollywood royalty to its European counterparts. Very simple answer: Hollywood was (and still is) a deeply middle-class community. Sure, when Edie Goetz went to the hairdresser, she brought her butler along so he could serve her lunch on a silver tray. But that wasn't Edie's innate taste, it was the result of a childhood spent watching movies. The fact is, Louis B. Mayer, like a lot of Hollywood heavyweights, spent money freely but never quite figured out how to turn it into style—he learned about class from twenties and thirties movies made by directors and producers who'd never really experienced it themselves. In comparison, I actually got around.

When I look at my date book from this glamorous era, it

Traveling with friends: At top, in Switzerland with Marian and Irwin Shaw, Harry Kurnitz, Martin Gabel, and a pretty woman whose name I can't remember. Bottom left, with Kitty and Moss. At bottom right, with Lee and Ira Gershwin and Harry Kurnitz.

seems there was a glittering party every night, each one more stellar than the next. In one week alone in 1952, I attended a party given by King Vidor and his wife, a farewell party that Jack Benny threw at Romanoff's for the vacation-bound Goetzes, and a huge black-tie affair at Dore Schary's home. And when I think of the talent who performed at these parties, it boggles the mind:

Mary Martin, Jerry Lewis, Michael Kidd, Howard Dietz and Arthur Schwartz, Danny Kaye, Kay Thompson, Donald O'Connor, Judy Garland, and Joe E. Lewis.

The formal nights blur. What you remember are the unchoreographed moments when someone who's had too much to drink or is in the grip of a private drama. Like the Christmas Eve party that the Bogarts gave in 1951. Oscar and June Levant were there, and Oscar was none too pleased that his wife was dancing with other men. Around one in the morning, Oscar pushed June rather violently out of the room. She started to cry, so Bogie heaved Oscar out on his ear. Oscar sat outside for about half an hour, then went home alone. Somehow it fell to me to take June home. Unlucky me. And unlucky June—a second after she closed the door behind her, it opened again and Oscar tossed her out. I helped her up and helped her in. And Oscar ejected her yet again.

This sort of thing was bound to happen in a closed society where you saw the same people all the time. Those nights were so "inside" you practically felt you were committing incest. The Bill Goetzes, the Arthur Hornblows, the Sol Siegels, the Danny Kayes, and the King Vidors—to cite just one of the industry's tight-knit groups—seemed to travel in a pack. They were madly devoted to one another, yet there was constant friction. Everyone would appear to be amiable, but the behind-the-fan conversations were so extraordinary you could easily conclude they all loathed each other. I'd leave these evenings thanking God for the facade of good manners.

The thing was, there were just too many parties. A prudent person would turn some down, or at least limit the number of nights he'd go out each week. But if there were such people, we didn't know them—we were addicts for events, even though we knew that the conversations we had at them weren't that interesting. After all, most of these people didn't have much to talk about outside of the movies. No wonder that Oscar Hammerstein would walk into a Hollywood party, look around and yawn, then mutter, "Same cast."

I remember a dinner the Bogarts once gave for Richard and Sybil Burton. There were about forty guests—like Frank Sinatra, Spencer Tracy, Groucho Marx, and Clifton Webb—and most anyone in America would have given a lot to be there. I wonder how eager my fellow citizens would have been if they'd known the topics of conversation. First and foremost, income taxes. Then that they have no money. Then that they're underpaid. Then income taxes again. I do recall that we talked about sex a bit, but the general conclusion seemed to be that no one was all that interested.

Life got a lot livelier when Bogie would be working or out on his boat and I'd escort his bride. Miss Bacall's idea of a good time was, after a few cocktails, to lash out at me—verbally and physically. In self-defense, I'd jerk back, sometimes falling off my chair, sometimes holding on to a dinner table for dear life. I'd want to slug her, but I'd remind myself that she was a lady. Then she'd launch into another tirade so explicit I was sure she was really a longshoreman.

Each encounter with Betty Bacall was like the first time, though, because when you called for her she looked like a dream. For a party at the Goetzes, I recall, she wore a dress that looked like something a demure Smith College girl might wear at graduation. It was all-white and starched, and it stuck out very nicely where it was supposed to and tucked in very nicely where you'd want it to, and the only color was a charming green collar. Betty wore pearl earrings and two simple bracelets. The effect was perfect.

But only for thirty minutes.

You know how it is when you go to the fights and you spot a prizefighter who looks like a god? A few rounds in, you bend down to retrieve a program you dropped. And when you look up—just seconds later—your god is on the floor, disheveled, eyes aglaze, hair askew. Well, that was our girl. She'd only had one twirl around the room, but she'd fueled it with two or three brandies, and now she'd lost her pearls and misplaced the starch in her dress. By one in the morning, Betty had danced with Jerry Robbins and Michael Kidd and me. Her hair was saturated. She'd lost one bracelet.

By then, I had heard Mary Martin and Jerry Lewis and Gene Kelly perform, so I was ready to call it a night. I suggested this to Betty, who told me she shared no such desires. Good for her! Because we stayed, I got to hear Judy Garland sing "Swanee" and "Melancholy Baby" so touchingly that even Richard Rodgers was crying. I began to realize this was a Significant Evening when Cole Porter said good night at two, left, and returned at three. "I went home, thought it was goddamned foolish, and I came back," he explained. By then, Betty was wearing Band-Aids instead of shoes. I finally got her out of there at four.

By the mid-1950s, Bogie was less kind about this repetitive merrymaking. I was once at a party Claudette Colbert gave, and Bogie summed it up perfectly. He walked in, went to the patio where dinner was laid out for thirty people, looked at the guest list, and said, "The same goddamn faces. I'm getting goddamn tired of it—and I'm not even drunk." Bogie then proceeded to correct that oversight. Once he was good and loaded, he insulted everybody. He even got riled at Betty for not being able to leave a party before 3 A.M.

Such merrymaking would wear anyone out, but a few nights later, we were at it again. This time Frank Sinatra and I were the hosts. We served several pounds of fresh caviar and gallons of champagne at my flat, then moved our forty guests over to Frank's house, where an orchestra played during dinner. And then Frank, Judy Garland, Dean Martin, Jerry Lewis, George Burns, and Sammy Davis, Jr., put on a show that didn't end until four in the morning. Not a bad night—until you remember that Frank and I sponsored this blast on a Sunday night, and a great many of our guests had commitments on Monday morning.

In 1950, after living at the Garden of Allah apartments and then briefly at the Bel Air Hotel, I moved to a duplex on Wilshire Boulevard in the Westwood section of Los Angeles. This place was my first real home since I left Brownsville.

My apartment was in a lovely complex owned by Gladys Belzer, a famed Hollywood decorator who happened to be the mother of Loretta Young as well as three other exquisite beauties. Mrs. Belzer was as engaging as her daughters. She took great pride in her series of two-bedroom duplexes, and lovingly furnished them with good antique furniture and appointed them with objets d'art and fine silver and china.

I was delighted to have this wonderful place. I went out and bought so much linen and towels with my initials monogrammed on them that, forty years later, I still had some I'd never used. Then I gave Mrs. Belzer six thousand dollars in cash for a year's rent.

"Why are you doing this?" she asked.

"Because I don't want to be billed, and I don't want you to have to come looking for me."

"What happens if you die?"

I knew she was a devout Catholic, so I told her in the event that happened and there was credit on my account, she should donate the money to the nuns at St. John's Hospital. That endeared me to her, and we became good friends.

Marguerite Lamkin was the first neighbor I met. She had a Southern drawl that even Tennessee Williams couldn't understand when he employed her to coach Elizabeth Taylor for the role of Maggie in *Cat on a Hot Tin Roof.* She went on to marry Mark Littman, one of the most successful barristers in England, and now has one of the most fashionable salons in all of London.

Even then, Marguerite was well-connected. She once had Dame Judith Anderson as her houseguest and gave a small dinner in her honor. That evening, she discovered that the sterling silver flatware was missing. She called Mrs. Belzer to tell her she had been robbed and the silver was gone.

"No, dear," explained Mrs. Belzer. "I borrowed it for Mr. Lazar, who is having a dinner party tonight. I'll return it to you tomorrow."

There were no holds barred. Joan Harrison, the screenwriter, producer, and Alfred Hitchcock's longtime assistant, was also a tenant. She once admired a table in Loretta Young's apartment. The next day, it was in Joan's living room. "I gave it to Joan. Somebody had to use it," Mrs. Belzer said when Loretta asked about it.

This complex soon became known as "the Boulevard," in recognition of the steady stream of characters that passed through here. Billy and Audrey Wilder lived there at one point, as did Audrey Hepburn and Peter Ustinov. I didn't go out of my way to stock the place with clients—for a while, Ustinov was enough.

I represented Peter from the time *Romanoff and Juliet* was on Broadway, having made a deal with David Merrick for him to produce and appear in the play. He received 10 percent of the gross profits as the playwright and another 10 percent as an actor. *Romanoff and Juliet* was to be directed by George S. Kaufman, but Peter wasn't satisfied with George. So out went Kaufman and in came a new director—guess who? Peter collected an additional 3 percent for his directing services. This gave him 23 percent of the gross profits. Nobody I knew at that point—Lindsay and Crouse and Noël Coward included—received that much. I was thrilled by 10 percent of all that. But do you think Ustinov was happy? Not by a long shot.

What made it even worse was that his wife was second-guessing me all the way. If I suggested something and it turned out well, she would say nothing. If my ideas didn't bear fruit, she'd say, "I told you so." I tried to stick it out, but this cycle got to be a bore. Finally, I said, "Peter, I will give up the commission. Let me step away from this project. I can't please your wife, and you seem to be very much influenced by her. The whole thing is getting to be too much for me." He insisted I'd made a marvelous deal for him and it wouldn't be fair. I suggested he could get another agent and pay us each 5 percent—and that's how we parted.

But when Peter was on the Boulevard, it was Ustinov night almost every night. It was during the time of the McCarthy hearings, and he was a genius at mimicking the witnesses. At night, a pack of us would go over to Bogie's and Peter would recreate the hearings, with the intonation and characterization so precise that it was uncanny.

Life on the Boulevard wasn't always that entertaining. Like the time Kitty and Moss were in town. Moss had written the remake of *A Star Is Born,* and as it was just about to begin filming, I gave them a party. Many of their friends were there: the Gershwins, the Oscar Levants, and Johnny Mercer. Johnny had had a few drinks too many. That was never a good idea—when lit, he wasn't very guarded in his conversation. And Johnny was glowing when Judy Garland walked in. "Why did you let your mother die in a parking lot?" he asked, before she'd even had a chance to settle in. With that, Judy began to cry.

"Go upstairs to the powder room and pull yourself together," I told her. "I'll ask Johnny to leave."

Dinner hadn't yet been served, and with the exception of this brouhaha, people were having a lot of fun. I got caught up in the festivities, so it was Lee Gershwin, a great friend of Judy's, who realized that Judy had been gone an unusually long time. Lee went upstairs to check on her.

Her scream stopped the party cold. Judy was lying on the floor, her wrists slashed and blood all over her. We called for an ambulance. The attendants gave her some temporary dressing for the wounds, put her on a stretcher, and off they went, sirens and all. Naturally, the incident was so macabre that everyone left.

Judy wasn't just an acquaintance, she was a real friend. As a result, I saw both sides of her persona. You know about the dark side, the one everyone writes about; that was just sheer desperation. But she was also a bright woman with astute opinions. When she was on a roll, she gave the most incisive, hilarious, and accurate portrayals of other personalities—Moss considered her one of the smartest people in Hollywood.

I was present at the birth of Joey, her son by Sid Luft. It was the night before the Academy Awards in 1955, and Judy was up for Best Actress in *A Star Is Born*. Betty Bacall, Frank Sinatra, and I had dropped by Sid and Judy's after dinner. As we chatted away, Judy began to watch the clock—and when the sharp pains started coming at ten-minute intervals, it became clear she was bound for the hospital.

The next thing I knew, we were all at Cedars of Lebanon Hospital. Frank ordered some pizzas, and then, for something to do, began to answer the phones in the Maternity wing. Suddenly the doctor was giving us the good news, and we were ushered in to see our groggy friend. Quite a night.

Judy turned to me a couple of times when she was in trouble. One time was in London, when she hadn't paid the hotel bill in weeks; I bailed her out. Another time she invited me to her house and showed me a stack of kinescopes. She needed money and wanted to sell the tapes of her shows. "How long would it take you to do a deal for all these?" she asked. I told her it wasn't that easy; people had to view them to see what the market was for them. "I can't wait. I have to eat, I'm broke," she said.

Judy's was a hopeless situation. She was working and married, but she felt destitute. She blamed Sid, but I found it hard to take sides. Sid was one of the first people I had met in Hollywood after the war. He was the first to take me to the Hillcrest Country Club. He encouraged me to take up golf. Sid wasn't exactly J. P. Morgan, but the fact that he stayed married to Judy for as long as he did and catered to her whims and illnesses made him nothing less than a hero in my eyes.

Bogie thought Sid was just a hanger-on. I remember a night at my house when Bogie started needling Sid. "Do you sing?" he asked. He didn't give Sid a chance to reply. "No, you don't. Then why the hell are you making a living off a singer?"

Sid was quite an athlete. When he lifted Bogie up, brought him nose to nose, and said, "I don't want to have to hit you," Bogie backed down real quick.

I had my first encounter with the guy who would later become my most unforgettable neighbor during my band-booking days, when Harry James told me about a singer at the Rustic Cabin in New Jersey. "I hear the kid's pretty good," Harry said. "Why don't you go out and hear him?" I went to the club. And the skinny kid did sing like heaven.

I went backstage, gave the kid my business card, and told him Harry James might like him to front his band. Soon enough, James hired him. The kid was so grateful he told me he'd like to sign with MCA. James was paying him only seventy dollars a week—it seemed silly to take a seven-dollar-a-week commission. So I suggested that the kid wait until he was making some big money.

After singing with James's orchestra, the kid joined Tommy Dorsey and recorded "I'll Never Smile Again." That's the way I soon felt. With that song, Frank Sinatra became a massive hit, and 10 percent of him meant quite a bit.

Now here we were, nearly twenty years later. Frank had just separated from Ava Gardner and was looking for a place to live, so I took him to see an apartment in the Belzer compound. He rented it on the spot, and, like me, paid Mrs. Belzer a year's rent in advance.

Now that we were neighbors, we struck up a close friendship. We spent so much time together that I coached him in the "I'll leave the light on" tradition of Ira Gershwin—although Frank was a loner, he didn't like to be alone. One night I returned home late, saw his light on and the door ajar. I went in and Frank was hunched down in an easy chair. He was shooting a BB gun at three faces of Ava that had been painted by the artist, Paul Clemens. As I started to tiptoe out, Frank asked me to stay for a drink. I don't drink late at night, but that didn't mean that Frank wouldn't. I held on to my glass and he proceeded to get drunk. It was a very revealing experience.

One of Frank's favorite pastimes was needling "Swifty." He knew what irritated me and enjoyed watching my reaction, so I guess I was the perfect foil. He put a great deal of effort into organizing these pranks. For instance, he knew I was a clotheshorse and meticulous about my things—the way they're hung, the way the shoes are lined up. Once when I was in New York, Frank teamed up with Harry Kurnitz and the screenwriter Charlie Lederer and hired a bricklayer to build a brick wall across the closet. Then they had it painted to match the rest of the wall. As a final touch, they took the furniture from the bedroom and put it in the kitchen. The minute I walked into the apartment, I knew who had done it.

Then there was the time I gave a dinner party, and, while I was upstairs dressing, Sinatra had his butler slip into my apartment and move everything over to his place. When I came downstairs, the bar and kitchen were seriously understocked, so all my guests ended up going to his house for the evening. He thought that was funny.

And it was. What I didn't think was so funny was when he stole my help—which he did on three occasions. I had a terrific butler who ran my domestic life. One morning he brought me my coffee and announced he was leaving the next day.

"Leaving? Why? What's the matter?"

"I can't talk about it," he said.

"How can you leave on one day's notice? I wouldn't throw you out that way."

I told him not to wait until tomorrow, right now would be fine by me. Then I began to wonder: Who would employ Mariano for more money than I was paying him?

Only Sinatra.

I called Frank to ask why he'd hired my man away from me.

"He told me he left you," Frank said.

"Well, considering that you live next door to me and I see you every night, don't you think the least you could have done is call and ask if I'd fired him?"

"I don't understand what difference it makes if he wants to leave."

The major difference in my mind was what would have happened if the tables were reversed. I didn't want to make a big deal of it; I just figured I'd hire someone else. Mariano went to work for Frank until the afternoon he forgot to pick up Frank's younger daughter, Tina. And that was the end of him.

But that didn't stop Frank from filching my next butler. This man was a good driver and valet, he could serve, and he was very attractive. He not only had a good sense of humor, he understood me. And we went on quite happily together for about three years. But then, just before Christmas, he made an announcement that was starting to sound familiar: "Mr. Lazar, I have to leave you."

"When do you want to leave?"

"Today," he said.

I knew Frank had struck.

Again, I called and asked Frank how he could do such a thing, and again, I got the same answer: "He told me that you fired him, so I figured I'd take him."

And then there was my secretary of sixteen years whom Frank took a shine to, and she, too, wound up working for him. Others who have seen this side of Frank like to say, "It's Frank's world—we're just living in it." Me, I say that Frank simply liked people who worked for me.

However you put it, it took a lot of resilience to hang with Frank in those days. You had to be a very docile person in order to cope. His friends—like Leo Durocher and songwriter Jimmy Van Heusen—would sit around while Frank talked. If Frank didn't feel like talking, nobody talked; it just became a staring contest.

Frank has mellowed with the years, but in those days he had a one-track mind. Not the track you think. Frank never got as far as other people. His obsession when he got up in the morning was this: What can I do today to enhance the life of Frank Sinatra? Self-absorption of that kind isn't unique to Frank. You see it in all superstars, and you ignore it because you understand that it takes self-absorption to soar so high. What was unique about Frank's incessant focus on himself was that he had immense style —I can't think of another superstar who entertained so lavishly. When Frank played Vegas, he'd have a dinner every night flowing with champagne and booze. He'd give the ladies five hundred dollars to play blackjack; if they ran out, he'd give them a couple of thousand more.

Many have commented on Frank's tendency to blow hot and cold to people who think they're his friends. It's true that he can be very close to a group of people and then all of a sudden, there's a new group and he may not see the first bunch for a long time, or, in some instances, ever again. Close as we were, even I found myself on the outs with Frank. And for months at a time. Then, out of the blue, I'd get a call: "Hiya, buddy." And Frank would pick up the conversation as though we'd seen each other only yesterday. Sometimes Frank didn't remember if he was on or off me. One night when he ran into me unexpectedly at "21," he turned to Jilly, his sometime boon companion, and said, "Is this the week I like 'Swifty,' or the week I don't?"

In Betty Bacall's first autobiography she wrote: "One day Frank Sinatra came over to our house. I don't remember how that happened." Well, I'll fill her in. Shortly after Frank moved into the Boulevard, he was without a plan one night. As I was going to dinner at the Bogarts, I took him along. Friendship ensued.

What Betty hasn't forgotten is how, after Bogie died and she and Frank became an item, I was responsible for their celebrated breakup. It happened because I was the one having dinner with Betty and Frank at the Imperial Gardens on Sunset Boulevard when he announced he was going to marry her. A few days later, Frank left town to play at the Fontainebleau in Miami.

I'd escorted Betty around town after Bogie died, and when Frank was away, it was only natural for me to continue taking her to parties. During this trip of Frank's, I brought Betty to a party at Zsa Zsa Gabor's. And Louella Parsons was there.

Top, Frank Sinatra serenading Betty Bacall from the stage in Las Vegas,
while Kim Novak, Cole Porter, Martha Hyer, and I look on.
Bottom, A dinner honoring Commander Alan Shepard (standing).

Louella was a terrific woman and a match for anyone, so she
went right up to Betty and asked, "What's happening between
you and Frankie?"

"Talk to Lazar," Betty said.

I didn't know the engagement was a secret, so I spilled the
beans to Louella. Then Betty and I left the party to have dinner
at Romanoff's. When we walked out of the restaurant at 11:30,
newspaper guys were hawking the *Examiner*. And the headline
read: "SINATRA TO MARRY BACALL."

Well, Betty wanted to kill me.

"He's going to be furious, simply furious. We'd better go
to my house and call him," she said.

She then did something that I thought was really curious.
As I was making the call, she said to tell the operator to charge
it to my number. She's got her life in her hands, and she's thinking about a sixty-five-cent telephone call!

Well, I got Frank on the phone and tried to make light of
the blunder without being too clear that I was the culprit. But he
was none too pleased. He had wanted to tell his ex-wife and kids
before they read it in the paper, and he was embarrassed. And
Frank doesn't handle embarrassment well—he broke off the engagement.

Betty was plenty pissed off at me. I could understand her
point, but I couldn't feel bad. If anything, she should have
thanked me for saving her from what would have been a terrible
blunder. Because she and Frank were ill-suited for one another.
In no way was Betty a subservient woman who could remain in
a man's shadow. Frank didn't realize that at the time because she
had been more than willing to let him think she would be a little
hausfrau. The first time she raised her voice on a night when
Frank was drinking, the odds are good there would have been
headlines—and they would have been ugly.

In this instance, I knew Frank better than Betty did. The
thing is, he's a cross between the most generous man on earth
and an absolute shitheel. The trick is to see him between mood
swings. You can do it, but it's a lot easier if he's not on the
booze. When he was sober, Frank had the potential to be a
pussycat; when he was drunk, he was the meanest son of a bitch
that God ever put on earth. It was Jekyll-and-Hyde time. I've

seen Frank throw a man through a glass door because he thought the guy was rude to him. And I've seen him drive a golf cart through a window in Palm Springs and end up in some innocent soul's living room at three in the morning. Jimmy Van Heusen once gave me some good advice on how to handle Frank if he's drunk: Disappear!

To his credit, Frank generally regretted his behavior the next day, and his victim would usually get flowers and a note of apology. A few years after he and Betty had split up, for example, I gave a party at the Bistro for my clients Larry Collins and Dominique Lapierre to celebrate their book, *Is Paris Burning?* By this time, Frank was with Mia Farrow, and Betty was married to Jason Robards. Still, this was the first time Betty and Frank had laid eyes on one another in six years.

Frank got drunk very quickly and decided to insult Lennie Dunne by telling her just what he thought of her husband, Dominick. Before I knew it, she was in floods of tears. At this, Frank looked at me and remembered he had a gripe with me too. "If it hadn't been for you," he snapped, "Betty and I would have been married!" Then he hurled a couple of chairs and pulled a tablecloth from under glasses and plates. Everything smashed to the floor. And, quite satisfied with himself, he left.

When Frank got to his car, he discovered his tires had been slashed. (Later, I found out the culprits were the musicians at the party, who were furious with his behavior.) According to Mia, he drove home on the rims of the tires. And like clockwork, he sent me a telegram the next day: "I think from now on you'd better send me a guest list or don't invite me at all, Frank."

Everybody knows about Frank the bully; there aren't so many stories about his quiet generosity. But I remember a time when I had an apartment at the Ritz Tower in New York and I invited Frank to join me for dinner at Le Pavillon, the restaurant that used to be in the hotel. He arrived early and had a drink at the bar until I showed up. While waiting, Frank asked the bartender what he did on his days off. The bartender replied that he played golf, and looked forward to buying a good set of golf clubs and getting better at the game. A week later, a fantastic set of irons and woods with two dozen golf balls arrived at the hotel in a golf bag with his name on it.

That's pure Frank. He can be unreasonable but rarely with little people. A mutual friend of ours once put it succinctly. If you expect nothing from Frank, you'll get a lot. If he knows you're expecting something, watch out.

But then, of course, there are Frank's phases, which have more to do with him than you. Like his cherry bomb phase. He was throwing them everywhere. Very late one night, he set some off at the foot of my bed in a Vegas hotel room, then hid behind the door so he could watch my lady friend and me jump ten feet up in the air. In Paris, he once used them as ammunition when he was mobbed by French journalists.

In the late forties and fifties, Las Vegas was the hot weekend spot. But it was never hotter than when Frank was playing the Sands. The usual routine was for a group of friends like the Bogarts, Charlie Feldman and his then girlfriend, Capucine, David and Hjördis Niven, Peter and Pat Lawford, Mike and Gloria Romanoff, Louis and Quique Jourdan, Judy Garland and Sid Luft, and Bill and Edie Goetz to fly up in a chartered plane. When we arrived, Jack Entratter, the Sands' entertainment direc-tor, would be waiting at the airport with two bell captains from the hotel. We weren't allowed to fuss with our baggage; it was limousines to the hotel and, once there, valets to unpack our clothes. The whole thing was very self-contained: Sinatra would occupy the Presidential Suite at the end of the hall, and we'd settle into two-bedroom suites along the corridor.

Once we were settled, we'd get our orders from the Chair-man of the Board: "We're meeting for cocktails at five o'clock." Over drinks, Sinatra would give each of us three hundred dollars in chips to get us started at the tables. He knew we could afford to buy them; he just didn't want to have his friends standing around for even a minute without being part of the action.

Away we went, giggling like a bunch of school kids while Frank got ready for the show. A while later, we'd take our seats in the first row of the showroom—an enormous sacrifice for a gambling casino to make, because, with the exception of Charlie Feldman and Mike Romanoff, we weren't heavy gamblers. It wouldn't have mattered, though, if we'd lost a bundle; as Mike Romanoff discovered, Frank covered any markers.

*A friendly face-off
with Sammy Davis, Jr.*

In those days, that wasn't the biggest of favors. The Mob
had a vital interest in the Sands, and Frank, who owned a small
piece of the hotel, was their idol. There have always been accusa-
tions that he was associated with the Mob, but it was really
about being friendly with the people who employed him. Frank
expressed his friendship by encouraging Dean Martin and
Sammy Davis, Jr., to play the Sands. They could have worked
elsewhere, perhaps for more money, but if Frank wanted them
to work the Sands, that was all they needed to know.

Once Frank put together the Rat Pack show, the Sands was
the hottest casino in town. When he was the attraction, it was
really jumping. After his second show, which ended about
eleven o'clock, Frank would settle into the lounge. The other
important stars in town would try and get over there after their
own shows, not only to pay court to Frank, but to perform for

him and his guests. When did these lounge sessions end? That was Frank's call. If he didn't want to go to sleep, everybody had to stay up. If he decided to go to bed early, the lounge emptied. That's the way it worked.

When I wasn't in Frank's entourage, I'd go out alone. Many of the guys I knew from my nightclub booking days were now running the hotels. And I still had a soft spot for showgirls. I'd visit Jack Entratter at the Sands and sit with him and the choreographer while they chose girls for a show—a smart move for me because it looked to the girls like I was involved in the selection process. In a town where schmucks were lined up ten-deep to meet showgirls, I had a great way to get a proper intro-duction.

In addition to the chorus line, casinos had what was known as "swing girls"—dancers who would fill in for anyone who was ill or on vacation. Every once in a while I'd latch on to a girl I liked; in order to see her, I'd have to pay the swing girl to take her place on the weekend.

Sometimes I'd take a lady friend from L.A. with me. One of these pals was Constance Smith, a fabulous English beauty who was under contract to Fox. She was classic in looks and had the quintessential English peaches-and-cream complexion. I began to represent Constance through an unconventional ar-rangement with an agent in London who didn't think that any-one in Hollywood could take care of her as well as I. I happily accepted the assignment and said I wouldn't take any commis-sion because there wasn't anything to do other than talk to her every once in a while.

Constance and I became good friends, and I suggested one day that we go to Las Vegas for the weekend. (This was a com-pletely innocent invitation; at the time, she was married to Bryan Forbes, the English actor and, later, director.) The first night, we wanted to see the show at the Desert Inn, so I called Angelo, the maître d', and asked for seats in the second row—the best row for those who, like me, don't enjoy throwing their heads back to see the show. When Connie and I arrived, I noticed that Jimmy Vernon, who was part of a dance act I had booked years before, was sitting in front of us. He now worked for Howard Hughes, and I assumed that Howard would show up any second.

Sure enough, when the lights went down, Hughes slipped into the showroom and sat down at the table. His back was to the audience; nobody knew he was there. As we watched the show, Vernon whispered something to Hughes, who turned around and took a look at Constance. He mumbled something to Vernon, and Vernon scribbled a note that the captain brought to Connie. "Meet me afterward in the bar," it said. And there was Hughes's name.

Connie tore up the note.

"What's that all about?" I asked.

"He's so rude. He didn't say that 'we' should have a drink. He just invited me."

Vernon watched Constance tear up the note and told Hughes, who proceeded to write her another one. Same invitation. Constance tore that one up, too. Just before the lights went up, Hughes slipped out of his seat and left the room. It was my impression he was gone for the evening. We said good-bye to Angelo, and I made sure he loved us deeply by giving him twenty-five dollars—headwaiters in Las Vegas are anything but subtle. And then, at the top of the stairs, we saw Howard.

He addressed himself not to me, but to Connie.

"Why won't you have a drink with me?" he asked, in his high-pitched voice.

"I think you are very rude not to invite Mr. Lazar," she replied.

"You're her agent, right?" he asked me.

I nodded.

"Well, I want to talk to this girl. I think I can do something for her."

"It isn't up to me," I explained. "If she wants to have a drink with you, fine. If not, that's her decision. I don't want to get involved."

And with that I marched off to the men's room, which was about twenty feet away. Connie apparently brushed him off, because the next thing I knew, Howard was standing in the next stall. He still couldn't understand why she wouldn't have a drink with him. He even asked if I would agent the drink.

"I don't think it would do any good if I were to ask her," I said. "If anything, it would make things worse. She would think you're operating on a level that I know she doesn't appreciate."

Howard replied that his intentions were purely professional, and that he would take care of the whole thing the next time he talked to Darryl Zanuck. "Fine," I said, and went to wash my hands. Howard did the same.

Now, as everyone knows, I have a legendary fear of germs. The problem isn't really germs, it's the proximity of dirt that annoys me, especially someone else's dirt. Hughes, on the other hand, did have a germ phobia. So that night, as I always do when leaving a public toilet, I reached for a paper towel to use on the door handle so I wouldn't have to touch it. Alas, there were none left. A few seconds later, Howard made the same discovery.

So there we were, two germ freaks both walking toward the door. I lingered, hoping to force Howard to deal with the door. But Howard saw that gambit and stepped aside, leaving me right in front of the door. Was I going to grab that germ-ridden handle? Not on your life. So we were at a standstill. Luckily, another man entered, giving us a chance to duck out before the door swung shut again.

Vegas was a place of public amusement, and while Frank and his friends sometimes got crazy there, they were always aware that they were on display. For that reason, the real action during the 1950s was in Palm Springs, and, in particular, Sinatra's house. The plan of attack rarely varied. There were no freeways to Palm Springs, but it took only a little over two hours if Frank was behind the wheel—three with anyone else. Halfway to the Springs, there was a little saloon which had pictures of him all over the place. The bartender, a great Sinatra fan, would have two vodka martinis waiting for us, straight up and chilled in a thin-stemmed glass, superbly made with just the slightest whiff of dry vermouth. We would always arrive there precisely at five o'clock, have our drink—and, more often than not, one for the road—and then be on our way.

At these weekend blowouts, the cast included everyone from Noël Coward, Terence Rattigan, Laurence Olivier, and the Bogarts, to the entire Rat Pack. But the highlight was the New Year's Eve when Rex Harrison and Kay Kendall were in town.

Frank planned several parties that were just sensational, and the festivities on New Year's Day started at noon with a mariachi band playing. It was "forget-the-world" time, and everybody got more loaded with each passing hour.

Being in Frank's atmosphere always seemed to inspire nutty behavior in others. About 5:30, with the sun setting and the temperature dropping, I went inside to change clothes. There were still a number of people around the pool, including Betty and Bogie. When I returned, now wearing a cashmere jacket and flannel trousers, I walked over to talk to the Bogarts. My back was to the swimming pool, and Bogie, who always liked to stir things up, saw an opportunity that was too good to miss—he pushed me into the pool.

I emerged looking a lot less elegant, to put it mildly. I went to my room and changed clothes. When I reappeared about twenty minutes later, Bogart was still holding court. Well, now it was my turn. I picked him up by the crotch and neck like a wrestler preparing to do serious damage to an opponent. And then I tossed him into the pool, strolled into the house, and sat down by the fire.

Noël Coward had witnessed this exhibition and found it highly amusing. Bogie didn't. He walked in bedraggled, wet, teeth chattering, and his whole body shaking from the cold. Clearly, he was angry. He glared at me, glanced at his expensive Cartier watch, then took it off and threw it in my lap.

"How are we going to get this dry?" he demanded.

I casually tossed the watch into the blazing fire and said, "Like this."

Bogie ran to the fireplace to retrieve the watch, almost putting his hands into the flames, but the blast of the fire made heroic measures inadvisable.

"What are you going to do about it now?" he snarled.

"I'll get you another watch," I said.

"When?"

"This very afternoon."

I had seen a Mickey Mouse watch someone had left in my room, so I enlisted the services of Sinatra's butler to get some boxes of various sizes. We wrapped the watch at the bottom of the tiniest box, then nested it in ever-larger ones. I then had the package delivered to Bogie's room with a card: "I never make a promise I can't keep. Here is your watch. This should make you happy. Love, Swifty."

I had met Humphrey Bogart and Betty Bacall at the Gershwins'. I liked him immediately. He had the least amount of pretense of any actor I've ever known. He downplayed everything, even the fact that he came from a fine family. You had to be very close to him to get him to say anything about his father, who was a physician, his mother, the artist, or his days at Phillips Andover Academy.

Although Bogie looked macho on the screen and sounded tough as a boot when he was riding a topic, he was, in fact, not terribly strong. Or athletically inclined. In ordinary hand-to-hand combat, he was a sucker for a left hook. One good reason for his surprising frailty was the cigarettes that seemed to live in his hand—and the cough they put in his chest. He wasn't easy to understand with his lisp, growl, and coughing, but what came out was usually amusing or interesting.

Bogie was cynical about life and people in general, and absolutely withering on the subject of Hollywood newcomers. He didn't gripe about actors or writers who arrived via a Broadway play or a best-seller. His obsession was the change that took place as each new star achieved status. He loved to trace the transformation. First, he noted, came the acquisition of two dogs, usually large ones. Then the star bought a big house with a swimming pool, and stocked it with several servants and a press agent. And yet, of course, the onetime New Yorker would maintain his disdain for Hollywood and claim he was immune to the California way of life.

Despite his tartness, Bogie was incapable of being mean. The way he hunched his shoulders and stalked a room and turned a lisp into a weapon made those who didn't know him fear him. But he was actually very civilized. His favorite sport, in truth, was pointed conversation. He was a provocateur extraordinaire who liked to start an argument on any subject just for the sake of arguing.

To some of his victims, he was a royal pain in the ass. To me, he was just a gifted needler and a worthy opponent. For once you got into his game and wanted to spar, Bogie was great fun. Brinksmanship was his favorite practice. He would go as far as he could to infuriate someone who could easily smash him with a single blow—but as soon as he reached that point, he would turn on the charm and convert a raging bull into a peaceful puppy. There would be a moment of calm. I mean a literal moment, for as soon as the tumult had died down, Bogie would start his routine all over again. And his debating partner would be, by turns, bewildered and enraged.

Everyone was a victim of his needling, not just me. And there was something about the way he punctured people that he always got away with it. Like the night Billy and Audrey Wilder gave a party upstairs at Romanoff's. There was a lawyer named Greg Bautzer who was an around-town guy in those days. Like Bogie, he was a nice fellow until he got drunk.

Bogie spotted Bautzer at the bar and suggested we go over and talk to him. I was reluctant, but as Bogie often used me as conspirator or savior, I went along. Even I was shocked by Bogie's opening salvo to Greg: "You shouldn't have fucked Doris Stein."

Doris was married to Jules Stein. She was both beautiful and highly respected. It was impossible to think she'd slept with Greg.

"Wait one minute," Greg snapped, his temper flaring. "You can't say things like that. It's not true."

"Look, Greg, I feel very protective toward Jules," Bogie went on. "I'm not going to tell him, I just want to get it straight. You shouldn't have done it, and if you'll admit it, I'll just forget about it."

"If you don't stop," Greg said, "I'm going to kill you."

Greg Bautzer was a strapping six feet two and could have annihilated Bogart with one swipe. This didn't prevent Bogie from asking him if he wanted to step outside. Greg had a few drinks under his belt and rushed downstairs. Wisely, Bogie stayed at the bar and ordered another drink.

A few minutes later, we heard some commotion downstairs. Bogie went to the staircase and saw Greg coming up.

"Greg, I'm glad you came to the party," Bogie said cheerfully. "I've been looking for you."

"I thought you told me to meet you outside. We were going to have it out."

"About what? You're my buddy. Come on, let's have a drink."

Greg didn't realize what was happening to him. He calmed down, came back to the bar, and joined us. When Greg was settled with a fresh drink, Bogart looked around the room and noticed Ginger Rogers dancing with William Holden. And, once again, he turned to Greg.

"You know, Greg," he said, "one of the things that I really regret is that you knocked up Ginger."

Greg looked at him in amazement: "Bogie, you better stop talking like that. She's a friend of mine. We were once engaged —I love this girl. Now cut it out."

"I'm not saying anything wrong," Bogie insisted. "I'm just saying you shouldn't have knocked her up, that's all."

"You say that once more and I'm going to hit you so hard you're going to land on the other side of the room," Greg warned.

"Greg, let me explain something to you. I'm trying to enhance your reputation for being a cad. I want you to know that everybody says,you're a cad and that you never took care of the kid Ginger had with you. Well, I think we ought to take up a collection. And I, for one, am willing to contribute."

Bautzer grabbed Bogie.

"Stop it! Right now!" Greg snarled. "If you want to fight, let's go outside—now!"

Once again, Greg raced downstairs. Once again, Bogart suggested we have another drink. This routine went on until we actually got Bogie to apologize.

You put up with these stunts from Bogie because he always kept a straight face. Once he was in the role, he never broke it. And he expected you to do the same.

One night we went to a dinner party together, and Bogie, ever on guard for bores, stepped into the dining room long before dinner to see where he was seated. "Christ! I'm sitting next to that stupid cunt Doris Vidor," he cried. "Why do they always do this to me?"

As Bogie intended, her husband, King Vidor, overheard his slam and grabbed Bogie.

"Oh, I wasn't talking just about your wife, I meant any one of these broads," Bogie said, making a very offhand apology. Vidor let him go. He completely missed that Bogie's remark was quite deliberate.

It was Bogie who dubbed me "Swifty." It happened on a day when we were having lunch together. Just for the hell of it, because he was amused by the way I hustled for deals, he asked, "How many deals do you think you can make for me and in what period of time?"

I thought for a minute about the movies currently being cast, and the books and plays being turned into scripts.

"I could make you three deals in one day," I said.

"No way," he said.

I looked at my watch, which said one o'clock.

"Let me loose at two and give me twenty-four hours."

Bogie was very modest about himself, and he didn't realize how much he was wanted. I went to three different studios and got three deals. Then I told him he was booked for the next three years. And, with that, he named me "Swifty"—though I much prefer to think the name was really inspired by a play called *Swiftly* that Bogie had been in back in the twenties.

When I got those deals for Bogie, it goes without saying I wasn't his agent. Nor did that hat trick lead to his becoming my client. Bogie's agent was Sam Jaffe, and I always told journalists that even though they often chose to write otherwise. On a technicality, though, I was—very briefly—Bogie's agent. Not that I knew it. Once, when I was out of town, Bogie had a beef with Jaffe, and, in a hotheaded moment, fired him and told him he was going to hire me. He tried to reach me by phone several times to give me the good news, but I was in San Francisco at the opening of a show and didn't return his calls. So I was immensely puzzled when I returned to Los Angeles to find this full-page ad in *The Hollywood Reporter:* "Dear Swifty, You're fired, Bogie." I called Bogie immediately and demanded an explanation.

"Well, I made you my agent yesterday and I couldn't find you," Bogie said, "so I fired you."

Although we didn't have a business relationship, Bogie liked to talk things out with me. One night I was having dinner with Billy Wilder, who had just made a deal for Cary Grant to star in *Sabrina* with Audrey Hepburn and William Holden. It was a fancy role and tailor-made for Cary. But Cary wasn't going to do it; he'd changed his mind for some reason.

I suggested Bogie, which Billy thought might be interesting and a good switch. So I went to Bogie and told him to get out of his trench coat and play the part of a wealthy East Coast patrician. He followed my advice and took the part. But he couldn't get along with the director. Billy didn't have time for Bogie's kind of bantering. Billy is a genuine great wit and Bogie was not. He realized very quickly that Billy was making mincemeat out of him. He hated the picture and soon hated me.

I had been listening to Bogie bitch and moan for weeks without comment, no small achievement. Then came the night I went to have dinner with him in his library, where he liked to watch television as he ate. "You son of a bitch," he began. "How did you get me into this picture?"

"You've got great lines, a great director, a great cast—what more do you want?"

"I hate this picture. I hate the whole damned thing. It's not my kind of action. Those fancy clothes and all that hogwash."

I was so exasperated by his complaining that I finally attacked him in a vulnerable area.

"Listen, you're lucky to be in this business," I told him. "Without an Aquascutum you couldn't get arrested."

That made Bogie so furious he banged his glass of scotch on the table, shattering it in his hand. Blood streamed down his arm. I called for the butler, who brought towels and bandages. Bogie was still cursing up a storm. I sensed trouble was far from over, so while the butler was tending to Bogie, I tiptoed out and ran for my car.

Just as I was backing out of the driveway, Bogie rushed outside and opened the passenger side. "Listen, kid, come on back," he said. "We'll never talk about it again."

Bogie had such fixed opinions about women, politics, and acting that you wouldn't think he could sustain a relationship with anyone. But his marriage to Betty worked—she understood he had to be the master of the house. She was pretty tough herself, but she never tangled with Bogie. He loved her deeply, liked her having a career, but he was the boss. They had dinner when he wanted, and they had guests when he cared to see people, and he wasn't interested in changing any of that.

Bogie drunk was a whole other cup of tea. At those times, he really was dangerous—because he didn't know what he was doing or saying, he was capable of anything. A singular example is an incident that took place at the home of Lewis Milestone, a fine director who did *All Quiet on the Western Front*. In Milestone's foyer was an eighteenth-century mirror. One night a well respected French writer named Joseph Kinsel was a guest at the Milestones'. Kinsel, a monster of a man, had mastered the art of eating glass.

Bogie had never met Kinsel. He couldn't speak French, and Kinsel didn't speak English very well. But they were fellow drunks and made for each other. It was early in the evening when Kinsel encountered Bogart in the foyer and asked him if he could eat glass. Bogart admitted he could not.

"I can," Kinsel boasted.

"Well, eat this," Bogie said, pointing in the direction of the eighteenth-century mirror. And before you knew it, Bogie had smashed the mirror and handed a piece to Kinsel. And Kinsel immediately swallowed half the piece Bogie had given him.

"If you can do it, I can do it," Bogie said.

He tried, but all he did was cut up the inside of his mouth. Betty spent most of the night trying to stop the bleeding.

Bogie drunk in Paris: that's a story with a few more beats than tales of Bogie getting sloshed in L.A. I remember that John Huston was in town as well, staying, like Bogie, at the Ritz. We had dinner together, then went to a Spanish nightclub that featured flamenco dancers. John fancied one of them, and at the end of the performance, he invited her to the table for a drink. The other dancers quickly followed when they discovered that Bogart and Bacall were there.

After a round of drinks, John informed his dancer that he was ready to take her back to the Ritz. At this, the club's owner reminded her she had another show to do and that if she left she was fired. The dancer ignored him and joined us as we piled into a limousine and headed back to the Ritz for another couple of drinks.

John, bless him, was controllable. He took the girl back to his suite and they made love. Then he fell asleep, and she took all his money, his watch, and anything else she could lay her hands on.

Bogie, however, was interested in a few more drinks, which made the evening into a race against time. Could we get him to bed before he did something nuts? I thought we'd accomplished that, so I made my good nights and went on to my suite at the George V. My head hadn't hit the pillow when Betty called—Bogie was gone.

"It's two in the morning," I said. "Where do you suggest I look?"

"He kept talking about the girls at the Lido. You've got to go and find him. He'll get hurt and into trouble."

I called Peter Viertel, who was staying at the Raphael, and asked him to help me. We met at the Lido, where the maître d' was only too happy to direct us to the dancers' dressing room. I asked Peter to wait outside in case Bogie made a run for it. Then I went to the dressing room.

This was the scene that greeted me: through a fog of white powder, Bogie sat with his feet propped up on the dressing table. In one hand, he held a scotch and soda. In the other was a giant-sized, two-foot-square powder puff, which he dipped into a huge barrel of talc.

Bogie was not alone. The dancers, known as the Bluebell Girls, had one more number to do, and here they were, stark naked, except for their headgear. The talc was their body makeup—because they had to look buffed and dry when they stormed onstage, they powdered each other just before they went on.

Tonight, though, they had an assistant. Surrounded by girls with their legs raised high on the backs of chairs, Bogie was wielding the powder puff. He was also giving the dancers a bit of direction. "Lift your leg a little, dear," he would tell them.

When he spotted me, he was delighted.

"Hey, have a seat and relieve me, 'Swifty,' " he shouted. "This is getting too tedious."

I joined in the fun for a while, then told Bogie I was taking him back to the hotel. He refused. By this time, the girls had finished their last number and were changing into their street clothes. The manager came down and told us we had to leave. Bogie wouldn't budge.

By now, the novelty of having Humphrey Bogart backstage had worn off, and the manager brought in two gendarmes to escort him out. One was pulling Bogie by the arm, and the other was walking behind me. As they were guiding us to the stagedoor exit, Bogart said, "Fuck the friggin' frogs." He thought that sounded funny.

"Quoi?" the gendarme asked.

"He said it," Bogie said pointing to me.

The French cop grabbed me by the nape of the neck, twisting a little harder than necessary.

After they threw us out on the street, I walked Bogie around to the main entrance. No sign of Peter. "Wait here," I told Bogie. "I'll find Peter, and then we'll take you home."

"Sounds good," Bogie said.

I should have known better.

In the time it took me to find Peter and return to the street, Bogie had made a new set of friends—he was sitting in the rear of the Lido's casino with a gaggle of hookers. They were drinking champagne, and Bogie was raising his glass to toast each and every one of them.

Once again, he seemed glad to see me.

"Ladies, I want you to meet your host!" he cried. "There he is!"

With that, he ordered more champagne and told the waiter to give me the check. Peter, who was thoroughly disgusted, took the opportunity and left. So here I was, sitting with Bogie and a dozen or so of these tarts. I can't say I hated every minute. Or that I rushed our exit. It was only after many more bottles had been consumed that I asked Bogie if he was ready to leave.

"Now I am," he said. "We've had a good time. Now sign the check."

I signed "Humphrey Bogart," and off we went to the Ritz, where I deposited him into Betty's anxious arms.

There's a system in Paris that's just perfect for guys like Bogart. If you're a well-known personality, you can spend a fortune at places like the Lido and walk out without paying, because they have an arrangement with the concierges at the top hotels. The next morning the club or restaurant presents the signed tab to the hotel; the hotel pays in full, then puts the charge on your bill. So the Lido had its money long before Bogie was awake.

When Bogie was advised that he was out $1,500 for his night at the Lido, he called me.

"Do you know they presented me with that bill you ran up last night?" he asked, sounding quite surprised.

"Bogie, I didn't run up the bill, you did. Did you have a good time?"

"Yeah, I had a great time."

"Well, you're paying for it. Are you still happy?"

"No, I'm not. I thought you were paying for it."

That was Bogart—he was not a philandering guy, he just liked entertaining women of dubious reputation and having his friends pay. I didn't care. As sins go, this was small change.

I hate illness. I hate dying. I hate death. When Bogie was wasting from cancer, I had a hard time going to see him. One day, though, Bogie said to Betty, "I guess I'm a goner. Swifty's stopped coming around." When Betty passed that along, I knew I had no choice—I jettisoned my fears and feelings and resumed my daily visits to my dying friend. Those were encounters of amazing courage on Bogie's part.

He used to come downstairs in his dressing gown and drink, smoke, and chat with his friends. The living room was his limit; by this point, he couldn't go anywhere. Later, as he got weaker, he was unable to walk down the steps. To get to the living room, he'd curl up into a fetal position in the dumbwaiter and have himself sent downstairs. Then he would get into the wheelchair, roll into the living room, and greet the steady stream of people who would come to see him.

Bogie never wanted to talk about dying. He wasn't going to make you a party to it. Just the opposite—he acted as if it wasn't going to happen. Unless you knew he was very sick, you couldn't figure it out by talking to him. He never said a word about life being taken away from him or wondered how his kids would get along without him. He was gallant beyond description.

CHAPTER

Eight

I WAS FIFTY-THREE in 1960, and, more than ever, I loved being an agent. Everywhere I looked, I saw talent and opportunity. I was beholden to no one, so I could come and go as I pleased. And because I also represented writers in Europe, traveling was a synonym for agenting. All this freedom made for a happy life—I was like a kid in a playground.

It was also not a small source of pleasure to discover that I was able to compete with large agencies even when I wandered off to Europe. People ask about discoveries I've made and expect to hear names of stars. The fact is, one of my best discoveries was about myself—that I could work just as effectively from a hotel room as from home. I had a lot of fun abroad, but I never went to a city where I didn't make a deal.

So London, Paris, Biarritz, and Klosters became my playgrounds. Particularly Klosters, a little village in the Suisse-Deutsch part of Switzerland that was a favorite among my friends and clients. Anatole Litvak told Peter Viertel about it; soon after he came to stay, Irwin Shaw followed. I could see why. During the fifties and on into the sixties, Klosters was not yet a ski resort where travelers met the chic and famous. Après-ski was no more than a change of boots. Vacationers didn't bring

More traveling: in Moscow with Harry Kurnitz (top right), and skiing in Switzerland.

their evening clothes and tiaras, as the wealthy and fashionable do when they go to St. Moritz or Gstaad. Klosters, in contrast, had an unhurried, countrylike charm. At Christmas, when my chums converged at the Chesa Grischuna, the small but enchanting hotel that was the hub of the village, the party was both low-key and nonstop.

When I got to Klosters, the first thing I did was engage a ski instructor. "I'm an absolute beginner," I said, "so start me at the beginning." That was how a forty-six-year-old man found himself with the three-year-olds.

I didn't care that I was in kindergarten. Skiing was a tremendous adventure for me, and the sheer exhilaration of staying upright on the gentlest slope was worth everything. And I did get better—by the third year, I made it from the top of the most challenging run to the bottom without disaster. This prowess mystifies me now. The rest of the year, my only exercise was golf and tennis. I did no muscle conditioning to prepare for Switzerland. And yet I never suffered any injuries.

Even before I became a competent skier, I looked the part. My ski clothes were custom-made in green, blue, and white, with hats, boots, and gloves to match. Some thought I looked ridiculous. Others applauded. But no one denied that it was a spectacle.

Bogart told me that the only way to go to a ski resort was to arrive with your arm in a sling and hang out at the bar. That way, everybody will buy you a drink, if not dinner, and you won't have to risk breaking your ass. I loved taking the risks, and, of course, taking over some of the entertainment.

I would have taken over more of the entertaining, but Irwin fought me all the way. I liked to give small dinners at the bar of the Chesa, where guests would gather late at night to listen to a fellow play piano and sing Gershwin and Porter in his Swiss accent. But Irwin loved to have people—lots of people—at his house. The burden of managing it all was not-too-timidly placed on the shoulders of his wife. I think Irwin fantasized that Marian possessed supernatural powers, for she could, on no notice, in the thick of a snowstorm, produce tables with bowls of spring flowers and a magnificent dinner.

Irwin's constant cry for "M-a-a-a-arian!" was like that of a

Tennis with Irwin Shaw.

beleaguered beast. And her name was only the prelude. What followed was the plaint of a man in the throes of helplessness: "Why didn't Marian leave the keys in the car?" "Why is Marian always washing her hair?" "Why isn't Marian ready for lunch?" Mostly, it was "Why isn't lunch ready?" Lunch was Irwin's fetish; he insisted that it be served on time, always with a fine wine. He thought nothing of having six bottles on the table for as many guests.

An outsized appetite for pleasure: that was Irwin Shaw in a phrase. The man was just bigger than life, both in stature and in sensibility. He was only about five foot eight, but when you sat next to him you felt you were sitting alongside the Woolworth Building. He seemed to envelop you and the space around you.

In a long life filled with more friends than I could ever sort through, I realize that there are fewer than a handful of people with whom you feel a real kinship. Moss, Irwin—in 1960, they were at the top of the short list. Not surprisingly, both came from backgrounds similar to mine. Moss was raised in the Bronx; Irwin and I were Brooklyn-bred sons of Russian Jewish immigrants. As a result of that upbringing, all three of us loved making money and spending it. The South of France, noisy dinners in good restaurants, big ideas and bigger deals—Irwin and I were like twins in our pleasures.

As a writer, Moss was a highly strung instrument, and you needed always to watch him for subtle, almost subterranean clues. In that regard, Irwin was simpler to understand—he wrote so he could make money and have the good life. No blockage in him; he wrote every day of his life, no matter how late he'd stayed up or how much booze he had consumed the night before. Because he was both prolific and accomplished, it wasn't hard to keep the money coming in for him. That made Irwin the perfect Lazar client: a plethora of talent, good work habits, and a winning personality with an attractive life in a fashionable, foreign setting. Between Irwin in Europe and Moss in New York, what more could I ask for?

Then, in December 1961, when he was just fifty-seven, Moss Hart dropped dead of a heart attack in Palm Springs. He and Kitty had moved there a few months earlier, after Moss had suffered a heart attack in Toronto while directing the out-of-town tryout of *Camelot*. Clearly, he needed a more peaceful environment than New York if he was going to survive a long life. Palm Springs was surely that, and I had every reason to think we'd have Moss around for years and years.

I was so confident about Moss's improving health that I didn't react dramatically when something happened that should have signaled trouble. That clue came on Sunday, when Moss complained of a pain in his upper left jaw. That is often the sign of an impending heart attack; it was, as Kitty and Moss and I knew, the exact symptom he'd had in Toronto. So we rushed Moss to the doctor, who took an electrocardiogram. It showed nothing.

With that, we cheered right up and went ahead with the long-standing plan to take the entire Hart family to the Racquet Club for the weekly Sunday night family buffet and dance—a Palm Springs ritual for couples with children. There was a grayish-green pallor to Moss's skin, though, and after a dance with his daughter Kathy and a quick whirl with Kitty, he wanted to go home. Fine, I said, and we went our separate ways, Moss to rest in bed, me to head back to L.A.

The next morning the phone rang quite early. You know how inanimate objects seem to signal emotion? This morning, the phone rang like that; when I heard it, I knew it was no good.

"Moss is gone," Kitty said.

I was at the airport twenty minutes later, chartering a private plane. The flight lasted little over an hour—more than enough time for me to relive decades in the sunlight of Moss's friendship. But we weren't just friends—we had spoken almost every day for nearly twenty years, and when Moss and Kitty moved to Palm Springs, I became a permanent weekend guest. There was a cottage on the premises which they repainted for me and made habitable by installing new furniture, phone lines, and a television. Using all the French at his command, Moss put up a sign outside the door of that cottage: LAZAR ICI.

Those were precious, lovely weekends. Moss blossomed in Palm Springs, and as he relaxed, he let the more capricious side of his character emerge. One day, as we were walking downtown, we passed a pet store with a huge, seven-foot-tall caged monkey in the window. Ignoring all objections, Moss bought it and named it Max, in honor of Max Gordon, the Broadway producer. Max the monkey had an obnoxious habit of spitting at everyone, but Moss cherished him and cared for him like a child.

Moss became crazy for canasta. He and Kitty loved to play, and it didn't matter who they played with: the grocer, the delivery boy. It always amused me that his canasta partners were so unlike his usual companions; I was in awe of his ability to feel so comfortable with people he had nothing in common with beyond cards.

Which isn't to say that Moss was isolated. The minute people knew he was in town—in Los Angeles, New York, Palm Springs, wherever—the invitations started flooding in, for his very presence somehow injected a spirit of anticipated fun. That was Moss in a nutshell: he lifted the spirits of people. And that was curious, considering that he suffered from depression.

Although I was well aware of the fact that Moss had been under the care of Dr. Lawrence Kubie, a somewhat controversial psychiatrist, he never betrayed the anguish that gnawed at him. It was as if he wasn't seeing Kubie and wasn't depressed. And I understood why: his face to the world was that of an enchanter, a dazzling host and storyteller with an inexhaustible zest for life.

His fondness for the pleasures of the world were only matched by his unwillingness to work. That was his idea of heaven—never to work. When he had a hit play and made money, he was the antithesis of, say, Neil Simon, who went right on to add the duties of a producer. Not Moss. Money was freedom for him, liberating fantasies of first-class travel, good servants, fine wine, toothsome food, and beautiful clothes. His great joy was to walk from his apartment on Park Avenue down to the Lyceum Theater, in which he had part ownership, meet another writer for lunch, and go on to the next social engagement.

A source of his malady was perhaps his hatred of having to write under pressure. I witnessed this in 1954 when I got him a five-picture deal with Fox. The crushing pressure to produce successful screenplays after he'd received the money caused him to turn down a substantial sum. It was not his way to put the Sword of Damocles over his own head.

But he had two children to consider and he felt the need for more financial security, so he asked if I would make a deal for him to write some screenplays for Darryl Zanuck. Well, the man said he didn't want to worry about money, so I asked Darryl for $1.5 million, plus a percentage of the profits, for five screenplays. This was a figure unheard of at the time. But Darryl was agreeable.

The Harts were visiting in Palm Springs, and I wanted to have the pleasure of taking the contract down that weekend as a surprise house present, so I asked Zanuck if he would do a special favor and have the legal department expedite the documents. On Friday afternoon, envelope in hand, I hurried to the pool at the Palm Springs Racquet Club. Kitty and Moss were sunning themselves, innocently enjoying their last moment of peace.

"You have a funny glint in your eye," Moss said.

"You didn't think we could do it? Well, it's done," I said, holding up the contracts.

"Terrific!" Moss said, getting up to hug me. "Leave the papers with me and I'll give them back to you over the weekend."

He didn't ask about the terms, and I didn't tell him. But I

knew when he looked at the contracts—the whooping and reveling began immediately. For two days, we celebrated, clinking glasses and toasting Moss's brilliance. But I could sense there was something gnawing at Moss, and, after the shock wore off, he told me.

"They're nuts to pay that kind of money," he said. "I hate to take so much. Can't I take less?"

"Moss, nobody in Hollywood has ever gotten that kind of money, guaranteed, to be paid over a period of ten years," I replied. "You have to do five screenplays. Each calls for a fifteen-week writing period, plus four weeks of revisions, so it will take roughly sixty weeks out of the next one hundred fifty-six weeks to do this. We can't accept less. More maybe, but not less."

Moss agreed, and off he went to write.

But after cranking out the first screenplay, *The Prince of Players,* he balked.

"I can't have that kind of obligation over me," he told me. "I want out."

I started to say that he was a master writer and a diligent worker, that he was inventing a problem. He cut me off.

"I'm an old hand at this, Irving. I've done screenplays. Sometimes they come off and sometimes not. This is great for the guys in Hollywood who can hack it, but I'm not one of them. I really don't want this deal."

"Okay, let's forget about it," I said. "Hey, it's just money."

Moss came over and kissed me on the cheek. "You're a real good pal," he said. And that was the end of it.

His sense of morality when it came to money was always the overriding factor in any deal I made for him. His philosophy was: "Don't get the best deal. Do what you think is fair, and make a deal that will let the other fellow be happy, too."

Those words, that generosity, the boundless love of fun—images of the vibrant, living Moss streamed through my mind as the plane landed in Palm Springs. Grief, as everyone knows, is not my thing, but coming off that plane, I felt entombed by it. And I knew I couldn't be, for Kitty was inconsolable and in no shape to organize a funeral. Somehow, I managed to make all the arrangements.

All these years later, there's hardly a day that goes by that I don't think of Moss. He was my hero. And if you must have a hero, what better one than Moss Hart?

Out of death came new life. In 1963, Irving Paul Lazar—the bachelor who joked that he would leave all his money to the wives of his best friends, and that these women, and not their husbands, would be the pallbearers at his funeral—surprised everyone and got married.

I had never had a live-in girlfriend. No woman was neat enough for me, not that I let anyone hang around long enough for me to explore her philosophy of domestic hygiene. But the issue was really simpler than personal habits—I just never wanted the responsibility of having someone in my life. I always felt that if I had to worry about someone else it would bog me down. It wasn't all joy living like that; of the many women I dated, there were some I could see myself liking a lot. But Mary Van Nuys was the only girl I ever wanted to marry, and I knew that the moment I met her.

Mary and I met at the end of 1962, on a plane bound for Paris. I was sitting in First Class, and decided to take a walk through the plane to stretch my legs. Sitting in coach were four fabulous-looking young women, laughing and having a great time. One of them was a model I had squired around New York a few times, so I stopped to chat. Her three friends, she explained, were also models; they were going to Paris to do a fashion shoot for *Vogue*.

One of these models was a dark-haired, fine-boned beauty, wearing a simple but elegant brown knit dress. We struck up a conversation, and I quickly learned that Mary loved to travel, adored the theater, and was a voracious reader. And I could see that she was genuinely fascinated by my being a literary agent.

The more I stared and listened to her talk, the more a refrain began to bubble in my brain: "I'm going to marry this girl." That kind of instantaneous knowledge is pure instinct and is really inexplicable. But looking back, I understand the spark: Mary was as bright as she was pretty. Before her, the women I dated were uniformly good-looking and fun, but none could be accused of being a great conversationalist.

I learned right away that Mary was thirty-one. I was fifty-six but the age difference was no more of a problem than two people being different because of their likes and dislikes or experiences. When I met her she had a successful career; in addition to doing fashion layouts, she had been the Coca-Cola Girl for a nationwide print campaign and also did television commercials. When we met, she'd been a model for ten years or so and she'd had enough; she wanted to quit and be a wife.

I didn't see Mary in Paris because the model I knew wanted me to take her out. I didn't want to cause trouble among the ladies, so I waited to call Mary until I got back to New York. For the next few months, I saw her every time I was in New York. By our fifth date, I knew enough to act on my instinct.

I took Mary to lunch at Le Pavillon, and, over the first course, dropped the bomb. "I'm getting married," I said.

Mary didn't miss a beat. "That's interesting," she said. "Do I know the girl?"

"You should—I'm marrying you."

She didn't say yes right away, but she didn't say no either. She suggested we go away for a couple of weeks, get to know each another beyond dinner and lunches, and take it from there.

Mary Van Nuys

And then I met Mary.

So we went to Klosters for Christmas. And Mary was not only as adorable and bright as she'd been in New York, she charmed all my friends. Now I was desperate to get back to America so I could marry her.

I am not a man who confides much in his friends. But in Klosters, I did tell Norman Krasna and his wife, Erle, that marriage was in my future. With that, Norman promptly organized an engagement party for us at the Chesa Grischuna with all my chums—Irwin Shaw, Peter Viertel, Anatole Litvak, Gene Kelly —and their wives.

This party was all it took. Overnight, the news traveled back to Los Angeles, and the impossible notion of Lazar getting hitched made a great many people extremely curious to meet the victim. In other circumstances, it would have been totally in character for me to "agent" Mary—to bring her to Los Angeles and show her off, as if I were eager to sell her to my friends. This time, I felt that approach would be not just foolish, but wrong. And, this time, I wasn't interested in anyone's opinion.

The news getting out did me a favor; it forced me to make a plan. What I came up with was the idea of going directly to Las Vegas and getting married without a lot of fanfare. We could do this at the Sands Hotel, where Jack Entratter would arrange everything, with Lee and Ira Gershwin as witnesses. Getting married like this fit into my basic philosophy: act fast. I don't like things to be left undone, or half done. I like to close the deal while the iron is hot. Mary agreed on the date. She had a little more trouble with Vegas—it wasn't quite the venue she had envisioned for her nuptials, but she understood my thinking. And she was able to set aside her preferences in order to become my wife.

And what a wife. From the moment we became a team, she made an enormous contribution to my life, personally and professionally. Her bright, beautiful soul was visible at all times, and her innate kindness was immensely appealing. In addition to being beautiful, charming, and well-dressed, she was a gifted hostess who created a welcoming home for me and a haven for my friends. In no time at all, Mary had made me the center of a glittering salon.

Beyond all that, she was key to my relationships with my

Our wedding day in Las Vegas, witnessed by Lee and Ira Gershwin.

clients. I had a nose for talent and a good way of hawking it, but I was not always as personable as I liked to think. Mary read and evaluated the material we got from writers, something I had neither time nor inclination for. Her keen perception of words and talent directed me to the excellence of material I might otherwise have overlooked. And because Mary could talk perceptively and enthusiastically about material, my clients—who, for all their fame, were often as insecure as first-timers—were crazy about her. That contribution alone made her instrumental in everything I did for the next three decades.

But Mary was no wispy flower child. When the moment called for it, she was fierce—woe be to anyone who dared cross her when it came to me. Was Mary aware of my shortcomings? Oh yes, and she wouldn't hesitate to tell me when I was being a pain in the ass. To the outside world, though, she was ferociously protective of me. And, in the process of defending me, she revealed me to myself.

What I only came to understand after I married Mary was that I—Mr. Life Enhancer, everybody's favorite fun-loving bachelor—had become not just a sidekick to my pals, but a bit of a joke as well. The way I looked, the way I talked, my chutzpah, my free-wheeling way of doing business: all these made me a comic folk figure. Before Mary, I didn't think too much about the jokes I inspired. I laughed harder than anyone when George Axelrod caricatured me as Irving "Sneaky" LaSalle—an agent who is supposed to be the devil in disguise and takes 10 percent of your soul—in his play *Will Success Spoil Rock Hunter?* After I married Mary, though, there were no more jokes at my expense. Everyone called me "Swifty" to my face back then, but Mary called me "Irving" and, over time, others acknowledged my existence correctly or paid the price.

As Otto Preminger found out to the tune of a slap in the face from Mary and fifty stitches from yours truly on January 7, 1966.

The setting was "21," where Mary and I had gone after dinner to meet Slim Keith and Truman Capote. Slim and Truman hadn't yet arrived, so we turned to the people at the next table—the German-born producer-director and sometime actor Otto Preminger, his wife Hope, the columnist Louis Sobol and his wife—and chatted for a few minutes.

After a while, Louis made the transition from pal to newsman. "Any news?" he asked.

"We just got into town," I said.

Then Otto inserted himself into the conversation. "Why don't you print that Frank Sinatra is going to punch Mr. Lazar in the nose and beat him up?" he said.

I knew why Otto wanted to make trouble. Two years earlier, when Truman was still writing *In Cold Blood,* Otto had wanted to buy the rights and have Frank star in the film. I'd given him some hope, but had carefully avoided saying anything binding. Which was just as well—when the book was finished, Truman decided we should sell it to Richard Brooks without inviting other bids. Left out in the cold, Otto was miffed.

"Louis, please don't print this," I said. "Otto thinks I promised him Truman's book. I never did. As for Sinatra being mad that he won't get to star in the movie, that's rubbish. I've seen him several times since the book was sold, and he was hardly violent. He even invited us to his opening at the Sands—if we hadn't planned to come to New York, we'd be there with him now."

"How about if I write that Frank and Otto wanted the book, but that you sold it to someone else?" Louis said, not wanting to see his story completely evaporate.

"Okay with me," I said. "How about you, Otto?"

" 'Swifty' sold it for five hundred thousand," Otto said. "I wouldn't have paid that much. It's not going to be that good a movie."

"Otto, it's academic," I said, wanting to end the conversation right there. "Let's drop it."

But Otto was just warming up. "You, Lazar, are a liar, a cheat, and a crook," he said.

"Otto, please, you've got to stop this or we can't be friends," I replied. "It's one thing to insult me—I can take it. But this is offensive to Mary."

Otto then turned to Louis. "I tell you right now: Sinatra is going to beat Lazar up when he sees him. And to prove it, I'm going to call him at the Sands." And Otto summoned a waiter to bring him a phone.

"Otto has been getting roles as a Nazi in the movies," Louis said to Mary, "and now he's trying to be one."

"Not at all," Otto said, as he tipped the waiter and began to place a call to Vegas. "Sinatra is going to tell me how he's going to beat Lazar up, and you're going to print it."

"You're making it impossible for us to remain here, Otto," I said.

Otto went on talking to the operator.

I motioned to the waiter, and Mary and I got up.

"You pitiable creature," Otto told Mary as she began to move away from the table. "I feel sorry for any woman who has to go home and go to bed with that crook."

"You're a dirty old man," Mary snapped—and slapped Otto's face.

And then Otto rose to his full height, which was a solid six

Otto Preminger complaining about me to the cops. Me in custody.

feet. He reached for Mary, so I reached for a glass. I could say that Otto's head hit the glass as I tried to get between them—I did say just that, a dozen hours later, to the police—but the truth is that I slugged him with it. Slugged him pretty hard, too, if I must say. Blood was streaming down Otto's face as Mary and I beat a retreat.

I was cut as well, a neat slice down my finger caused by the broken glass. My wound required eight stitches. That was nothing—Otto's required fifty. The doctors even gave him a tetanus shot, on the theory that I might have bitten him as well.

The following afternoon, I was arrested at my hotel and charged with felonious assault. My lawyer got me out on bail and brought me uptown in a Rolls-Royce. Otto, meanwhile, was considering civil charges against me. (In the end, the police case became a misdemeanor, and, to placate Otto, I made a contribution to his favorite charity.)

The papers had a field day. "One of the tiniest of manhunts for one of the tiniest of men ended without a shot being fired

My favorite picture of Mary and me.

yesterday," one article began. It concluded: "This is not the first time Swifty Lazar has drawn blood from a producer. He does it every time he negotiates. This is merely the first time he used a deadly weapon."

Those newspaper stories got it almost right. The thing is, the deadly weapon was not the "21" drinking glass. It was, I'm proud to say, my dear wife.

CHAPTER

Nine

By the sixties, I had perfected my sales technique. Along the way, I had learned that the most important facet in selling is energy. So I poured it on—I energized a project and made it whirl. If the outside world hadn't come to me by two in the afternoon, I went to it; I discovered where the action was and jumped into the fray. And not always into eager arms, mind you.

A competitive spirit was just as important as energetic promotion. I am so competitive that, no matter how profitable my year was, I was still agitated when I read that another agent had sold a property. However lowly the book or play, however small the deal, I always felt that something I might have handled had escaped my grasp.

Ty Cobb, a special hero of mine, was one of the toughest competitors—and meanest guys—in baseball. A reporter once told me that, during the 1947 Old-Timers Game in New York, the sixty-year-old Cobb stepped up to the plate and cautioned the catcher to step back. It had been a long time since he'd swung a bat, he said, and he was concerned that it might slip from his grasp. The catcher thanked the old duffer for his thoughtfulness and moved back from the plate. And what did Cobb do? He laid down a perfect bunt right in front of the plate and made it easily to first base. That's one of the oldest wiles: an old man asks for a favor, you oblige, and then he hits you right in the kisser. And that's my kind of guy.

This fifty-three-year-old gent started off the decade with what would be the most interesting, trickiest, and difficult deal in my long career. It's also the one I'm most proud of. The movie rights to *The Sound of Music* went for more money than any play or book in the history of the movies. And the deal I structured for its authors, Lindsay and Crouse, was also unprecedented. When a key player in a film gets a percentage of the gross, that doesn't usually begin until the movie has earned back its costs—but Lindsay and Crouse received 10 percent of the gross from the first dollar.

This masterstroke of a deal all began at the opening of *The Sound of Music* on Broadway. Spyros Skouras, who was then president of Twentieth Century–Fox, was sitting next to me. I couldn't help but notice that many of the scenes and most of the songs moved him to tears. And there is nothing like a Greek in tears.

Not long after the opening, I was in Europe when Howard Lindsay called to say that Warner Bros. had offered $1 million for *The Sound of Music*. Although that was a fortune, he wanted Leland Hayward, the show's producer, to hold up the deal until I returned. That was a smart move because I felt certain I could do better.

I came back a week early. And the first thing I did was call Skouras. "How would you like to buy *The Sound of Music*?" I asked.

"Come right over," he said.

I told him we'd been offered a million but I really wanted $1.25 against 10 percent from the first dollar. Skouras didn't flinch. All he wanted was to confirm the terms with Buddy Adler, who ran the studio in California. Buddy didn't wince either. I called Lindsay and Crouse, and, verbally, we shook hands—a record deal in record time.

The Sound of Music sold quickly and on my terms because Fox was in trouble and Skouras and Adler thought this film would save the studio. As it happened, once they'd purchased

In Spain with Mary, Nadia, and Larry Collins, and Dominique Lapierre, circa 1965.

With two of my favorite people, Adolph Green and Betty Comden.

the rights, Fox's board of directors deemed the property too
risky to make. It languished at the studio until Jack Warner asked
me to represent him and offer Fox a $250,000 profit if they'd

transfer the rights. By this time, Skouras had been deposed and
Darryl Zanuck was at the helm.

Thanks to the prodding from Warner, the picture got the
green light at Fox. Once set in motion, it was nothing but a cash
cow. Decades after it was made, the families of the authors still
get checks. And, of course, so does their agent.

The sixties brought so many deals that it seemed at one
point every major literary or theatrical property passed through
my hands. I sold Truman Capote's *In Cold Blood* for $500,000,
plus a third of the profits. I moved *How to Succeed in Business
Without Really Trying* for $1 million. Jack Warner paid $1.4 million, plus a percentage, for *Camelot*. And I was involved in the
sales of *Is Paris Burning?*, *Barefoot in the Park*, *The Odd Couple*,
On a Clear Day You Can See Forever, *Catch-22*, and *My Fair Lady*,
among others.

The reason I did so much high-level business was that I
never stopped believing in my right to represent a project—with
or without authorization. A producer asked me: "Who do you
represent in this deal?" My reply was easy: "I represent you."
How could it have been otherwise? Everyone else was fully
agented.

I represented Paramount, for example, when I sold Neil
Simon's *The Odd Couple* and *Barefoot in the Park*. Simon was
represented by the Morris office, and as I told him, there was no
reason to disrupt his relationship with his agent. "Let them have
their 10 percent, I'll get mine from the studio," I said. Could the
studio have called the Morris office directly and cut me out?
Easily. Why didn't they? They liked doing business with me.

Over the years, my usefulness to studios became so great
that I created another niche for myself: I was, I think, the only
agent in town who got a yearly retainer from studios. Under
the terms of those arrangements, I could sell a particular studio
anything and represent it for any property—except for material
that involved my clients. That made sense. It would, of course,
be unethical for me to steer a client's work away from the open
market to a studio where its sale might do more to enhance my

relationship than produce top dollar for my client. But, then again, I had no signed agreements with clients and tended to "represent" people who had other agents. Who, in that thicket, could say what a "client" was for Irving Lazar?

Over the course of my career, I had deals with Columbia, Fox, Paramount, United Artists, and Warner Bros. My so-called steady clients hated the fact that I had these deals. They saw it as a conflict of interest. They had no way of knowing if I was showing their material to the studio where I was on retainer. From their point of view, that particular studio may not have necessarily been the place they wanted their material to go.

There were times when clients said to me quite directly: "Irving, you have a conflict of interest." But whatever anyone said, it always seemed that when they saw the deals I got for them they had no trouble cashing the check. Me? I just saw the arrangement as an offshoot of being an agent.

Success is rarely a pure testament to skill and intelligence. It also helps to be lucky. An exemplary bit of good fortune came my way when I happened to be in New York at the same time as Noël Coward and he invited me to the theater. Noël would rather see a play than do anything else. No matter what country he was in, the theater came first. He looked at the listings, checked off what he hadn't seen, and arranged his evenings accordingly.

"There's a play that has been running here for more than two years called *Come Blow Your Horn,*" he said. "Know anything about it?"

"Someone told me it's funny," I replied. "But I don't know anything about it or the author."

"Well, it must have something to have run all this time," he said. "Let's go."

We got to the Brooks Atkinson Theater, where we joined a scant audience of fifty or sixty people. The curtain went up, and there, before me, was a very familiar scene: a Jewish family in the Bronx. As the story began to unfold, I started to laugh. And, to my astonishment, Noël—this distinguished Britisher who had no knowledge of that culture—was laughing as hard as me.

"You know, this chap Neil Simon is a wonderful writer,"

Noël Coward.

Noël said at intermission. "He knows how to construct a play. He writes wonderful jokes and knows how to use them. He has a great sense of the dramatic and poignant, a rare combination. Get on to him, 'Swifty.' It seems from the program that this is his first play. But he is major stuff, I'll tell you that."

I took Noël's advice, and, the next day, sent a note to the theater asking Simon to call me. Over lunch at Le Pavillon, he told me that his agents, the William Morris Agency, had sold *Come Blow Your Horn* to Paramount for very little money and that he had just completed a new play. I asked to see it—and, the next day, he sent me *Barefoot in the Park.* True to my code, I read just enough to know that it was hilarious. I called him immediately.

"What did you get for your last play?" I asked.

"Seventy-five thousand."

"Well, I am going to get you five-hundred thousand for this one."

"But I've promised Bud Yorkin and Norman Lear, who produced *Come Blow Your Horn,* that they'll have first look at it."

"And they will," I promised.

Both Mary and I loved the bullfights, as did many of our friends. That's me below in the arena, trying my hand with the cape.

I sent *Barefoot in the Park* to Lear. And waited. And a full week went by without a word. So I called him.

"We read it and don't think it's deep enough," Lear said.

"If you're looking for a funny play, Norman, this is it," I told him. "If, on the other hand, you're looking for oil, you're right—it's not deep enough."

My next move was to give the play to Jack Warner. And Jack did something which was unusual for him: he read the play himself. And thought it was terrific. And wanted to buy it. Which is how I made a deal with Warner Bros. for $500,000. Neil was to write the screenplay, which would give him a total of $750,000, as well as profit participation. I secured a two-year wait so the play could go on the road and have foreign productions before filming commenced.

Simon couldn't believe it. To him, I had made a miracle. Paramount, as it happened, thought the same thing. Almost. What they felt was that I was about to pull off a miraculous crime —according to Jack Karp, head of production at Paramount, his studio had first refusal on *Barefoot in the Park*. I told him that I had already been turned down by Norman Lear. No matter, he said; the obligation was to Paramount, not to Yorkin and Lear. The unhappy part of the story is that I had to go back to Warners and break the deal. The happy ending is that the film wound up at Paramount under the same terms as the Warner deal.

About eighteen months later, Neil called with much alarm in his voice, to ask if I could rearrange the Paramount contract. The play had been beautifully directed by Mike Nichols, and cast superbly with Robert Redford and Elizabeth Ashley, and it looked as if it would run forever. But there still hadn't been a road company, and, although it was eagerly awaited in Europe, it still hadn't opened there. If the film could be held up, Neil stood to make an additional million dollars or more in royalties.

I explained the situation to Jack Karp, reminding him that he had bought *Come Blow Your Horn* for very little money, that the movie performed well, and that he now had another Simon smash on his roster. Yes, he'd paid a lot for *Barefoot in the Park,* but, increasingly, it looked as if he'd scored another bargain.

"Why don't you be big-hearted and give us the time?" I asked.

"I'm working for the studio," Karp said. "Give me a reason, other than a sentimental one. Has he got another play or idea that we can buy or option?"

Neil told me he was working out the story for another play. When I passed that news on to Karp, he suggested that Neil come out to Hollywood for a story meeting; if the idea was even halfway something Paramount liked, they'd give him the time he wanted for *Barefoot*. So, the following Thursday, Neil flew out.

The morning of our meeting, I was in the shower when Mary rushed into the bathroom with the news that President Kennedy had been shot. I called Neil at the Beverly Hills Hotel and asked him to come right over. Like everyone else, he was undone. I called Karp to suggest that we cancel the meeting.

"Come on over and tell us the story, anyway," he said. I understood; he wasn't being insensitive, he was just a conscientious man running a big studio. But Neil was in no mood to relate a funny story when the President of the United States had just been assassinated.

Three days later, when the country went back to work, we met with Paramount. And Neil related, in five sentences, the germ of *The Odd Couple*—the relationship of two friends, both recently divorced, who move in together and find that living with one another is more difficult than being married to the wives they've just left. He didn't have much of a story, but there's nothing like having a hit on Broadway to make others think whatever you're saying is funny.

Neil's summary was enough for Karp and his associates to give him the same deal he got on *Barefoot,* no small feat considering the latter had been a finished play and this was merely an idea. They were smart. *The Odd Couple* turned out to be one of the best plays Simon has ever written, and one with the greatest longevity. And all of it, for me, was the result of going to the theater with Noël Coward!

I also learned over time that it's sometimes necessary to lay siege to your prey. An extreme example of this occurred when I was having a rough time trying to sell *Camelot*. Considering its success on the stage, I felt this was insane. What could I do, though, but shop it around?

At long last, Jack Warner expressed interest. Alan Jay Lerner wanted Joshua Logan to direct the film—a double pleasure, as Logan was also my client. But Jack Warner didn't want Logan. I tried to convince him by showing him some footage from *Paint Your Wagon,* Logan's most recent film, but he still resisted me. I realized that traditional methods wouldn't move Jack. I would have to devise a scheme.

I knew that when Jack was in Palm Springs, he went for a workout and a massage at the Spa. So I went to the Spa one day. This was putting myself at a great advantage, as Jack was an extremely shy man. He was comfortable in just two places: his home and behind his desk at the studio.

I waited for him to finish exercising. In the shower, I knew, he always wore a rubber cap. It made him look ridiculous. If he had to deal with me in his altogether and his bathing cap, I reasoned, I might just do some good work.

Jack had just stepped out of the shower, dripping wet, when I blindsided him. "Well, what about Josh Logan?" I asked.

Panicked, Jack looked around for a towel, but I was ahead of him—I'd planted myself in front of the stack. Now he was feinting like a fullback, hoping he could make a successful end-run around me. In the midst of all that, he tried to end this conversation.

"I've already told you no on Logan," he said.

That's when I laid out my threat: "Jack, I'm going to come here every day at this time until you agree to him."

"Okay, okay," he said, almost in desperation. "I'll take Logan. But promise me—you'll never accost me again when I'm naked."

My name is so associated with blockbusters and celebrities that it sometimes surprises people that I have also represented literary personages. The biggest shock for the uninitiated is that I handled the writer who is often regarded as the supreme literary figure of the middle of this century: Vladimir Nabokov. Granted, I would only hear from Nabokov infrequently, and even then his requests would come through Vera, his wife. Once a year, though, Mary and I would visit the Nabokovs at the Montreux Palace Hotel in Switzerland, where they lived.

I have never met a more modest man than Nabokov. Quite

With Vera and Vladimir Nabokov.

rightly, he held himself in high esteem, but when it came time to make a deal he never thought his talent required editors to pay him a specific price. Rather, his sights were on the people—he wanted to know the creative forces behind the project.

And, like his wife, Vladimir was extremely sophisticated about business. Years before it became common practice, Vera asked me to include a "Cost of Living" clause in Vladimir's contract. This was such an unfamiliar request I had to go to an economics manual to see what she was talking about.

From the day he met me until the day I sold *Catch-22* to Columbia Pictures, it was touch and go as to whether Joseph Heller would fire me. Because I didn't ask him to sign an agency contract, he could, in theory, dispense with my services whenever it suited him. Joe's situation was that he was Jewish, nervous, and, worst of all, broke. A Jew who is broke is not only nervous, he's frantic. So Joe kept firing me. And, each time, I convinced him that we were on the verge of making a deal and he was making a big mistake; with that, Joe would agree to stick it out with me.

I've had only one client leave me in a way that truly hurt. Maybe that was because I'd just arranged for George Cukor to

I was fortunate to be able to count as friends some of show business's most interesting and durable personalities. Among them, clockwise from the top: George Cukor with Sherry Lansing; Carol Channing; George Burns; Jack Benny.

direct the film of *My Fair Lady*. At a moment like that, you're expecting bouquets, not the ax.

Cukor was one of the great directors, but getting him that plum assignment was far from simple or quick. The marathon began with Alan Jay Lerner, Jack Warner, and me having lunch in Jack's private dining room. The topic was possible directors and actors for the film. Jack was extra-picky about his choices, not only because we were talking about a prestigious project but because he had a vision of the film as the crowning glory of his career. For that reason, Jack was favoring Vincente Minnelli—who had sensitively and successfully directed *American in Paris* and *Gigi* for Alan—to hit a third home run.

Jack had a habit of whistling between his teeth, which he thought was very clever. Because he never listened much to what anybody was saying, he tended to whistle at random moments in our conversation. I, for one, found this highly annoying.

"Stop whistling," I said at last.

"I've got to whistle," Jack said. "It's how I think."

"Well, you've got one whistle every three minutes. No more."

"Okay," he said. "I'll take three." He was a very funny man, actually. "Who do you want to direct?"

"Minnelli," Alan said.

"All right," Jack said. "Who do you want for the leads?"

"Julie Andrews and Rex Harrison," Alan said.

"I don't think Julie Andrews means anything at the box office," Jack said. "I prefer Audrey Hepburn. She gives me protection. This is the last film I'll ever make. It's my swan song to the movie business, and I want it to be a big hit. Audrey is British, a good actress, the right age, and she can add weight to the film."

Audrey was a very fine actress, and a friend, but she couldn't sing. I knew that. Alan knew that. Reluctantly, we had to agree with Jack.

As we were leaving, Jack had a question: "By the way, if I have a problem with Minnelli, who's your second choice? You guys are all going to New York and I'm left here with these agents."

"George Cukor," I said at once.

"Fine with me," Alan said.

"Cukor's great," Jack agreed. "If we don't make a deal with Minnelli, we'll go with him."

Vincente Minnelli soon heard that he was Jack Warner's choice to direct *My Fair Lady*. He passed that news on to his agent, who somehow assumed that Jack Warner had no bargaining position. And so, at the behest of the then-Mrs. Minnelli, the agent asked for a big salary plus a percentage—"or we don't take the deal." Jack didn't have to add the numbers to know this was more than he wanted to pay. But Minnelli's agent, thinking that was just a ploy, wouldn't budge.

It was at this juncture that Jack called me in New York.

"What do you want for Cukor?" he asked.

"Whatever you say, you've got him," I replied, well aware that George Cukor had never earned more than $150,000 a picture.

"I don't care what Cukor gets," Jack said, "but I'll give him two hundred thousand—no more."

"Then you've got Cukor."

"He'll take two hundred?"

"Jack, you've got a deal."

When I called Cukor with the news, he thanked me profusely. There was no question that I had made a valuable contribution to his career. Later, I went to see George and told him I was going to the Orient to see Run Run Shaw, the most prominent film producer in the Far East. George wished me well, we embraced, and I left on my trip.

When I arrived at the Peninsula Hotel in Hong Kong, there was a telegram waiting from George's lawyer: "George Cukor has authorized me to advise you that you are no longer to hold yourself out as his representative. You are hereby discharged immediately."

I had done a great job for him—and here I was, fired! I was shocked and hurt. We had been friends long before I represented him. If there was a problem, I felt the call should have come directly from George. Instead, I was the one who had to get on the phone. What went wrong had nothing to do with *My Fair Lady*—someone had called my office to inquire about George for another film, I wasn't in Los Angeles, and George was teed off.

A day or two after I returned to Los Angeles, I saw George at a dinner party given by Laurence Harvey. He came right over to Mary and me as if nothing had happened. "When did you get back?" he asked.

"George, I'd rather not talk to you," I said. "I'm too angry. And I have too much respect for you to insult you, so let's forget about it."

George started to bluster, but nothing he said had any effect on me. He then turned to Mary, who also refused to speak to him.

Several months went by before George called and said, "I've got to see you. We're old friends."

"If you're in trouble, I'll help you," I said.

I went to his home for lunch, and he apologized. He'd done the wrong thing, and, because he was a gent, he wanted to correct it. Which he did. We remained friends until he died.

□

More friends (some of them clients as well): Gore Vidal with Shirley MacLaine; James Jones and Irwin Shaw (and someone I don't remember).

With Slim Keith and Truman Capote.

"Either we make a deal now, or forget about it," Charles Bluhdorn, the chairman of Gulf and Western Industries, told me when we were discussing Alan Jay Lerner's *Coco*. Of all the lines you hear as an agent, that's my least favorite. That is, it's one I sometimes use myself but hate to have used on me.

Like many complicated situations, this had started simply, with Alan mentioning to Robert Evans, the head of production at Paramount Studios, that he and André Previn were working on a Broadway musical about the famed couturiere Coco Chanel. Evans expressed an immediate interest in buying the film rights. Alan suggested that he call me to work out a deal. So far, so clean.

Alan was aware that the play's producer, Frederick Brisson, was also my client. He was unaware, however, that Brisson had promised "first look" to William Paley, chairman of CBS. For his part, Brisson seemed to be unaware that the film rights to the play were owned by the author, not by the producer.

It was clear that Paley would have more than a passing interest in *Coco*—having bought *My Fair Lady*, he had great faith in Alan. He liked fashion. He liked Brisson. Without doubt, *Coco* would work for Mr. Paley.

One evening later that week, Truman Capote had a reading of *In Cold Blood* for his friends in New York. I attended, as did Bill and Babe Paley. Afterward, we all went to Le Pavillon for supper. And, inevitably, Bill asked, "Where is the play?"

"Bill, Alan Jay Lerner is sitting right here," I said. "I can't give you the play without his permission. Why don't you ask him for it?"

I knew something Paley didn't—he'd never pay the advance I was seeking. While he was knowledgeable about the musical theater, he was not in the picture business. He had bought *My Fair Lady* when it was already a tremendous success—he knew what he was buying. But *Coco* wasn't close to being ready for an audience. It was a kit in the bag. It might be a hit. But while Chanel was a familiar name to the rich, the American theater-going public was far less aware of her. Selling her to the masses might be an uphill swim.

I, for one, could see *Coco* as a gigantic flop—which is why I didn't want to sell it to Paley. I tried to suggest the play's uncertain future to him, but Paley wasn't accustomed to many people giving him advice. He was sure I was tricking him.

The next day, I was to meet with Charles Bluhdorn, who also wanted to buy the play before it opened. Before I went to see him, I dropped in on Bill Paley. "Bill, I'm in a trap," I began. "I'm meeting with Bluhdorn at five o'clock. If you want *Coco*, you can have it—but you've got to make a deal now."

"I haven't read it," he said. "I need time to think about it."

"What would you like me to do if I get an offer of two million or more from Bluhdorn?"

"You'll have to wait," Bill said.

"You know Bluhdorn—he doesn't want to wait," I pointed out. "If he wants to move fast, I'm in trouble. I don't want to lose the deal with him because I'm waiting for you—and then lose a deal with you because you walk away. As you know, you've done that before."

I was, as he knew, referring to a blowup we'd had after he made $12 million on *My Fair Lady*. I had proposed that he pay $1 million for the film rights to *Camelot*. And Bill thought that was over the moon. Remembering that, there was no way I was going to put Bluhdorn on hold while Bill read and thought.

At any rate, at about five o'clock, I was in Charlie Bluhdorn's office with Alan Jay Lerner and Robert Montgomery, Brisson's lawyer and a very sophisticated negotiator. Bluhdorn also had several of Paramount's lawyers and business affairs people present. He got right to the point.

"What do you want for the play?" he asked.

"I want one and a half million for the film rights and a million to finance the play," I said.

Bluhdorn said yes to every demand.

And yet I found myself saying, "Charlie, you know that Bill Paley has been a good friend to Alan and me. Well, he's interested in *Coco,* and we don't want to make a deal without talking to him."

Seismographs don't hold numbers high enough to register Bluhdorn's outburst. I mean, he hit the ceiling. I mean, plaster fell.

"You either sign this deal now, or else all of you get the hell out," he shouted. "Don't come back to me, because I'm through with it."

I saw $2.5 million floating away.

"Will you give us a few minutes?" Bob Montgomery asked.

"Why?"

"We have to call Freddie Brisson in California."

"What for?"

"It's only fair that we call him," I said.

Bluhdorn couldn't fault that, and we went into the next office and called Brisson.

"Don't take it," Brisson advised. "It's worth more."

"You're talking fairy tales," I told him. "You're talking 'if' money."

"Let's take the deal," Alan Jay Lerner said.

Bob Montgomery agreed. Brisson went along. And we made the deal with Bluhdorn.

The next day, a lot of stuff hit the fan. With Paley, for one. He was furious. Alan went with me to see him.

"Don't lay into the agent," Alan said. "I am the principal, and I'm telling you: I have to take this deal."

As the world now knows, the play opened to ghastly notices. If it hadn't been for Katharine Hepburn, it never would have run. She even said, "I'll take it on the road until you fellows break even." And that's exactly what she did. She toured until everybody recouped his investment. Paramount eventually retrieved its money, but the movie was never made.

Sometimes the fault for a disastrous deal doesn't lie with the producer or the studio. Or even with the agent. Sometimes the trouble can be traced right back to the client—especially when the client was that famed shit-stirrer Truman Capote.

Truman was a very good friend, and I'd represented him on a number of projects, including the sale of *In Cold Blood*. So when Truman told me that he needed some money, I called David Brown, now the celebrated motion picture producer and then vice-president of Twentieth Century–Fox.

"Is there anything on paper?" David asked.

"No," I told him. "But Truman's prepared to pitch an idea."

At our meeting, Truman told David an elaborate story. And David, a shrewd fellow, transcribed the story as Truman told it. He then presented the story to Darryl Zanuck, who liked it enough to pay Truman two hundred thousand dollars.

But when Truman handed in the screenplay, there was something off about it—namely that it wasn't written in his style. David Brown, ever the gent, felt that perhaps Truman had been unwell and to avoid the embarrassment of repaying Fox, Truman had somebody else write the script for him. Other Fox executives were less concerned with what had happened to Truman than with their money—they advised him they wouldn't accept the screenplay until he rewrote it in something closer to his own style.

Truman stood his ground, insisting that the work was indeed his. Fox then asked for its money back. At first, Truman refused again. Then he decided it was wiser not to have the studio bad-mouth him all over town. But he wasn't willing to repay the entire payment—according to Truman, he owed Fox $180,000. The remaining $20,000, he said, would have to come from his agent. The legal department at Fox wasn't slow to

approach me. But I dug in my heels. "I actually performed the service I was supposed to," I said. "I'm not going to pay it back."

Truman was unhappy about that. But he paid Fox, turning his quick-money project into a $20,000 loss for him. He deserved that. The truth was that he'd had a singularly untalented friend write the screenplay, and, although he knew it was no good, he'd decided it was "good enough for Hollywood."

CHAPTER

Ten

I NEVER THOUGHT the day would come when Darryl
Zanuck, Harry Cohn, Sam Goldwyn, Louis B. Mayer, and Jack
Warner would leave the movie business. Or that I'd miss them.
Or that they'd be replaced by men they would never have hired.

But in the 1970s, the business that I had grown up in
changed so radically it might as well have died. Longevity? A
thing of the past—I found myself dealing with studio executives
who didn't know where they'd be working the next week. Big-
name authors? It was the era of the original screenplay. Big-
ticket productions? All anyone seemed to want was the next *Easy
Rider,* a film that cost a few hundred thousand and grossed a
fortune.

In my forty years in Hollywood, the moguls had such firm
control of the business that the average executive kept his job for
almost three decades. Starting in the 1970s, the average stay was
around three years. It seemed as if being chosen to head a studio
was like being appointed the president of a Central American
democracy—each day, you wondered if this was the day you
were going to be shot.

Very quickly, I came to feel that no matter which button I

Mary and I had many wonderful evenings with a variety of friends.

pushed the elevator was going down. The men who ran the studios now were professional executives or, worse yet, lawyers. They didn't care about relationships. They didn't even seem to care about movies. If they had any passion, it was for the bottom line.

One class of talent now ruled the town: the box-office star. No longer a glorified contract player under the thumb of a mogul, the free-agent star was a combination megawatt god and thousand-pound gorilla. He might not be able to assess material as well as a producer or director, but he suddenly had the power to hire and fire writers at will. This was great for the Dustin Hoffmans of the world. It was, however, hell for my clients and me.

From the forties through the sixties, I had handled a series of distinguished playwrights whose hit plays had become hit movies. In the seventies, it became tough to sell plays to Hollywood. The plays that were written weren't intended for the movies—face it, you weren't going to get a worldwide movie attraction from Harold Pinter.

In this new climate, it seemed that if something sold it was an accident. As studio heads played musical chairs, I got the sense that a great many people were hanging on by their fingernails over a ledge eighteen stories high. Fear ruled. And when no one can step up, make a decision, and back it up with a big check, there isn't much for a guy like me to do. Except, perhaps, to forget about these chaps and concentrate on books.

In the 1970s, I turned my eyes back to New York. I'd done a lot of different things in my life, but I was still pretty much a virgin when it came to publishing. Where could I fit in? Well, what did I know? I knew people. Famous people, accomplished people, controversial people.

It was a short step from that realization to a new career based on selling the autobiographies of celebrities. In that change of life, I guess you could say my past became my future. I had seen my share of Hollywood stars, knew what had happened in those lives, and sensed how much truth these stars needed to tell for the public to feel it had gotten its money's worth.

Arthur Rubinstein, John Huston, and Betty Bacall—her

Betty Bacall has always been one of my favorites.

With Jackie Onassis, Liza Minnelli, and Bianca Jagger.

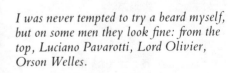

I was never tempted to try a beard myself, but on some men they look fine: from the top, Luciano Pavarotti, Lord Olivier, Orson Welles.

memoirs sold for $350,000 in 1975—proved that the public was interested in celebrity memoirs. Their success confirmed what I suspected: it would be much easier to sell a dozen celebrities to publishers than to close a single studio deal. During the next two decades, I went enthusiastically after Angie Dickinson, Joan Collins, Ali McGraw, Jesse Jackson, Michelle Phillips, Kirk Douglas, Carol Matthau, Michael Caine, Cher. Although most of them never thought they could write a book, many of them needed the money.

There was also a straightforward way of doing business with the publishers that was reminiscent of the way I had worked in Hollywood. By comparison, the new Hollywood characters were as slippery as the decks of the *Titanic*. In 1977, I had arranged for the publication of approximately thirty books.

What I figured out early on in the book game was that writers were heavily underpaid. I never saw a publishing house that didn't get three or four times more money from a hit book than it paid to the author. That was an intolerable inequality, unless you subscribe to the theory that, for a publisher, successful books support the losers. Well, that wasn't my problem—I wasn't selling them the losers!

Ratcheting up the advances wasn't just profitable, it was fun. I thrived on the cross-fire between agent and publisher. And it was great delivering Christmas at contract time to a writer like Bette Bao Lord, who never failed to tell me she was crazy about me. Or Larry McMurtry, who continually lavished praise on me for my efforts on his behalf.

Books weren't yet like movies, with the betrayals that the film business breeds—there was still, in the 1970s anyway, a gentleman's code about the enterprise. And there was so much more to do! During the day, I dealt with an eclectic mix; at night, we'd go to the theater or a dinner party where the guests —unlike their California counterparts—wore civilized clothes and exchanged civilized views on a raft of topics. A little of that, and I was hooked on New York all over again. And so, while maintaining our Beverly Hills home and office, Mary and I bought an apartment at 1 East Sixty-sixth Street.

The flat had good bones—a pleasant, eighteenth-floor view of Central Park, a wood-burning fireplace, and a separate bed-

More memorable friends.

room wing—and Ahmet Ertegün's wife, Mica, and her partner, Chessy Rayner, did a great job decorating it. We hired a wonderful chef, and, for big parties, there was a restaurant in the building, just for tenants. As a package, this was a great launching pad for a much more agreeable life.

And there was no end of fun. That is, fun defined as getting clients bigger advances than they ever dreamed possible. Bette Bao Lord was startled when I told her I could get her a million dollars for her second book—a substantial leap from the high five-figure advance she had received for her first novel, *Spring Moon*. Okay, I didn't get a million. But I came very, very close. And I might have scored the full seven figures if Bette hadn't decided to go with Knopf because her favorite editor was there.

Bette had a finished manuscript to sell, but I soon found there were equally potent ways to sell books that didn't even have a written outline. Richard Nixon is the classic example. It wasn't too long after Nixon resigned from the presidency that I was asked to represent him. I visited him for the first time at San Clemente in September 1974. I was first briefed by Ron Ziegler and then ushered into Nixon's office. When I emerged, three hours later, I was impressed by his resilience—he was in much better form than I had expected. The only evidence of the battering he took was an occasional remark, like "I'm quite fatigued, as you can imagine."

As our conversation drew to a close, he sent for his appointments secretary and had him write—in longhand—a full and complete authorization for me to represent everything that he would do in conjunction with his memoirs, including television appearances. It was a great coup and a complete surprise.

Selling Nixon wasn't going to be hard—the challenge was getting $2 million in 1974 dollars. Before I could concoct a battle plan, I happened to be on the telephone with Frank Wells, then head of Warner Bros., about another project. And, offhandedly, I mentioned that I was representing Nixon on his memoirs.

Warner Bros. had recently formed a publishing division, and, quick as a flash, Wells said he wanted to buy the memoirs. The big ticket price bothered Wells not at all. He saw the situation realistically: Warner Books was a paperback house with no cachet whatsoever, and here was some potentially great publicity for the house. Howard Kaminsky, who then ran Warner Books, saw the upside. But he also knew he'd be staring at gallons of red ink if the book bombed, so he quite legitimately expressed the opinion that the money was high.

"It's way high," I cheerfully agreed, "but buying the Nixon memoirs will take you to a new level and put the house on the map."

Which is exactly what it did.

The only glitch in the entire Nixon deal occurred when *The New York Times* took my client and me to task for making a television deal with David Frost instead of a network. I saw Lew Wasserman shortly afterward, and he said, "I always knew you were a juggler but that was fantastic." He understood: I had swivel-hipped around three networks and a couple of independent TV producers to pull off a tremendous deal that was quite extraordinary.

There was a funny incident attached to the taping of the Frost interview. The terms were quite straightforward: Frost got ten hours of conversation, Nixon got six hundred thousand dollars. Frost was more of a showman than a businessman, so, at the end of the taping, he went over to Nixon and dramatically handed him the check. Seeing my commission disappear right in front of my eyes, I sprang like a cobra. "Mr. President, that belongs to me," I said. "You get yours later."

Nixon held on to the check. "Why is that?" he asked.

I explained the first law of agenting. I get the check, then deduct my commission and send the rest to him. Nixon had no problem with that. He wasn't greedy, just curious.

The world is divided into two: half the population thinks they're agents, the other half thinks they can write. Agents are frequently confronted by the assertion of an author that their lawyer, or a friend, or perhaps their barber, has said to them, "That book's worth a million dollars. You shouldn't take a dime less." It's easy for an amateur to comment on the value of a literary property—if challenged, he doesn't have to produce results.

On the other hand, sometimes writers are underpaid be-

With Deborah Kerr and Mary in Switzerland.

Mary and me with David Brown and Lily and Richard Zanuck.

cause they don't know how much they're really worth. I once promised Elia Kazan—the great director who went on to become a novelist—that I could get a million dollars for his book, *Acts of Love*. Gadge was skeptical, but I felt this lovely novel, which was something of a prelude to his autobiography, would be a surefire hit. So I asked for $1 million. And got it. I was, however, wrong about its appeal, as it turned out to be not such a big hit. But the publisher, Warner Books, never complained.

Another client who was far too modest in the beginning was Larry McMurtry, who had never received more than $25,000 for a book before he came to me. It wasn't in his nature to ask for more money. He also didn't like to accept a dime until he finished a book. I couldn't allow that.

Simon & Schuster had published all of Larry's novels, so when I sent over the manuscript of *Lonesome Dove*, I asked Michael Korda, the editor-in-chief, for an advance of $500,000. Michael liked the book a lot, but he didn't think he could pay more than $200,000 for it. After some negotiations, he went to $250,000—and wouldn't go higher. I decided to go elsewhere. I offered the book to five other publishing houses. They all wanted the book, but $250,000 seemed to be everybody's favorite number; no house would pay more. So, feeling like a fool, I crawled back to Michael and accepted the $250,000.

Some months later, at a dinner party at the home of Marietta Tree, the conversation turned to current books. Joseph Alsop, not knowing I represented Larry, said he had read *Lonesome Dove* and declared it one of the most remarkable books he'd ever read. Well, I just glowed. Joe was a perceptive critic and a good barometer of informed good taste. His praise was, early on, a harbinger of *Dove* becoming an enormous success and winning the Pulitzer Prize.

While McMurtry was writing his next book, Simon & Schuster offered him a $500,000 advance. Now it was Larry's turn to be difficult. Once again, he announced that he didn't want *any* money until he had finished the manuscript; this time, however, I convinced him that this was childish behavior and that I should grab some cash.

Within three years, I had his price up to $2 million a book.

□

When I'm negotiating, I prefer as brief a meeting as possible. Lengthy meetings divert the buyer's attention. If your customer is the head of a studio or the editor-in-chief of a publishing house, his time is limited. Even if he wants to have a long conversation, you're better off keeping it short.

Once you've named your price—let's say $1 million—the ball is in the other fellow's court. He has to come back with a counter proposal that at least acknowledges my demand. So he suggests $500,000. In point of fact, had he known all of the facts or if I hadn't been so bold in my demands, he might have offered $50,000 or $100,000 at the outset. That is the genesis of any important deal: ask for the moon.

It never failed that when I asked for a large sum and publishers declared it was more than they expected to spend, they almost invariably ended up meeting me more than halfway—not because they came to agree with me, but because they were embarrassed to give me less. One of my favorite tactics when I dealt with the head of a studio or publishing house was to say, "I can't go back to my client with what we've been discussing. It's demeaning." Most of the time, that was less salesmanship; the offers were low. By the time I felt I could take an offer to my client, though, it was generally close to what I had originally asked for.

Which isn't to say a good agent doesn't compromise. For example: the first time David Wolper, an independent producer, called to ask me what I wanted for a book I was representing, I told him I'd like to get $200,000.

"That's out of my league," he said. "I've only got twenty thousand."

I reconsidered and announced we had a deal.

That, too, was integral to my strategy. No matter what I asked for, I was always prepared to accept a lower figure. Thirty years after that call from Wolper, Jeffrey Berg, the president of ICM, called to ask me what I wanted for the rights to Larry Collins and Dominique Lapierre's book, *Or I'll Dress You in Mourning*.

"I'd like five hundred thousand, but I might accept less."

"What about fifty thousand?" he asked.

We settled on a slightly higher figure.

At the marriage of Charlie Feldman to Clotilde.

I tell this story not to show I'm reasonable. Just the opposite. During the negotiations, Jeff said, "You've got the guts of
a lion. This book is twenty years old, no one wants it, and you
ask for half a million dollars."

"I said I'd take less," I replied.

Another reason I never like to delay a deal is that often the
person I'm doing business with doesn't have final authority. It
always makes me crazy when someone says he's wild for a book
I'm representing—and then I discover that this guy has to kick it
up to his superior. More often than not, that's death to my cause,
for the subordinate is sure to present the idea in a less convincing
way than I would have presented it to the boss. But I generally
take revenge: once I learn that the person I'm dealing with
doesn't have final word, I rarely go back to him again.

In this respect, publishing is easier than the movies. When I
deal with the head of a publishing house, I'm usually negotiating
with someone I know well and have made deals with before. For
that reason, top editors tend to keep close associates in the room,
to stretch the proceedings out and get a few points back in the
process.

I remember a phone call when I was going over deal points
with Michael Korda on the telephone. I thought I was doing well
—and then he said, "I have Joyce Andes here." Joyce is the
head of the contract department and, believe me, whenever a
publisher brings his attorney in, it begins to resemble an operating room. In this case, Joyce functioned as the anesthetist.
When she got me groggy enough, Michael took out his scalpel
and went to work on me. By the time I woke up, my client and
I had emptier pockets than we would have liked.

And the deal is just the beginning. There are umpteen different ways for them to screw an author. They can underpublish
the number of copies. Or they don't sell the book hard enough.
Or—and this is so common that it's almost a surprise when it
doesn't happen—the book won't be in the stores when the
writer's on tour. With these cut-out points, publishing is an
almost risk-free system, which is why very few publishers have
ever gone broke.

I find contemporary publishers quite different from the days of Horace Liveright, when publishing was an honor and editors sat in dusty little offices and read every book that crossed their desks. Except for the men and women who are line-editing a manuscript, I don't think publishers really read any book anymore. If they say they do, they're lying as much as anyone at movie studios. Publishing today is show biz. It's the same as the world of entertainment.

Publishers like to say that the reason their business is now in a somewhat precarious state is because of agents like me who, starting in the mid-eighties, demanded outrageous advances. Well, nobody was forcing their hand. They paid because they thought they were going to make a profit. It wasn't a charitable contribution.

The fact is, most publishers aren't good business people. They're neither showmen nor entrepreneurs. They're not as smart—and certainly not as wily—as the fellows who ran the movie studios. With notable exceptions, I've found them easy to manipulate. The way to do that: give them a carrot, which is to say, a book with a very high profile.

I've always loved the challenge of a tough sale. But even I was surprised by the difficulty of the negotiations I conducted for Ambassador Jeane Kirkpatrick. I had been briefly introduced to her at a party given by Lally Weymouth for Lord Weidenfeld, the eminent British publisher. I had seen the ambassador on television from the United Nations and was impressed with her tenacity. While I didn't always agree with her, there was no question that she was an impressive, effective speaker. I thought that when she left the U.N., she could have a significant book.

After our meeting, I wrote to her and told her what I thought. An aide to the ambassador called soon after and suggested that I meet her for lunch at Lutèce—a rather astute choice on her part, as it's one of the most expensive restaurants in America. The locale seemed to set the tone for a discussion in which big money was sure to be a main topic.

Over lunch, as Mrs. Kirkpatrick and I discussed her book, she advised me that in no way would she consider meeting with any publishers. She thought it belittling to "hawk" her book. A sophisticated approach, I thought. Also naive. She refused to use

Our twenty-fifth anniversary party.

as a selling tool the considerable charm that made her so attractive to me. Her plan was to submit nothing more than a written outline. Her aim was for me to effect a sale in a matter of only a few weeks. And she left me to ponder what I could do for her, given those conditions.

Thus began a gavotte over the next few weeks that wasn't to be believed. I kept telephoning her office, but she didn't return my calls. The ambassador was in eighty different places each week, and here I was, trying to pin her down. I couldn't find her, much less her outline.

"I'd like to have one more meeting with you even though I don't think you're going to let me represent you," I said, when I finally reached her. "Whatever happens, I'd like to give you some advice."

So she invited me to her office at the United Nations.

"Apparently, you are being dissuaded by someone from dealing with me," I said, "and I think that someone is Lord Weidenfeld."

She admitted that it was indeed Weidenfeld. The ambassador respected him and didn't know that he was looking out for himself. He didn't want me to be her agent because he knew I'd be asking for more money than he wanted to pay for the English rights to her book.

"There are a lot of fat publishers, but there are not a lot of good agents," I told her. "You're not going to find a better agent than me. Weidenfeld scoffed at my telling him that I would get a million dollars for you, saying I was 'looney and ridiculous,' but I don't think he knows as much as I do about the American audience and what the public wants."

In all fairness, Weidenfeld & Nicholson is a fine publishing house. I've always liked doing business with George, which is more than I can say for some of the other English publishers. And—this matters almost as much—I enjoy his company. I later confronted him with the Jeane Kirkpatrick problem.

"You ask for too much," he replied. "I overpay you. So if you're not the agent, I'll have an easier time of it."

I wouldn't have been bothered by this seeming lack of loyalty so much if George didn't act as if he loved me. His embraces were always torrid. But he was myopic. He attributed his lack of judgment in buying certain books which didn't eventually pay off to some brutality on my part, instead of a lack of judgment on his.

I was about to leave the ambassador's office when she said, "What makes you think I'm not going to give you the book?"

"Because you haven't said that you would and here we are parting company."

"No, we're not," she said. "You take care of the book. I'll give you until next Wednesday to sell it."

How about that for consolation? The ambassador was going to give me *one week* to get her a million dollars for her book—with no outline. Fortunately, I learned from a mutual friend that she had had a meeting with Si Newhouse and Howard Kaminsky [who was then president of Random House], advising them of her plans for the book and asking them to communicate with me. Kaminsky and Newhouse were very impressed with the ambassador and wanted the book. But Kaminsky didn't think it was worth a million.

As it happened, I had spoken to Michael Korda of Simon & Schuster about Kirkpatrick—before her meeting with Random. "You can't go to another house," he'd said. "We have a contract with her for the next book. We must see the book and determine if we want it." That presented a whole new twist.

I promptly called the ambassador and told her that she was in no position to sell her book at all—it was already under contract to Simon & Schuster. But once again, she was ahead of me. It seems that she had already written the book she owed Simon & Schuster, she just hadn't presented it to them yet. "I'm going away soon, Mr. Lazar," she said, "and I don't have much more time for this. If you're going to obtain a suitable contract, please do so immediately."

Pulling out all the stops, I convinced her to give a day of her time to meetings with several publishers; that's all it would take, I assured her, to close a deal. I delicately explained that if she gave a verbal pitch—I'm sure I said "explanation," for she would have thought "pitch" fatally vulgar—the million would quickly be forthcoming. This was news to her. She really thought that if an agent said, "I have a book by Jeane Kirkpatrick," publishers would line up with bags of cash.

Once I had her cooperation, though, it really didn't take much more than that. At lunch not long before, Nelson Doubleday had asked if I had any books that he might be interested in. Now I told him about the possibility of the Kirkpatrick book. He said he'd like to meet with her.

Over the years, I'd learned that Doubleday & Company took too long to make decisions. I often thought an agent would have to hang the Doubleday editorial board by their ankles to get prompt attention. This time, I told Nelson, your team should move more quickly, for the book would be sold by the end of the week.

When Ambassador Kirkpatrick finally agreed to meet with publishers, she allotted just three hours. Clearly, we couldn't hop all over town—the publishers would have to come to my house. This was going to be a French farce. I couldn't very well hide Nelson Doubleday in a closet; he's too big. And he was bringing Sam Vaughan, his editor-in-chief, along.

An hour into a productive conversation with the ambassador, Doubleday and Vaughan found themselves eased out of the apartment. A few minutes later, Richard Snyder and Michael Korda arrived for lunch. There, Ambassador Kirkpatrick was at her most brilliant—so full of ideas, notions, and opinions that you knew what the book would be about. It was one of those fortuitous as well as rare times, when the author had a clear position of where she stood and what she wanted to say. And having rehearsed with Doubleday, she was in top form for Snyder and Korda.

Snyder and Korda had brought along an editor who had experience with political writers of the same persuasion. He was a big factor in helping Kirkpatrick decide between the two publishing houses. I was sure that Random House would have topped Simon & Schuster's offer of $850,000, but she didn't feel as comfortable with the Random House executives, who didn't share her view politically. She felt they would be looking over her shoulder and perhaps criticizing her.

Selling the Kirkpatrick book proved to be a great adventure. And a learning experience. After that, when I had a major client, I settled him or her in my living room and had the publishers in. So much better, don't you think, to have "home team advantage"?

☐

For years I had been urging David Brinkley to write a book. His reply was always the same: "Someday." Finally, one afternoon he called and told me his ideas. I got right on the phone to Bob Gottlieb at Knopf to see if this might interest him.

"Do you think I'll like Brinkley?" he asked.

I assured him that Brinkley was a wonderful man in anybody's world. Then I hit him with my price.

As all of America had known for thirty years, Brinkley was an excellent writer with an easily identifiable style. His personality shone through every sentence. So Gottlieb, without so much as a piece of paper from Brinkley, gave me his offer. And within an hour after David's exploratory call to me, I was returning the call with a deal.

To say the least, Brinkley was startled.

I loved every minute of that hour. It was a shocker, it was smart business, and it was the kind of great tennis that very few editors can play. In fact, it could only have been done with Gottlieb. I don't know of another editor who would have done that.

One evening at Noël Coward's home in Switzerland in 1972, Noël regaled Mary and me for two hours about his experiences with George Bernard Shaw, Somerset Maugham, Judy Garland, Sir John Gielgud, the Duchess of Windsor, Harold Pinter, and a host of others. It was the most marvelous collection of reminiscences I'd ever heard.

"Noël, if I'd had a tape recorder tonight, you would have had a book," I told him at the end of the evening.

"How about *Name Dropping* by Noël Coward?" he offered.

"I'll get you a hundred twenty-five thousand for it," I countered.

"No, you can't, Swifty. I've never gotten more than twenty-five thousand pounds."

"Nonsense. This is worth a hundred twenty-five thousand, or I'm no agent."

Noël wasn't well—this was a year before his death—and he had carried on with his stories only to please and entertain us. He was hunched over and in pain. Though he wore a beautiful dressing gown and was immaculately turned out, he was not the

With Noël Coward.

same Noël I had known from years gone by. At length, he admitted as much: "Why don't you try for it? I really could use an elevator in this house."

I called Bob Gottlieb the next morning and told him about our evening.

"Tell him if he'll take a hundred fifty thousand, he's got a deal," Gottlieb said.

Sadly, this project never came to fruition. A few weeks later I received a letter from Noël. While he was grateful for the offer, he didn't think he was up to writing the book, and he wasn't comfortable with accepting payment in advance—he had only done so once in his life. It would, he wrote, "put me under obligation and I would rather feel free to write, and then get paid."

The publishing deals I've done are, in the end, more the result of osmosis than calculation. My idea of planning is to go to a dinner party with a notebook and pen. And I carry a tape recorder in the car so as not to forget an important thought.

When you're working on twenty to thirty manuscripts or proposals every day, you have to prioritize. You also have to let go. It's like your body—if you don't make too great a fuss about it, it's inclined to cure itself. So I see myself, in a way, as a natural healer. If I'm confronted with a hopeless manuscript or proposal, I don't tangle with it. I let it be. And, three months later, it's over. The pain is gone, and so are the people, and that's that!

You'd think the bulk of those doomed projects come from old friends who are convinced the story of their life requires hard covers. Not at all. My friends produce the liveliest books of all. Like John Huston—when he asked me to represent him, nothing gave me greater joy.

It wasn't, after all, as if John's book was solely his idea. I'd been badgering him for a while to write about his colorful life. Finally, when he was in his early seventies, he agreed. Again, there was no problem getting a publisher. And again, it was my good friend Bob Gottlieb who bought it for a sizable advance.

I had first met John at the Gershwins'. Right off, he was a true hero and that rarest of Hollywood events: a renaissance man. He inspired me with his insatiable appetite for life. He burned the candle at both ends, the wax melting in the middle, too, if that's possible. Of course, his pleasure in being alive meant too many marriages, too much imbibing, risking his life and the lives of those who worked with him in locations no one else would have tolerated. But that was because John's mind was always restless.

I loved talking to John about his work. In the summer of 1985, just after the opening of *Prizzi's Honor,* he came to see Mary and me at our New York apartment. Pauline Kael had written in *The New Yorker* that if she didn't know Huston had directed the film she would have thought it was the work of a much younger man. As John and I were the same age, I told him how proud I was that he had made this movie at this time of his life. He lowered his voice, although there was no one within hearing range, and said in his courtly growl: "I think we got 'em."

John's gallantry during his final illness reminded me of Lou Gehrig's farewell speech at Yankee Stadium after learning that his disease was incurable: "I'm the luckiest man alive." Huston never admitted that he was failing, even after a conference in which we discussed his directing *Lonesome Dove*. Although he was clearly in bad shape, he told his companion to put the breathing equipment away because he didn't want McMurtry to be dissuaded by the trappings of his illness or to think he wasn't well enough to shoot the picture. He was practically panting throughout the meeting, but he tried to create the impression that he was sturdy enough to take on a Western, a massive undertaking for any director.

I knew it was difficult for him to speak without the oxygen. After the meeting, I told him I thought this project would be too much for him.

"I can do it," he said. "If they'd just forget about this apparatus, I can do it." He was eighty and dying, but he wasn't going to let go.

If John cherished the relationship he had with you, he kept in touch. He never let go. John Foreman, his producer and friend, told me that at a dinner party at John's manor in Ireland, he had stood up and said: "I want to drink a toast to someone who isn't here, who has made a great contribution to my life and to others. Let's raise our glasses to 'Swifty.' "

A few weeks before he died, John called to say he wanted to see me. He didn't want me to visit him, he said; his son, Danny, was going to drive him over to my house. When Mary and I heard the car pull up, we went out to greet him. He wasn't strong enough to get out of the car. He had his oxygen equipment with him, and on his lap he held a superb bottle of Château d'Yquem.

"I've brought this for you. You'll love it, just love it," he said.

We chatted outside by the car for a few minutes. He told us he was leaving in a few days to film *Mr. North,* which he cowrote with Danny. We kissed him good-bye and then he drove off. And that was the last time we saw him.

I can't think of a more appropriate exit. John showed me that there are two ways of dying: with gallantry and acceptance, or as a coward. I've had friends who died angry at the world, blaming others, jealous that their friends would live past them.

With Peter Viertel, John Huston, and David Niven on the set of The African Queen.

But even though John was burdened by the constant fear that this breath would be his last, he was cheerful, observant, and kind right up to the end.

There are, I'm sure, a great many people who, if they think about agenting at all, believe it's a lead-pipe cinch to sell the work of name-brand writers. Let me tell you, it's not that easy. At a certain level, it's more difficult selling the work of a well-known client—which may explain why, even at the high end, agenting is a profession with more quitters than survivors.

You have to remember that a writer doesn't hit a home run every time out. As often as not, therefore, you're asked to sell a book or a play that hasn't been very successful. It's pretty hard to be passionate about the future of a project that's carrying its past around on a ball and chain. How do I sell properties for which I've had dim expectations? Well, let's just say I'm not the fella to dissuade the buyer. Thanks to that selective myopia, I've sold any number of things I would not have bought.

It's just as disheartening—maybe even more so—to try and sell a client's work that you alone believe in. Here's everyone in town turning it down, and yet you must retain your faith in the work until it's sold. Let me tell you, it's not easy keeping at it when the writer is badgering you with phone calls that, just below the surface, suggest the problem has less to do with his material than his agent's inattention.

The book that eventually became the basis of the first and most successful miniseries in television history (next to "Roots") made it to the small screen with a behind-the-scenes story rich in agent-client conflict. I'm talking about Irwin Shaw's *Rich Man, Poor Man,* one of the roughest projects to sell I've ever encountered. You wouldn't have thought that when the novel was published in 1970—the thing looked like an easy movie sale. It was Irwin Shaw at his best: a good straight story with fascinating characters and a colorful background. And yet nobody was interested.

After I struck out with every studio in town, I turned to the independent producers. I struck out with them as well. I even put it to the self-test that Jules Stein taught to me when I was first starting out: "If you needed this one sale in order to eat,

Sailing with Irwin Shaw.

With Mica and Ahmet Ertegün and Marella Agnelli.

where would you go with it?" But I couldn't think of anything I
hadn't tried.

After the book had been out for about a year, and had done
very well, Mary and I were having a luncheon in the garden of
the Hotel George V for our usual Paris bunch of pals: Marian
and Irwin Shaw, Gloria and James Jones, Deborah and Peter
Viertel, Sophie and Anatole Litvak. Champagne and caviar were
being consumed in quantity, and everyone was having a very
gay time. That is, until Irwin spoke up and stopped traffic.

"What kind of fucking agent are you never to have sold *Rich
Man, Poor Man*?" he said, in a tone that was much more of an
accusation than a question.

I was stunned. Before I could remind Irwin of all my efforts
to place the book, he lashed out with another derogatory remark
about my expertise. I was inclined to get up and leave, but I
refrained—this was, I thought, the booze talking.

When I got back to Hollywood, I was more determined
than ever to sell the book. I went to Barry Diller, who was then
at ABC. Barry was an extremely inventive thinker who had
more or less invented the idea of the movie of the week; it didn't
take much salesmanship to convince him that *Rich Man, Poor
Man* could be spun into TV. As he saw it, the book merited four
or five hours of prime time, spread over several nights. We went
to Frank Price at Universal, who liked the idea and was keen on
joining forces with Barry.

The sale of *Rich Man, Poor Man* to TV marked the first time
that a major novel had been sold for a miniseries. (In fact, the
production of the show was grist for a second book, *The Making
of Rich Man, Poor Man*.) The miniseries itself was a revelation. It
turned Nick Nolte into a star and sold untold copies of the book.
In addition to the $1.2 million which came Irwin's way from a
new burst of book royalties, he enjoyed an international acclaim
beyond anything he'd ever experienced.

When I sold *Rich Man, Poor Man,* I made a great mistake—
and, over time, it cost me my friendship with Irwin. The lowli-
est writer who sells his book to television gets, by union contract, at least a guaranteed minimum for repeat showings and
spinoffs. In Irwin's contract, there was no such provision. I
know what I was thinking—I'd had such a struggle selling it that

There are never too many beautiful women.

I believed it would never get beyond the option stage—but I should have protected Irwin better. I had no excuse.

Irwin never read the fine print in his contracts. That was my job. But you can believe he hauled that document out and put a magnifying glass to it when the cash register started jingling for that miniseries. Did I say jingle? It was more like a fire alarm— "Rich Man, Poor Man" was shown around the world at least seven times, by my last count.

And it was even worse than that: according to the contract, Universal owned and controlled the rights to the book's characters. When I made the deal, I thought nothing of this clause; at the end of the book, after all, the hero died. How could they turn him into a sequel? Well, in television, they can do anything. And in the case of the sequel to "Rich Man, Poor Man," Universal planned to resurrect the dead protagonist. If they were going to take that step, I reasoned, they could also resurrect Irwin's royalties. So I went to Lew Wasserman, and, on bended knee, succeeded in getting Irwin a great deal of money.

There was, however, a price for this bonanza—to get it, Irwin had to work on the sequel's story for a month. Being a hired hand on a project that should have been an annuity for him was a bitter pill for Irwin to swallow. One night, when I called him in Switzerland, I made yet another blunder: I said I'd never made a mistake for a client. And if he thought so, I added, it was because he had changed since he became rich.

This was, I soon realized, like waving a rag in front of a bull, for Irwin promptly wrote me to let me know how very wrong I was. He wasn't rich by any standard, he said, and he hadn't changed. And he was still livid about *Rich Man, Poor Man.* "Sure, I like and need the dough—but I'm not only in the marketplace," he wrote.

Although directing harsh words to a man who'd been a central figure in his life for decades troubled him, he felt he had no choice: "We've done very well for each other, and we've developed a long-standing profound friendship which nothing can shake, at least for me. But that does not mean that I suspend my critical faculties or my desire to defend my name when necessary."

That last sentence has an ironic ring, as I consider how our relationship played out over the last eight years of Irwin's life. He had never read through a contract before, but after *Rich Man, Poor Man,* he became suspicious of my negotiating abilities. I continued to make terrific deals for him, but he constantly worried that something about them was off.

This anxiety came to a head over the movie deal for *Nightwork*. We had optioned the book to director Frank Perry for five years, and in that time, Perry had been unable to get a screenplay he liked. In exasperation, he wrote his own script. By then, however, his producer had lost interest, so he took the property to Elliott Kastner.

In 1981, with Kastner on board, I steered the project to CBS theatrical films, and was, for my efforts, rewarded with the title of executive producer. For those services, I was to be paid $120,000, plus a percentage of net profits. To me, it was money earned, and not a penny of it came out of Irwin's share. To Irwin, it would become a conflict of interest, pure and simple.

In 1983, relations soured between us. At a lunch that winter, I grandly announced that I'd just sold a Joan Collins novel for a fortune. Irwin was enraged: "It is demeaning to be represented by you. Do you understand? Demeaning!" He called me afterward to apologize, but that summer, his bitterness and paranoia reached new heights.

The focus of Irwin's hostility was *Nightwork*—specifically, his belief that I had gotten him to sign the CBS contract when he was in an intensive care unit in Columbia-Presbyterian Hospital. According to his version of events, I had showed up at his bedside when he was heavily sedated and took advantage of his drugged state to get him to sign the contract. His son, Adam, also believed this. I say there were no papers drawn at that time, and that Irwin signed them later in 1981, when he was completely lucid.

But it was impossible to reason with him on this subject. All he saw was my executive producer credit, and that convicted me. In the summer of 1983, he had his lawyer send me a terse letter advising me of his desire to negotiate a fresh deal with CBS —with another agent representing him.

I think I know what Irwin was feeling. He was, I believe, looking back on his life and concluding that he had wasted a lot of time on well-paid hack work. In his view, that wasn't his fault. He had been tempted by that old devil, Irving Lazar, who knew his fatal weakness: he was hungrier for money than for critical acclaim. In Irwin's construct, he was just a junkie and I was his pusher.

I don't feel that I took an artist and bent his talent for commercial purposes. The choice was always Irwin's, and although he was sometimes divided, his choices were always consistent; he went for big advances that require big sales. And I, on my side, was equally consistent; I always looked for ways to maximize my income. We were, Irwin and I, well matched.

CHAPTER

Eleven

Y<small>OU'D THINK</small>, at a certain age, that people who might otherwise want to propose alliances would look at the actuarial tables and decide not to, on the theory that the old horse was statistically bound for the glue factory any day now. Not in my case. In my fifties, in my sixties—hell, even in my seventies —I got offers.

One day in the mid-1960s, I was at the Colony Restaurant, a now-defunct but formerly stylish New York watering hole. A few tables from me, Jules Stein was having lunch with his brother-in-law, Charlie Miller. Jules and I had remained friends over the years, so it wasn't unusual that he asked me to stop by on my way out.

But what he had to say was surprising.

"I'd like you to think about coming back to MCA," he told me, as we settled in for coffee.

"Jules, this makes the second time you have asked me to come back. What do you have in mind?"

"I'm disappointed in the pictures that Universal is making," he said, referring to their low-budget, "Ma and Pa Kettle"–type films. "No one has a grip on choosing good material. I'd like you to advise us on what we should and shouldn't buy."

I had been a very well-paid consultant to United Artists for about three years and hadn't yet signed a new contract, so I was free to go elsewhere. His proposal sounded interesting. I promised I'd call after I returned to California.

"Here we are," Jules said, when we next met. "You're the bride, and we're the bridegroom. Why don't we get married?"

"You'd have to pay me a great deal of money," I said.

Money wasn't an issue for Stein and Lew Wasserman. All I had to do, they said, was name my figure. Best of all, they assured me I would have no surveillance and could work any way I pleased. I realized, however, that my contact with Lew would be infrequent, as he didn't do a lot of the day-to-day work. I'd have to deal with people I didn't know—which was exactly what I didn't want and why I had shifted my business to publishing.

Mary and I discussed the offer over the next few days. If I didn't cherish my independence above all, perhaps I would have chosen otherwise, but I finally called Lew and said I couldn't do it—just as, in the early 1980s, I declined an invitation to join what many consider to be the best theatrical agency in California.

And I was, at various times, asked to head studios. I never paid much attention to those offers, either. A classic was one during the mid-1950s, when I got a call from Charlie Feldman.

"I just spoke to 'The Greek,' " he began.

He meant Spyros Skouras, president of Twentieth Century–Fox. Skouras had called him to ask if he was interested in running the studio now that Darryl Zanuck was moving to Paris. He told Charlie he could have anything he wanted.

"I told him I didn't want to do it alone," Charlie continued, "but that I'd do it with you. What do you think?"

"Charlie, you know that anyone who runs a studio has got to be there by nine o'clock in the morning, or earlier. Which of us is going to do that?"

"Not me!" he exclaimed.

Well, it certainly wasn't going to be me either. And that's how I got to not run Fox.

I don't regret my decision to stay my solo course. I could have been richer, very much so, but I don't think that would

have made me any happier. I mean, I did everything I wanted, and I did it first class all the way.

And, most important to me, I've done everything my way, perhaps selfishly—which is why, in my eighties, I look back at my life with few regrets. Oh, how I wish I were younger. I wish I were about forty now and terrorizing all the young agents in the business today. But then I think: there are a few today who still consider me a thorn in their side.

Mike Ovitz, for one, didn't appreciate it when I went after some of his clients—Cher, Faye Dunaway, Michael Caine—and negotiated their book deals. And then there is the agenting duo of Mort Janklow and Lynn Nesbit, my main competition. They found me a damn nuisance because I attempted to poach from them on several occasions. Because a leopard doesn't change his spots? Sure. But also because I think it's outrageous that they take a 15 percent commission from their clients. From my point of view, if you're getting $3 million for a book, it's pure greed to take more than 10 percent on domestic earnings.

The larger problem with contemporary publishing and movies is that the guys today take themselves too seriously. I never represented anyone I didn't like—and there were a lot of best-selling commercial writers I could have handled if their personalities hadn't irritated me. Mine was a simple test: if I didn't want to have dinner with a writer, representation was out of the question. For me, it had to be fun. Agenting was a business, sure, but it was also a vehicle for personal growth.

In the glory days, when books and movies weren't regarded as software and people tended to stay put at one company long enough for the ink to fade on their Rolodex entries, manners counted. As did wit and style and an appreciation for the good life. Wealth was important—but it was still on the lower end of importance. Today if you're not rich, you're not as good as the next guy. And that makes agents and producers somber. Think about the bottom line long enough, and fun goes out the window. My basic philosophy, which is more balanced, has never had to be changed: Get the money, run for the train, leave town, and have some fun.

"Isn't this an ignoble profession?" an important Hollywood agent said a few years ago.

I was astonished. "You mean to tell me you're not having the time of your life?" I asked.

"No."

"Well then, get out of the business," I suggested.

What my colleague was missing was the obvious reality: this is the greatest time in the world to be an agent. As the studios have weakened, the agents have become more powerful. They're the showmen, or they at least have the power to be. In the old days, a strong studio could reject an agent for any reason they chose. And when you were barred from one, it worked like a daisy chain. There were only five studios in those days, so if you were cold-shouldered from one or two it was hard to stay in business.

Tough-guy talk aside, I know I'm much, much closer to the end than I am to the beginning. Still, I can't start a sentence with a phrase like "As my life draws to a close . . ." I feel too vital for that. I'm reminded of what the late Elsie Woodward, one of the grandes dames of New York society, told me when I was hitting seventy: "I know you're well, because I keep hearing about all of the interesting things you're up to. And it boggles the mind." One would think that boggling the mind of a ninety-two-year-old lady would be easy, but I assure you, such was not the case with Miss Woodward.

"What are your plans?" she asked.

I told her we were leaving soon for New York, London, Paris, and St. Moritz.

"Keep going," she urged. "You're at the top of your form."

"Elsie, you've never missed anything in your life."

"You bet I haven't. And my advice to you is never miss a thing while you can get around, because there might come a time when you won't be able."

I thought about what she had said and saw it neatly matched my own philosophy, which has been never to miss a trick and to be in as many places simultaneously as I can. I've never lost my zest for travel, and the frenzy of an airport, which is tedious to some, is a quasi-sexual experience for me. I find flying romantic. Hearing departures announced for Karachi, Bombay, and Papeete makes me salivate. It does not pain me to stand in line at the ticket counter, or to be charged overweight for my luggage, nor does it discommode me if I'm bumped from my favorite seat in first class: Number One, Row One. Traveling around the world has enabled me to meet so many people and to engage in so many enterprises that I've always felt part of the scheme of the world rather than the city where I lived.

A few years ago, I received a charming note from Irving Wallace's wife, Sylvia, who had just returned from a safari in Africa. She wrote, "One night, we were having pre-dinner drinks alongside a muddy river. And Dennis Zaphero, our British guide, told us about the world-famous people he had escorted: 'There was Ernest Hemingway, and there was Clark Gable, and there was Irving Paul Lazar, and then there was Prince Charles.' "

I rather liked that.

So if I had to do it over again, I don't think I would change a thing. I've successfully fought off boredom and restlessness, even though I've had some close shaves in my attempts. After a two-week stay with Mica and Ahmet Ertegün at their home in Bodrum, Turkey, a dozen summers or so ago, Barbara Howar joined me on a charter flight from Kos, an island in Greece, to Athens. We were twenty minutes out of Kos when the left engine of the small plane caught fire. We could see the flames eating at the fuselage.

The pilot sent out a Mayday signal. "We're turning back," he told us.

"I have an appointment in Athens," I said. "Go right on."

"We'll never make it."

The plane began to sputter and spin a little, and we were told to put on our life jackets. We were relieved when we spotted the airport at Kos with its fire trucks at the ready. The pilot shouted for us to dash out of the plane as soon as we landed, for fear the plane might explode. But his landing was perfect, and our sprint was unnecessary. Still, we didn't complain when Olympic Airlines sent two pilots and a twenty-passenger plane to collect the two of us and fly us to Athens.

When we landed in Athens, it was almost sunset. We went directly to the Hilton, dropped our bags, and chorused, "Let's get drunk!" And we went right over to the best restaurant in Athens. It was jammed. I gave the guy at the door fifty dollars and asked that he find us a table for two. Barbara ordered a drink and I had three martinis in a row, straight up. When I finished ordering dinner, the waiter asked how many people would be joining us.

"Just the two of us."

"But you have ordered enough food for six people."

"Don't you worry about it. We just want to taste everything. We were almost never to taste anything again."

Over the years, my good friend Peter Viertel tried to kill me every chance he got. His first attempt at an early demise for me was in 1947, when he put me upon Bourbon, a horse of his that only his stepdaughter had been riding. No sooner was I in the saddle than the horse reared and headed for the barn across the road at a clip of about eighty miles an hour. On the approach to the barn, there were about fifteen cars parked in the driveway. Bourbon knew his way back to his stall, but wasn't accustomed to the cars of Peter's Sunday guests, so, at near-full speed, he sharply zigzagged his way between them, with me hanging on to the reins for dear life. Fortunately, I ducked as the horse entered the barn; a taller man sitting upright would surely have been decapitated.

Irwin Shaw was Peter's equal in testing—and breaking—my limits. The classic Irwin dare occurred at his house on Escondido Beach, when I ventured too far into the ocean on a small raft. The waves were high, the raft capsized in the rough waters, and I disappeared from view. The Shaws and their guests stood on the shore, unable to help, certain they were witnessing the end of a life. After a great while, though, I came in with the tide; had it been going out, this book would not have been written.

"You're fearless!" Irwin used to say. Never correct a writer, but I would say "daring" is the better word. For it never occurred to me that these exploits were life-threatening. I believe that when one's time is up, somewhere, somehow, there is a beckoning—and then you go, ready and well-dressed for the occasion.

Epilogue

I N THE SPRING of 1992, with his wife, Mary, very much alive and his days filled with activity, Irving Lazar cornered me at a dinner party given in his honor by Tina Brown and Harold Evans.

"Remember me?" he asked.

"Who could forget Irving Lazar?" I replied, looking down at all five feet three inches of him from my five-feet-eight high-heeled perch.

"I remember you, too," he exclaimed, smiling that mischievous, self-satisfied smile. "You're the girl who's always turning me down."

His eyes, though camouflaged by the signature black insectlike glasses, were gleaming with fun. He loved twitting people, and the fact that I had declined to coauthor the books of two of his clients made me fair game.

"I'm not always turning you down," I said. "We just haven't found the right project."

Irving Lazar wasn't known as a hesitant man, and there was no hesitation now.

"What about my book?" he asked.

In other circumstances, I might have had a snappy come-

With Slim Keith.

back. This time, I was truly surprised. For I had recently coau-
thored the memoirs of Slim Keith, whose forty-year friendship
with Lazar had ended abruptly when he undertook the sale of
her book. She had found him less than stellar, and, rather than
go forward with the deal he'd made for her, she'd returned her
advance and started fresh with Lynn Nesbit as her agent. None
of this had appeared in the book itself—in my telling of her

story, Slim was charitable about Lazar, going no further than poking fun at his well-documented eccentricities.

Because I assumed that feelings ran deep on both sides, it made me uncomfortable to banter with Lazar. And it was natural for me to conclude, knowing a few things about the man, that the reason Lazar was offering me his book was that he'd never read Slim's.

Lazar promptly punctured that assumption. "You made Slim sound . . . ," he said, pausing to search his mind for a rare word of praise, ". . . like an intellectual." The implication was clear. He hoped, in my hands, that he'd come off as the Kissinger of agents.

And so, in the late spring of 1992, Irving Lazar and I began a mating dance. It was quite instructive. For the man who had separated publishers from millions of dollars for his authors turned out to be his own worst client. No sooner did I agree to his terms than he began to renegotiate. This process was continual, insulting, and counterproductive. I had no choice but to bow out.

That fall, Mary was diagnosed with bone cancer; two months later, in January of 1993, she was dead. In February, desperate for a way to fill his days, Lazar agreed to be profiled in *Vanity Fair*—a piece that, as he saw it, would take the place of the memoirs he had been working on for more than a decade.

For me, it was a fine irony when the magazine selected me to write that profile.

Lazar also saw the irony.

"You had a chance to make a fortune on the same material you'll be writing about now for only a few grand," he said, a few minutes into our first interview in Los Angeles. "I don't understand it. How silly of you. You know, kid, you were the only one I ever wanted to do my book."

His flattering comment didn't make me want to rekindle the project. I took it as his way of trying to charm—or perhaps disarm—the interviewer. But this typically Lazar way of reducing a relationship to its financial component was, alas, only a tease. This wasn't the Lazar I'd met in New York; this was a grieving, distracted man.

Lazar's focus for himself that season was his annual Academy Awards party at Spago. His commitment to his epic profile in *Vanity Fair* was something less. It did not, for one thing, involve spending much time sharing his memories with me. For that material, he said, I should consult several large file boxes, where, he promised, I would find all the stories and anecdotes I'd need for the article.

There was a surprising amount of material. I found dozens of folders with subject headings that ranged from the logical to the comical: *Childhood, Clients Who Turned Down $1 Million, Death and Mortality, English Tailors, Hollywood as Middle-Class Community,* and my favorite, *People I Don't Like.* I also unearthed files on moguls, movie stars, musicians, and writers from the last five decades. Though he had been unable to complete a manuscript with a coauthor he thought was suitable, it was clear that Lazar had, since 1984, devoted substantial time to recording material for his memoirs.

The incomplete manuscripts written by Chris Chase and Michael Shnayerson, Lazar's two previous collaborators, were not the only ones I found. Linda Jones, who had been a devoted Lazar assistant for fifteen years, had meticulously transcribed his musings and constructed a rough-draft manuscript based on those tapes. The combined efforts of those three suggested to me that Lazar was closer to the completion of his memoirs than he knew. When I expressed my amazement at the work that had already gone into this project, he merely shrugged. Was it possible that Lazar, famous for not reading, had not even read his own material? Highly possible.

Lazar may have regarded a magazine profile as a summing-up, but mortality was not a subject he wanted to discuss. It was difficult extracting information from him in the winter of 1993; his attention span was minimal. But far from being annoyed, I was sympathetic. As I saw over and over again during our talks, Lazar was clinging to the last shreds of a life that had, in his words, been "one constant party."

Now I understood his single-minded concentration on his Oscar party. Another man might have mourned privately; Lazar's way was to deny his pain and cast himself as the showman

THE OSCAR PARTIES.

The Oscar Parties.

The Oscar Parties.

The Oscar Parties.

he had always been. Some of his friends were shocked by this decision, but it made sense—even to this comparative stranger, it was obvious that Irving Lazar was not emotionally equipped to deal with grief.

It had simply never occurred to him that he would have to confront the loss of the woman he called his "guiding light." The twenty-five-year age gap between Mary and him was supposed to be a built-in security system—once he passed on, Mary would be there to protect his reputation in death as she tried to do in life. For him, the Oscar party was a way to delay the mourning process, as if to say he had devised a new plan that would allow him to go on.

But after a few days of steering around the subject of Mary's death, Lazar broke down and admitted that his interest in life was practically nil. Now the man who had always boasted that he had no regrets was consumed with one: "When Mary was dying, she never once whimpered. She never cried, never said 'Why me?' Instead, it was me who wept, kicked, and screamed when I realized she was going to die. So Mary found my presence oppressive in her final days. She urged me to go out at night with friends, the way I'd done all my life. And because I couldn't accept that she was going to die, I followed her instructions, leaving her to prepare herself—alone—for the end. I regret the way I handled Mary's death. I wasn't by her side during those last months, and we never said our good-byes. I never got to hear her say, 'I had a great time, I love you.' And I never got to thank her for all she had done for me or tell her that, even though I know I wasn't always the greatest husband, she had been the focus of my life."

If Lazar shared similar thoughts with close friends, I'm unaware of it. It seemed, on the contrary, that he was spiraling out of control, surrendering to rage, spite, and greed. In the weeks before his Oscar party, New York gossip columnists noted with interest that Lazar was demanding the return of a diamond necklace bequeathed by Mary to Karen Lerner, her dear friend and the former wife of Alan Jay Lerner. Lazar told her that he was required to pay a gift tax on the necklace and that he needed it back so he could have it appraised. Friends on both coasts speculated that the real reason he wanted it was that he planned to give it to the wife of one of his more socially prominent friends.

That accusation certainly had a ring of truth. During the last two decades of his life, Lazar's social climbing had reached epic proportions. Through the years, as he's written, his social and business lives were intertwined. But since the 1970s, his desire to hobnob with the swells began to overshadow his professional concerns.

Because Lazar had turned himself into a Social Figure, he was, that season, subjected to the snide judgments of other Social Figures, who found it not quite correct that Teresa Sohn, a beautiful young woman who had been hired to assist Mary in her final illness, was still on the premises. At the same time, Lazar's business acumen came under scrutiny when Alan Nevins, Lazar's protégé for the last several years and the real workhorse of the operation, bolted to start his own agency and took some Lazar clients with him.

None of that seemed to matter, though, on Oscar night, when Hollywood royalty and New York society settled themselves at Spago at the ungodly hour of 6 P.M. to toy with dinner and watch the Academy Awards. Lazar entered slowly but confidently, wearing perfectly tailored dinner clothes. His cane and Teresa Sohn at his side were the only signs that anything had changed since last year.

Lazar made his way from table to table, shaking hands, hugging, kissing. For those who knew him only through the media, it was a star's entrance—Moses parting the waters. Insiders knew better. A few days earlier, I had asked Jack Nicholson what was the most telling thing about Lazar. "What he's doing right now," Nicholson said tenderly. "Going ahead with his party. That's very gallant."

That was not the majority view. Even as they were eating his food, many in attendance at Spago were complaining that the seating lacked Mary's touch and that the party was really a bridge too far. If his friends had had their way, Irving Lazar would have retired right then and there, and, like other Hollywood figures of advanced age, wait to be wheeled out on ceremonial occasions.

□

I returned to New York, wrote the Lazar profile, and handed it in to *Vanity Fair*. It was at this point that Lazar asked me again to write his book. This time, he came as a supplicant, not as a benefactor. And this time, having seen the riches in his archives, I had no trouble accepting.

For I no longer saw Lazar's story as just the self-aggrandizing tale of a single-minded flesh-peddler; in context, his life seemed like an archetypal twentieth-century American saga. Lazar was someone out of Odets and Schulberg and Runyon, a self-made son of Eastern European Jewish parents who fought his way from the slums of New York to success and prominence. That breed had all but disappeared. Through Lazar, I thought, I could make that era come alive for a generation that hadn't read Odets's *Golden Boy,* Schulberg's *What Makes Sammy Run?,* and Moss Hart's *Act One.*

In July of 1993, I arrived in Los Angeles expecting to spend the summer working with Lazar. But the intervening four months had taken a considerable toll on him—he seemed tired, frail, and diminished. My presence did not revive him. Lazar now had real physical problems. A circulatory blockage in his left foot made it difficult for him to walk. And because he also required four sessions of at-home dialysis each day, he was now virtually immobilized.

For another eighty-six-year-old, working on his memoirs might have constituted therapy. But Lazar's therapy had always been travel. In the past, when he was restless, he took a trip; it depressed him that it was no longer realistic even to plan one.

To add to the frustration, his social calendar was all but empty. In March, when many craved an invitation to his Oscar party, that calendar had been as full as ever. Now Teresa Sohn and his assistant, Cindy Cassel, had to generate invitations for him. Because Lazar was both grieving and dying, it was increasingly hard for them to fill his evenings. As an old friend put it, "Having dinner with Irving has become a cottage industry."

Lazar was all too aware that his social life had lost its glitter. And the reality that he was no longer A-list material made him angry and resentful. "I'm not lunch, I'm dinner," he sternly told the beautiful wife of a famous actor who was one of his closest friends.

In March, when I had gone to dinner with Lazar and a few friends, he was the king of the table, painting pictures of a long-vanished Hollywood. Bogie, Goldwyn, Sinatra—he was the proverbial walking encyclopedia. When the dinner ended, he was just hitting his stride. Remembering that, I organized dinners with him and my husband, whom he liked enormously. It was my hope that in this setting I could get him to perform, so I could capture his voice and get some fresh revelations. But Lazar was just not up to it.

I had only been in Los Angeles for two weeks when the end began. Mary would have been sixty-two on July 18, and Lazar intended to visit her grave that day. But as he was leaving the house, flowers arrived from a friend in memory of Mary's birthday. That brought her death home to him again; claiming he was ill, he retreated to his bed and refused to leave the house. The next morning, he was hospitalized with a severe case of pneumonia. And then, while hovering near death, he suffered a minor stroke.

As Lazar recuperated, I turned my attention to the unexplored boxes that filled several closets and made, to my delight and relief, a valuable discovery: Irving Paul Lazar had been a prolific letter writer. In the years before people routinely made long-distance phone calls just to chat, he had composed lengthy letters to friends and clients and saved all the carbon copies. Because his intent was to be accepted into his clients' social circles, these letters went beyond discussions of deal points and business opportunities. Lazar had, in essence, typed an ongoing journal of his social life—he had turned himself into the Samuel Pepys of Hollywood. Through these letters to Moss Hart, George Kaufman, Irwin Shaw, Harry Kurnitz, and many others, he painted a portrait of Hollywood glamour far richer and more candid than anything he had recorded for his book.

Among these carefully preserved gems, I found his extensive correspondence with his family. These letters not only provided insight into his early days in Hollywood, they revealed a more human and accessible Lazar than most people knew. As the principal wage-earner in the Lazar clan, he supported his father and helped his younger brothers financially. Lazar had told me and others that, after he left home, he had little contact with his family. But here was proof that he was a devoted son and brother.

To cheer him up, I showed him home movies he had forgotten about. Across the screen we traveled to Klosters, the South of France, the bullfights in Pamplona, and far-flung places like Cambodia. It was too much; he had to go to bed. After that, I stayed away from the past and finally adhered to the command he'd been repeating since my arrival. "It's all in the files," he said wearily. "You'll find everything you want there."

Lazar came home from the hospital in a wheelchair. His stroke had left him with some slight paralysis which physical therapy could have cured. Instead, he developed an irrational obsession with money.

Although he was insured for most of the cost, the expense of his two-week stay in the hospital unnerved him. He would fire his domestic help only to reinstate them and call his office to threaten his assistants with salary cuts. After a long life of fighting to rise above mediocrity, Lazar was now a victim of a classic old-age worry: financial insecurity.

For that reason, he suddenly turned his attention to this book—if we proved to Michael Korda that we were making progress, Lazar was entitled to another check. "Let's get cracking, kid," he said. And so we spent several afternoons together, during which he would call New York to let our editor know we were bulling through the material.

Mostly, though, Lazar was rewriting his will. His beneficiaries were constantly changing. With Mary gone, Lazar's greatest fear was of being alone, so he used his will as a weapon. According to the attentiveness of his assistants, they rose and fell in the rewards they would receive after his death. This was a far cry from a will he'd made in 1958, when he was still a bachelor. In that last testament, he'd left all his money to the wives of his closest friends and clients—Kitty Hart, Joan Axelrod, Leonora Hornblow, Marian Shaw, Betty Bacall, and Audrey Wilder—with the instructions that they were to have a three-day party.

"Go home and write the fucking thing," Lazar instructed me on the day I left Los Angeles. As I worked on the book in

New York, I called him from time to time to let him know I was making progress. These were brief conversations; he didn't always remember who I was.

On several occasions, he called me: "Listen, honey, I think you better come out here. There are a lot of things we didn't talk about." And then he would give me a preview of stories I'd heard before. I didn't tell him that. I just listened, knowing that his urge to see me would pass.

His concern with his will had not subsided. But by November, the focus was slightly different. Five weeks before he died, he summoned his assistants, his attorney, and a witness to his bedside to make some changes. This time he was sobbing, struggling to gain control. "I don't have any children, I might as well leave it to the people who have made my life more comfortable," he said. And then, just as he started to sign the document, he stopped and looked up. "Who would believe *this* scene?" he asked.

"Neil Simon," someone suggested.

But he wasn't finished. "I like kids, who else is there that I've forgotten?"

For months, friends and assistants had been urging Lazar to have surgery on his left foot. By November, the circulation was so sluggish that the only alternative to an operation to install a synthetic artery was amputation. But his condition was not good, and his chance of surviving the surgery was only 50–50. Moreover, amputation was repellent to him. And I knew why. His mother had had her leg amputated as a result of diabetes, and he had cringed when he told me of the horror of visiting her in the hospital afterward.

Although it was clear that surgery was inevitable, Lazar refused to give his approval until the very last minute. He survived the surgery and was home in five days, but the operation was far more painful than he'd been led to believe. When I called to wish him a happy Thanksgiving, he sounded weaker than ever before, but for the first time in our relationship, he asked me about my children. And for the first time, he seemed genuinely happy to hear from me.

That unprecedented appreciation made me realize that Lazar

wasn't going to last much longer. Three days later, I flew to Los Angeles to say good-bye. Lazar greeted me from his bed. He was, if possible, even smaller; swaddled in his bed, he looked like a large baby. His voice was one tone above a whisper.

Although he was groggy from the painkillers, he made a considerable effort to talk to me. And this time his one and only subject was his mortality. He said he didn't particularly care how he was remembered. He had no thoughts on an afterlife. He wanted no epitaph. Even as he was making his exit, his thoughts were on the here and now.

"I never had any turmoil in my life," he told me. "I've had a fair shake for eighty-six years. I can't complain. You can't do any better than that. After Mary died, there wasn't much left for me. I had done everything, traveled the world, seen everything I wanted to see and had more friends than I could ever sort through. There is nothing left for me to do. Curiously, I'm not unhappy. I have a few more days to express my gratitude."

I realized then that Lazar had spent the last eleven months getting up the courage to make the decision to die. From the moment he lost Mary, he knew that was what he wanted. But even as I said good-bye to him for what we both knew was the last time, it was apparent that he was still somewhat conflicted. He wasn't prepared to live, but he wasn't quite ready to die—there was one more beat left to be played.

The thought that oil tycoon Marvin Davis and his wife, Barbara, would take over his Oscar party seemed to revive him. And he was still willing to joke about the casting of Irving Paul Lazar in some future dramatization. "I want Cary Grant," he said.

"Irving, pick someone who's alive," I said.

After rejecting Warren Beatty, Tom Cruise, and Robin Williams, he finally gave me the thumbs-up sign when I suggested Jack Nicholson.

During the last month of his life, painkillers distorted his sense of time. He didn't, as many do, return to days past; rather, he traveled. One afternoon, he had a nurse take him out for an ice cream cone; on the way, he asked him to stop and buy a *New York Times,* as he wanted to go to the movies. Another day, he ordered Teresa Sohn to book airline tickets; they were, he said, going to London.

Two weeks before the end, he pondered his career. "No one has ever written that I was brilliant," he told his bookkeeper. With that, he asked her to read the profile that Michael Korda had published in *The New Yorker* the previous spring. If Korda had said he was brilliant, he wanted her to read it aloud to him; she was silent when she finished the piece. Then he had her check for any mention of his genius in an article about him in *Buzz,* a Los Angeles–based magazine. Again, there was none.

"See, I told you so," he said. "No one ever wrote that I was brilliant."

By the end of December, his right foot was starting to turn blue—the sign that he'd need another operation. A few members of his inner circle encouraged him to take the chance. What, after all, did he have to lose? If the surgery was successful, he'd buy more time and, perhaps, even recuperate enough to get around. If not, he'd die on the operating table, which wouldn't be the worst way to go.

Lazar wanted neither to endure more pain nor the uncertainty of the operation. And so on the evening of December 27, in the presence of Janet de Cordova and Gene Kelly, Gene's wife, Pat, and his staff, he announced he was going off his dialysis. This quiet form of suicide would take no more than three days.

But unlike that jaunty final paragraph he had hoped would end this book, Irving Lazar did not have the luxury of dying painlessly. Once the decision was made, he was scared. His body convulsed from the pain and the medication. He did not want to die alone. Like a child, he asked Pat Kelly to cradle him in her arms.

As the hours progressed, his body relaxed. He didn't talk much, but rather was content to know that there were people around him who cared for him. And though he was on painkillers, his tolerance to them was extraordinary; once he decided to die, he kept his eyes open until his muscles refused to work. He wanted to know what was going on around him, he wanted to hear what people were saying.

The end came in the late afternoon of December 30, sixteen days short of the one-year anniversary of Mary's death. It was as

if he had purposely tried to time it so that the death year on his
tombstone would be the same as Mary's.

You would expect that Lazar's funeral would be a star-studded, multigenerational event. It was anything but. A week after
his death, a service was held at Pierce Brothers Westwood Village Chapel. The consummate event planner had left the vaguest
instructions—the same kind of gathering that he had organized
for Mary almost exactly a year earlier.

Although admission was by invitation only, this wasn't a
daytime version of the Oscar party. Rather, it was a role call of
Hollywood's old guard—Frank Sinatra, Gene Kelly, Don
Rickles, Jack Lemmon, Walter Matthau, and Kirk Douglas—
sprinkled with a few relatives, clients, business associates, and a
handful of stalwarts from New York. The seats of honor in
the front pew were reserved for Lazar's domestic staff and his
assistants, a gesture that gave him a kind of Proustian grandeur.

Emotions were complicated. Most of those present knew
that Lazar had led a rich and full life, and many of them had
created the work that enabled him to live that life. They had
celebrated and fought, and some had grudges that time wouldn't
erase. Nonetheless, there was real sadness in the air, not only for
the clichéd "end of an era" reasons but because of the specific
loss of a unique character.

Over and over in the eulogies, I heard variations on that
theme. Chris Hart, Moss's son, spoke on Lazar's ability to transform himself from a rough Brooklyn boy to the ultimate Hollywood host: "Of all the big deals, and celebrated clients, and
dazzling parties and movie and television packages Irving put
together, the invention of himself was his greatest coup." Bette
Bao Lord wondered what writer "would dare stuff every last
scintilla of *joie de vivre* in a hero bald, four-eyed, and maybe five
feet two in heels." Larry McMurtry saw him as "a larger-than-
life figure in a town that, but for the great magnifying glass of
the screen, would be in most ways smaller than life."

The topic of Lazar's uneasy last year was almost universally
avoided: in this company, death was like a flight by Concorde to
Mary. So it fell to George Stevens, Jr., to acknowledge that
Lazar had indeed gone to that place where fame never comes.

"Irving said to me more than once that he would sometimes become restless in Los Angeles—but everything would be fine just as soon as he had scheduled a trip that he could look forward to. This last year and a half was difficult. The trips were planned but not taken. I like to think that during this time he was packing up, knowing that a journey was ahead. . . . Travel well, little friend, travel well."

As I sat in this company, I felt strongly that these speeches, though well-intentioned, had very little to do with Irving Paul Lazar. A roast would have been more appropriate, with liquor flowing, and bawdy jokes, and a stream of the classic Lazar stories. At some points, it would have been difficult to tell if the speaker had been praising or attacking Lazar.

That was Irving Lazar: smaller than a minute, but bigger than life. God knows he was pretentious. And arrogant. And far from truthful. He got away with schemes and deals that would have been the ruination of any other agent. But he was also fearless and irrepressible, privately sensitive and publicly profane, capable of quirky loyalties. As Ahmet Ertegün, his closest friend in the last decades of his life, told me, "He wasn't who he pretended to be, and that was a large part of who he was." A complicated man, in brief, who never quite understood his greatest achievement—in his long march to model himself on men he considered classier, he somehow turned himself into a far more original creature than his betters.

—ANNETTE TAPERT

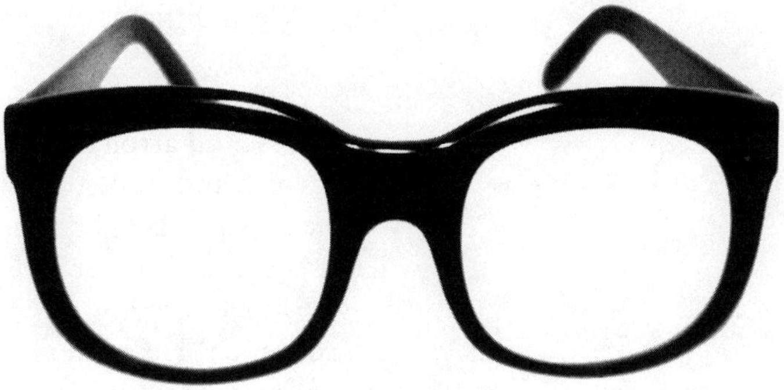

Index

Picture Credits

The photographs in this volume are all part of the Irving Lazar collection.

PAGE
  15:   Photograph by Horst
189:   *Both photos:* AP/Wide World
190:   © Skrebneski 1977
193:   *Bottom:* © Helen Marcus
198:   *Top:* Cano
199:   *Top:* © Paul Slaughter
212:   © Helen Marcus
217:   *Bottom:* © Sonia Moskowitz
221:   *Bottom right:* © Ron Galella Ltd.
244:   © Ron Galella Ltd.
251:   *Top:* Douglas Kirkland/Sygma
279:   Photograph by Hurrell 1981
        214–15, 230–31, 260–69:   Photos courtesy of the following photographers: Alan Berliner, Peter Borsari, Ron Galella Ltd, Michael Jacobs/MJP, Bill Nation, Frank Teti, Aloma/Jim Frank Photography.